What People Are Saying About MEGASHIFT

"I could only read a few pages at a time before I had to take a deep breath and wipe my eyes! Great inspiration!"

> Domenic Fusco,
> President, Image Artistry Video

"I've read a thousand books, but nothing ever moved me so powerfully as *MEGASHIFT*. I wept my way through page after page, miracle after miracle. Now I see how I've been placing God in a box. It's made a radical change in my way of thinking, and I'll never be the same again. Nobody could, after reading this book of wonders."

> Michael A. McGrath,
> Author, *The Epiphany of the Body*

"Jim Rutz has compiled an enormous amount of thrilling information and presented it in a brief, concise, and very readable form. I'm astonished at the amount of research that went into this exciting work. It certainly needs to be read and applied. It's a valuable reference that I'll come back to over and over."

> Dr. Jim Montgomery,
> Founder, Dawn Ministries;
> Author, *DAWN 2000: Seven Million Churches to Go*

"*MEGASHIFT* is an upbeat, optimistic, faith-filled look at what God is doing today and what He will be doing tomorrow around the world. Jim Rutz helps us to hear what the Spirit is saying to the churches. You cannot afford to miss this book!"

> Dr C. Peter Wagner,
> Chancellor, Wagner Leadership Institute;
> President, Global Harvest Ministries;
> Author of over 60 books

"I picked up your book at 12:30 A.M. on my way to bed and read it through in one sitting—couldn't stop! It certainly enlarged my view of God."

> Linda Reddick, Teacher with Open Church Ministries

"This 'new Christianity' is bursting with life, having exploded the brittle old wineskins of traditional Protestantism. Jim tells the story with grace, excitement, and humor. You cannot ignore this book."

Dr. Dan L. Trotter, Editor, *New Reformation Review*

"Jim Rutz has done it again. His book *The Open Church* was for thousands their first glimpse into what interactive Christianity could look like. Now he pushes the door open further with this clarion call for nothing less than a 'new Christianity.'

While the church around the world is growing at an astounding rate, the church in the West has been experiencing equally rapid decline. The answers lie not in more programs, but in a fresh infusion of the Holy Spirit's power. This is nothing less than another Reformation.

Historically, most revival movements have influenced church doctrine, but they have not had much impact on church practice. *MEGASHIFT* issues a call for a completely new paradigm, a new structure."

Dr. Tony Dale, Editor, *House 2 House* magazine

"God is catching us all by surprise, doing things around the world without asking anybody's permission! Churches are growing in places and styles we think should be forbidden because it upsets the status quo.

The Lord is bypassing some of our most cherished heroes and using housewives, teenagers, and faceless nobodies to prophetically guide the church. So fasten your seat belt as Jim Rutz takes you on a roller-coaster tour of some of the most exciting and groundbreaking developments on the planet today. If you can remain completely unperturbed and unchanged by what you are about to read, I honestly would like to meet you."

Wolfgang Simson,
Author, *Houses That Change the World*

"*MEGASHIFT* is must reading. A life-changing book."

Dr. Ted Baehr,
President, Christian Film & Television Commission

"This is one of the most compelling books I have ever read, and I usually have three or four going at the same time...As an aside, I often had to pick myself off the floor from laughter."

Doug Grills,
Financial Advisor, San Diego

Mega Shift

Igniting Spiritual Power

James Rutz

EMPOWERMENT
PRESS
Colorado Springs

MegaShift: Igniting Spiritual Power

Empowerment Press
2 North Cascade Avenue, Suite 1100
Colorado Springs, Colorado 80903 • (719) 277-6635

ISBN: 0-9669158-5-2
Library of Congress Control Number: 2005920116

Printed in Canada

Second Edition: July, 2006

Scripture quotations are from *THE WORD: The Bible from 26 Translations*, Mathis Publishers, Inc., Gulfport, MS 39506-6685. Used by permission.

Dedication

To the millions of intercessors and church planters who are turning the world into a temple and covering the land with God's glory as the waters cover the sea.

On your shoulders you bear most of the weight of the kingdom of God on earth. The deeper your travail and the tougher your work, the greater your reward. Every tear you shed will be a diamond in your crown.

You are my heroes and heroines.

Challenge

This book will draw you into a higher life, a new way of living that is beyond what you have experienced so far. If you read it with an open heart, I promise you will be changed forever.

Make no mistake: The path you are starting on will lead you farther above and beyond traditional, institutional church life than Luther and Calvin went above and beyond medieval Catholicism.

The high adventure you are beginning today will change you and bring you benefits that perhaps you never dreamed of. Yet it will require you to get serious about life in new ways, taking on a burden of responsibility for the world around you—and changing that world.

But don't be daunted. With the new burden comes new power. And I have it on Good Authority that the burden is light.

Contents

1

The New Kingdom Explosion
Exciting Miracles and Church Growth

"Be astonished! Be astounded! For I am going to do something in your own lifetime that you will have to see to believe." —Habakkuk 1:5

A leper is healed in the marketplace.
A paralyzed man leaps from his bed.
A small bit of food feeds a large group.
Storm clouds turn on a dime.
The gospel is preached in one language, but heard in another.
A desperate woman with a flow of blood is healed.
A demonized man chained up for years is delivered and set free.
The sound of a mighty, rushing wind is heard during a meeting of believers... yet there is no wind.
Withered limbs are restored.
The deaf hear; the blind see.
A girl is raised from the dead.
And Jesus appears in a vision to one of His chief persecutors.

Great historic events by any measure. And all have happened in the last twelve years.

After 2,000 years of people praying, "Thy kingdom come," it has. And you are about to dip your toe into it.

You Are Taking a Giant Step Up

If you read this book with your heart, you will have to refocus your eyes—on a wider and higher horizon.

You will start to do things you thought were out of your reach.

You will become able to handle problems that would flatten you today.

You will have a kind of freedom you thought impossible.

You will solve personal problems you expected to carry around for the rest of your life.

And you will no longer face a daily routine, but a daily adventure, perhaps even a world-changing pilgrimage on a spiritual frontier at the very edge of what's knowable, what's doable, what's imaginable.

There Has Been a Megashift in Your Status

Very few people realize that the nature of life on Earth is going through a major change.

We are seeing a megashift in the basic direction of human history. Until our time, the ancient war between good and evil was hardly better than a stalemate.[1]

Now all has changed. The Creator whose epic story flows through the pages of Scripture has begun to dissolve the strongholds of evil. This new drama is being played out every hour around the globe, accompanied sometimes by mind-bending miracles.

For reasons we know only in part, God has handed down a somewhat revised set of rules, delegating greater authority to more people. He has apparently decreed that plain folks like you and me are now a central part of an accelerated plan for a total transformation of the world.

That plan is centered around small clusters of loosely networked but highly committed Christian people who have been empowered to do extraordinary things. *These open, participatory fellowships are the subject of this book*, starting with chapter two.

Brace Yourself for a Barrage of Realities

But lest you get the idea that *MEGASHIFT* is about my pet theories of how things ought to be, chapter one will pepper you with

40 brief sketches of miracles of today, absolutely none of which were my doing. God is the one behind all this, and I'm just the pencil pusher He picked to scribble them down.

You may have a hard time believing some of these reports, but I've done my best to nail them down with almost 400 footnotes and endnotes plus a few photos. Be assured, I know nothing about flying saucers, crop circles, or the Bermuda Triangle, nor am I interested. I'm presenting to you the new world, the *real* world composed of granite facts.

Yet if you look carefully, you may see yourself in between the lines, doing things you always wanted to do, living a life you always wanted to live. Hang on tight, it's going to be a bumpy ride, but fun.

I'll start off here with an event that may cause you to rethink everything:

As I was leaving New Delhi, India, in March of 2003, I phoned a friend who leads a huge and growing network of house churches, Rodrick Gilbert.[2] I confessed to him, "Rod, I've got a credibility problem back in the States when I teach about resurrections. Could you send somebody over here to the hotel before I leave, somebody who's come back from the dead, so I can get a picture?"

So he graciously brought ...

Savitri and Arjun

At six o'clock on an April evening in 2001, five-year-old Arjun Janki Dass died in New Delhi from an accidental electrocution.

His parents took him to a medical clinic where they worked on his body for two hours—without success. The doctor charged them 5,000 rupees (about $110) and told them to call a mortician.

Instead they called Rodrick at the nearby Deliverance Church. He then called upon Savitri, one of his staff members.

Savitri brought two other Christians to Arjun's home, and the five of them began praying over the dead body about 10:00 P.M. They prayed their hearts out for six hours. Then at 4:00 A.M. the next morning, Arjun snapped back to life—no brain damage, no problems.

Today, he's a normal eight-year-old kid. I met with Savitri, Arjun, and his mother, Mina (see photos), and the boy is A-OK except for a nasty scar behind his left ear where the wire hit.

Savitri is a 60-year-old widow, a Dalit ("untouchable") from the lowly Dom caste. She spent her life as a street sweeper, which made her, in the caste system, the lowest of the low. The broom was her livelihood, and she remains today a fine, humble lady, a former Hindu turned to Christ.

As we were parting, I asked Savitri through an interpreter, "How many resurrections have you been involved with in the six years that

3

you've been doing ministry?"

She answered quietly, "Sixteen."

For a moment, my brain froze. Then I began to re-evaluate my life.

I would give you Savitri's e-mail address so you could check her out for yourself, but she doesn't have one. She can't read.

See photos in photo section.

You're in a New World

How long will it be before you start working some miracles yourself? That depends.*

1. It depends mostly on God's timing. Since about the mid-1980s, a tide of miracles has begun to engulf the entire planet. As time goes on, miracles are multiplying like loaves and fishes.

(By now, so many people have seen actual miracles that it has almost become more difficult to doubt than to believe.)

2. It also depends some on where you are. Robert Edwards, a local friend, once prayed and brought a very dead baby back to life on a visit to India, but in the twenty years since has done nothing like that.[3] And you may recall that Jesus himself was almost completely stymied by the unbelief in his home town. (Mark 6:5)

3. Finally, it depends a lot on *you*—which is the quiet theme behind this very noisy chapter.

It depends on your **obedience**.

It depends on the strength of your **faith**—or your desperation!

It depends on your faithfulness in your **mission**. Many miracles happen in the process of evangelism.

It depends on your **ears** as you learn to listen to God.

The rest of this chapter will illustrate these four factors. Vividly.

Grind-It-Out Obedience

The first catalyst of miracles is simple obedience.

• A distinguished Indian evangelist named Sadhu Chellappa was on a mission trip to a village north of Madras, when in the middle of the night he suddenly sensed God speaking to him: *Leave this house quickly and run away!*

Not exactly a convenient thing to do. But Chellappa was used to accepting even strange instructions from the Lord without discussion, so he dressed quickly and ran into the darkness.

---

*Pro forma note: The power for all true miracles comes from God, not people.

4

After a while, he was in open country. Then as he passed beneath a large tree, he felt God tell him, "Stay here and start to preach!"

Now, even for an experienced evangelist, this was puzzling—there was no one to be seen. Why did God want him to preach to an empty field in the middle of the night? But he stopped under the tree and began to preach the gospel.

Finally he reached the point at which he called on his unseen listeners to give their lives to Jesus. He was surprised to hear a voice from the top of the tree and see a man climb down, crying.

He tearfully give his life to Jesus. When Chellappa asked why he was in a tree out in the middle of nowhere, the man admitted, "I came out here to hang myself."[4]

Obedience is everything.

• For 21 years Mrs. Chang had lain in bed at her home in China, unable to move her arms or legs. Finally, the pain got to be too much, and she asked her eldest son to take her to the hospital, 40 miles away.

The doctors there discovered that some of her organs were almost dead, so they advised her son, "Take her home so she can die with your family."

But before she left, a Christian nurse came by her bed and slipped her a copy of the Gospel of Mark. "Read this when you get home," she whispered.

When Mrs. Chang got home, about the first thing she did was to ask her son to read something from the booklet. Opening it to page one, he began: "This is the good news of Jesus Christ ..." Before he could read any further, Mrs. Chang's bones started to move. Within moments, she sat up, completely healed! She promptly gave her life to the Lord.

The next day, on her way to the village well to draw water, she was asked by everyone, "Say, aren't you Mrs. Chang? What doctor healed you? We want to use him too!"

Mrs. Chang invited all the women to her simple home. When a large group had assembled, she stood and began speaking: "This is the good news of Jesus Christ ..."

In only four weeks, all 600 people of the village decided to follow Jesus!

From there, the story gets even more interesting: When the report got around, a police force arrived to stamp out this "new sect." They beat the villagers, shot their animals, burned the crops, and left, thinking that would be the last they would ever hear about this Jesus Christ.

They were oh, so wrong: The 600 converts remained steadfast, and within four years, *70,000 turned to Christ throughout the whole region.*[5]

The star of this story? The faithful nurse. Unlike Chellappa, she was not a famous evangelist responding to a startling voice from heaven. She was a nobody responding to the love in her heart, reaching out (despite the risk) to a withered, unimportant old lady. May her obedience be sung and celebrated by millions.

• I have a good friend named Barclay Tait who sells vacation real estate in Niceville, Florida. (Yes, Niceville.) Back in 1977, he was a 36-year-old Florida basketball coach. That summer, he decided to hitch-hike to a Christian conference in Front Royal, Virginia.

Arriving four days early, he went to a nearby forest and pitched his tent by a stream. On the last day, a tall, thin hiker with a notebook under his arm suddenly appeared, startling him as he read his Bible.

They introduced themselves, and Barclay explained his presence: "I came out here to fast and meditate."

The hiker, whose name was Dave, replied, "Well, I'm an intercessor What would you like me to pray for?"

Feeling somewhat overwhelmed, Barclay said, "Uh, frankly, I'd like prayer for a wife—one that God would choose for me."

It was a very brief conversation. The man wrote the request in his notebook, promised to pray, and walked on.

Fast-forward eleven years to 1988. Barclay has been married for a while, and he and his lively wife, Sherry, have been divinely guided to move to Asheville, North Carolina, though they don't know anyone there. Within three hours, however, Barclay has a house and a job. Also, a chance encounter in the Holiday Inn parking lot leads them to a Christian group on a hilltop outside of town at the home of a UNC professor.

Arriving just before the 7:00 P.M. meeting, they see about fifteen cars parked by a rustic log house. They walk in and find the people chatting—all strangers to them. But just then, the host walks in from the kitchen and stops dead in his tracks.

"I know you!" he exclaims, pointing his finger. *"You're Barclay Tait!"*

Barclay draws a blank.

"Just a minute. I have something I want to show you," the host announces. He scampers upstairs, leaving the puzzled Taits standing in the middle of the suddenly hushed room. In a moment he reappears with a well-worn ledger book. "See here? This is where I wrote your prayer request in column one when I met you in Front Royal in 1977: 'Barclay Tait: God's choice for a wife.'"

Barclay looks. It is the most detailed, methodical prayer journal he's ever seen.

"I prayed for you for seven years," proclaims Dave. "Then in the middle of the night on December 30, 1984, God woke me up out of a sound sleep and said, 'Write in your journal, *Prayer Answered.*' So I did. See? Here in column two, *Prayer Answered.*"

Barclay and Sherry look at each other with their mouths open. They sit down, and their eyes fill with tears. Quietly, Barclay tells Dave, "That was the day we were married."

Dave had learned how to talk with God, faithfully and obediently. You can too.

Five Stories of Faith and Desperation

The second factor in miracles is a desperate faith:

• In June, 1999, two Korean women came to pray for a village in Uzbekistan. Although they spoke only Korean, they were invited (by gestures) to enter a home and pray for an old man who was unable to move.

One of the ladies, Kim, said later, "The lame man began to wriggle, and then stood up as though someone had just cut his chains. He was healed!"

But as he got to his feet, the Koreans suddenly realized that the impressed bystanders had no idea *why* the man was healed. So in desperation, Kim began explaining the gospel in Korean, hoping they would understand a word or two and catch the drift.

To their amazement, the people listened in rapt attention for the next 20 minutes—because they were all hearing her in their own language! More than 40 people became followers of Christ that day.[6]

> *And they were all amazed and marvelled, say-*
> *ing one to another ... how hear we every man*
> *in our own tongue, wherein we were born?*
> Acts 2:7-8

• On a Sunday morning in 1996, Thai missionary Lun Poobuanak was conducting a quiet service for the few Christians in a Buddhist village in Kalasin Province, Thailand.

He was interrupted by the arrival of the village leader, who challenged him, "Because the monsoon rains have not come, the harvest in our fields is almost ruined. If you will ask your God for rain this month, all 134 families in the village will worship your god and become Christians."

Lun warned them not to play with God. But the leader replied, "We're serious. We swear we will follow your God. If not, He can judge us."

So the Christians prayed and fasted for three days. (Imagine the spiritual pressure.) On the fourth day, there was a cloudburst so heavy that all the canals and rice fields were flooded. All 134 families became Christians.

Not in Kansas Anymore

We're stunned.

Even those of us who are veteran leaders in the church are walking around with our mouths open, saying, "Things like this have never happened before."

We're like Dorothy in *The Wizard of Oz*, telling her dog, "Toto, I don't think we're in Kansas anymore."

Miracles are happening like popcorn starting to pop. That alone is amazing. But they are also attracting global numbers that no movement in history has ever seen.

Back in 1970, the world had **71 million** *core apostolics*, born-again Christians with a vision to reach out to the world. (The term is explained in endnote 15.) As of mid-2000, it had **707 million**.

That comes to 11% of the planet. And it doesn't even count the more than one billion Christians who are growing too slowly to fall within the fast-growing core. Their ingrown cultures, spiritual inertia, or liberal beliefs have stunted their growth.

But surprisingly, it *does* include North America and Europe, where the overall growth rate for Christians is nearing zero. We've gotten so used to being on a no-growth treadmill that it comes as a major brain-shock whenever a yankee, euro, or canuck hears these numbers for the first time.

THE BOTTOM LINE: True, free, Biblical Christianity is at last on the loose, and it is rapidly displacing all the other religions of the world. This is the new reality. Christ is the Creator, and He is swiftly taking over the planet, primarily because He is free to work through all of us, not just certified officials.

Any religion that denies His sovereignty is begging to take up residence in a museum.

Rain incidents are fun! You'll find four more in this endnote.[7]

• In the small Southern Mexico village of Chiconamiel, an epidemic of black measles swept through in 1998 and quickly killed about forty people.

Two of the victims were teenage girls, daughters of a widow who was a fairly new Christian. By the time the girls died, there was no one left in town healthy enough to help her carry the girls' bodies to the graveyard. So the poor woman had to drag both bodies there herself.

Because of the plague, there were only two young men still strong enough to dig graves, so there was a line of 21 corpses waiting to be buried. The woman tenderly laid the bodies at the end of the line, and since it was hot, sprinkled a lot of white lime powder over the bodies as a disinfectant. Then she set off walking down the mountain.

The next morning, after eight hours of walking, she reached the town where her Christian contacts lived. But since the men were in the midst of a heavy prayer and fasting meeting, she had to wait two hours more to see them. By that time, they didn't think they could climb back up the hill to Chiconamiel before nightfall, so they waited till the next morning.

When they finished the uphill trek, it was evening again, and the girls' bodies were only three or four away from being buried.

The men gathered around the bodies in a circle, as the disciples did for Paul when he had been stoned and left for dead in Acts 14:19. They prayed in the authority of the Lord Jesus Christ, and they called the girls by name.

Both of the dead girls sat up!

The young men then had a good laugh as they watched the girls trying to spit the lime powder out of their mouths.[8]

This is but one of the many highly varied occurrences in southern Mexico (plus the highlands of Guatemala) that have sprung from the work of the Freedom Ministries staff. To date, they have seen over 300 come back from death. (They've stopped counting.) This is the world's major epicenter of resurrections.

Freedom Ministries was founded and is led by David Hogan, a boisterous but very cautious American who has been present at 22 of these events. He no longer rushes to the scene of a reported death when they send for him. Like Jesus with Lazarus, he often delays in order to complete previous ministry assignments God has given him. And when he does arrive, he preaches a sermon to the bystanders. Gospel first, resurrection afterward!

- **"BONNKE RAISES MAN FROM DEATH IN ONITSHA"** screamed the banner headline in Nigeria's *Post Express*.

Actually, Reinhard Bonnke was upstairs preaching to an auditorium full of conference attendees at the time and knew nothing about the resurrection occurring downstairs in the children's department of the church. Other than that, the writeup was accurate.

The event is a welcome touch of verifiability because some of it was caught on videotape, and you can order it from Bonnke's organization, Christ for All Nations. What follows is my condensation of the website report by Robert Murphree and George Canty, which you can view in full at www.cfan.org/offices/usa/testimonies/resurrection/page1.htm, which in turn is a condensation of the video.[9]

On the morning of November 30, 2001, Daniel Ekechukwu, the pastor of Power Chapel Evangelical Church in Onitsha, Nigeria, with his friend Kingsley Iruka, took a Christmas present of a goat to his father in a village near the town of Owerri.

Why Don't They Put These Things in the Papers and on TV?

The short answer is, they can't.

Readers/viewers and industry critics would tar them with accusations of sensationalism, gullibility, fomenting religious hysteria, promoting cults, falling for frauds and hoaxes, yellow journalism, etc.

Another reason is that very few reporters are evangelicals who like to attend healing crusades. That means that reports of miracles come to them second-hand and thus are suspect.

Biblical religion does not occupy a revered position in most big-city newsrooms. So if an evangelist rents a hall or sets up a tent, the typical editor will not be motivated to assign a reporter, much less a camera team, to spend three hours filming the healer's every move in hopes that a clear miracle will happen. And any reporter who would promise his editor a splashy miracle ahead of time would receive a smile normally reserved for the village idiot.

On one notable occasion, the national press *had* to report on a miracle. It was when Cheryl Salem (née Prewitt) was chosen Miss America 1980. They don't award that crown to limping girls with a left leg that's two inches short, which was her condition after she almost died in a car crash at age 11. But at 17, on October 21, 1974, God instantantaneously lengthened her leg to normal in a Kenneth Hagin healing meeting. The Lord did such a perfect job that five years later in Atlantic City she even won the swimsuit preliminary. The judges hardly noticed her less-than-great bustline because her legs were so stunning!

At the big press conference the next morning, the first questions were about the faith healing. As Cheryl launched into her story, she commented later, "a wonderful thing began to happen. Incredibly, faces that had been hardened by years of skepticism began to soften into those belonging more to curious children. Hardly hostile, the press was fascinated!"

The soft-but-hard ambivalence of media people was revealed precisely in a comment afterward. As reporters were leaving, Cheryl overheard one say to another, "You know, it's the darnedest thing. To hear her speak, she could almost make a believer out of me!"[10]

Almost, but not quite.

On the way home, going down a steep road, the brakes failed on Daniel's 20-year-old Mercedes 230. Gathering speed, it hurtled downhill and smashed into a stone pillar.

Without a seat belt, Daniel was catapulted violently forward. His head hit the windshield, and the steering wheel knob punched into his body. Iruka, shocked though not badly hurt, turned to Daniel, hoping all was well. But the sight appalled him. Blood was pouring from Daniel's nose from a head injury, and then he began vomiting blood from heavy internal hemorrhage.

Rescue presently came. Marvelously, Daniel held up until he was placed in the local hospital's intensive care, or the best Nigerian equivalent of it. His wife, Nneka, was sent for. She found Daniel still alive but just barely. He hung on to life to ask her to have him taken to his family doctor's hospital in Owerri—a very serious mistake. It meant anything but a smooth ride of one and a half hours.

Within minutes of being lifted into the ambulance, Daniel felt himself dying. He tried to whisper his last words and instructions to Nneka. But his speech slurred, became incoherent, and stopped as he drifted into unconsciousness.

The ambulance driver pushed on at full speed, however, warning sirens blaring. Reaching the Owerri Regional Hospital, they ran in shouting, "Emergency! Emergency!" Daniel's doctor was not on duty, so a member of the medical staff took charge and checked Daniel's limp form. He turned to Nneka with a sad face. He could only certify that Daniel was already dead.

Naturally, Nneka was shocked. But a Bible verse had been ringing in her mind from Hebrews 11: "Women received their dead raised to life again." Then a non-rational conviction seized her: This meant *her!*

The text in Nneka's head made it impossible for her to accept the plain evidence that Daniel had gone or allow him to be buried. Her agitation dictated that something must be done. But at 11:30 P.M., when they brought Daniel's body to Dr. Jossy Anuebunisa at the St. Eunice Clinic, he confirmed the death.

From there the body was taken to the Ikeduru General Hospital Mortuary, not far away. The resident mortician, Mr. Barlington R. Manu, carried out the normal checks at 1:00 A.M. Saturday.

The mortuary having no cold storage facilities, the mortician administered the usual chemical preservative injection and prepared the body for embalming on the following morning. With a staff member he laid the body out on a mortuary slab between two other dead people. Everyone then retired for the night.

Convinced her husband would live again, Nneka wanted the body taken to the church in Onitsha where Reinhard Bonnke was to speak at a dedication ceremony of the Grace of God Ministries. So the next morning, Sunday, December 2, they went to take the body from the mortuary.

But the mortician was worried about their intentions. To hide the fact that a body was being taken away, he dressed it for a funeral as a pretext, placed it in a coffin, and shut the lid. They took Daniel in his coffin and set off on the long drive to Onitsha.

11

Arriving at the Onitsha church compound, the state security officer and the ushers saw them driving up with a coffin and ordered them to turn around and leave. But Nneka pled and persisted, so after checking the coffin for a terrorist bomb, they relented and allowed the body to be taken out and carried into the church, but only the downstairs part.

The church bishop's son Paul and another pastor on the church staff, Bathcomery Nkwando, laid the body on a table and found that rigor mortis had made the limbs "stiff as an iron rod," they said. Two other staff pastors, Lawrence Onyeka and Luke Ibekwe, joined them to guard the body. Upstairs, meanwhile, Bonnke went on preaching and praying with no knowledge of the body downstairs.

Before long, the pastors noticed a slight twitching of the stomach of the corpse. Then they saw the corpse draw a breath and begin breathing "in short bursts." Encouraged, they called for a video camera and threw themselves into powerful petitionary prayer, stripped the body of the mortuary gloves, socks, and shirt and began massaging it from head to foot. As this news broke out in the sanctuary above, it created pandemonium. Then at 5:15 P.M., nearly two days after his death, Daniel opened his eyes, sat up, and leaned on Pastor Lawrence.

People began crowding into the hall to see this resurrection man. Lawrence was worried Daniel would not have enough oxygen, so he carried him into the church sanctuary where Daniel spoke for the first time since his death: "Water! Water!" They gave him sips and then warm tea.

To give him a clear space, they seated him on a chair on the platform, where hundreds of people saw him slowly recovering. He had not yet collected his thoughts, and for a while could not recognize anyone, not even his own son. By evening, however, he was fully coherent. And as you will see on the video, Daniel is 100% lucid today.

This was a very public event and has been documented like no other resurrection. See endnote 9.

See photos in photo section

• A markedly different kind of resurrection was seen in South Africa in 1999. I spoke with South African pastor Jimmy Crompton to verify the news report about a friend of his named Ronny Sampson.

Sampson is a retired businessman who was enjoying a quiet visit with his daughter in Johannesburg when loud screaming sent him running into the street.

He met a totally hysterical woman carrying the body of her daughter, which had just been found at the bottom of a swimming pool. Sampson commented later, "Nobody knew how long she had been there, but she was completely blue, had no pulse, and had ceased to breathe."

While others called an ambulance, Sampson took the woman and child into his daughter's house and started to pray.

After twenty frustrating minutes of fruitless prayer, he finally became quite angry and started shouting loud commands at the "spirit of death" that held the girl.*

That made the difference. Suddenly, the child turned over, regurgitated a huge amount of water, and started to scream. In fact, her screams, combined with those of her still distraught mother, helped the ambulance find the house quickly.

The paramedics pronounced the girl completely healthy, and examinations showed there was no brain damage. A Dutch television team came from Holland and made a docudrama of the event.[11]

None of these five events had a star who set out to engineer a miracle. They were all people who got boxed in by circumstance and fought back with the only thing they had: their faith. The next time you get boxed in, think about that.

How Do You Resurrect Someone?

There is no one "technique" for resurrections. The "methods" run the gamut:

• I think of one missionary in Guatemala who simply read all of Isaiah 53 over and over to a circle of Indians silently mourning the death of a boy until he came back.

• I think of Duad, Manu, and some other members of the Indian Pentecostal Church in Dunger, Northern India, who simply prayed in Jesus' name and placed their Bibles on the body of a six-year-old boy who was near to being buried—whereupon he opened his eyes.[12]

• I think of a handful of Christians in Chilengo, Mexico, who spent long hours praying for a 20-year-old believer who had suddenly fallen dead from a massive seizure. In one corner of the living room, the ladies were decorating her body with small flowers, while the men prayed and talked in another. When one of the men went outside to relieve himself, he was alarmed to encounter a large, evil-looking black man and a big, black dog. (There are zero black men in that area, so this had no racial meaning for him. It was just plain scary.) He ran back inside to get help. When one of the men came out and said, "In the name of Jesus Christ, leave!" the dog took off running into the

---

*Lest you think you've discovered "the method" for bringing people back from the dead, let me say that yelling angry orders at a spirit of death is kind of unusual.

woods and his master followed. As the men walked shakily back into the house, they found the girl sitting up, brushing the flowers off her arms. They then understood that what they had seen running away was not a man at all, but a manifestation of the spirit of death.[13]

So other than a lot of prayer* there is no method but God. Resurrections are His show, not ours.

Now you've seen some examples of how *obedience* and *faith* are factors in the miracles you may perform in the future. Before we continue, let's take a break to look at ...

The Great Reversal

The direction of world events has made a sharp turn. Before the mid-1980s, Christians were growing about 2% a year, barely above the world population growth rate. Now God has stormed onto the scene like a tornado. Compare today's annual growth rates:[14]

- World Population   1.2%
- Buddhists   0.9%
- Hindus   1.1%
- Muslims   1.8%

- All "Christians"   1.1%
- All Protestants   1.4%
- Core Apostolics   8.0%

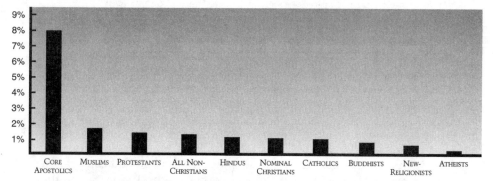

Why the World Will Soon Be Christian *Not only are core apostolics growing far faster than Muslims, Hindus, Buddhists, and new agers, but in fair and even encounters, spiritual power prevails and Jesus wins perhaps 99% of the time. The main defenses of other religionists are not theological arguments, but violence, persecution, legal barriers, and propagandistic falsehoods.*

Core apostolics are the new saints who are at the heart of the mushrooming kingdom of God. The term and the category are both

---

* An hour's worth of prayer is not uncommon. The most I've heard of was a lady who prayed at the bedside of her husband's emaciated, cancer-ridden corpse for 13 hours in a hospital. Kneeling on a pillow, she rebuffed all staff attempts to get her to go home. When her husband finally came back, he said, "I wish to go home." The doctors threw up their hands in horror: "Why, that could kill him!"

mine, but they're not at all subjective. They stand for a very real and countable movement of more than 707 million switched-on disciples.

As you can see, the growth rate of Protestants (and Christians in general) are so terribly low that they had clouded the picture, hiding the white-hot growth of the core apostolics. But now I feel you have yet another cause for celebration: the clear identification of an extremely strong center of the new Christianity. If you don't mind some tedious reading, you'll find my long-winded explanation of core apostolics and their numbers in this endnote.[15]

If you don't care for statistics, here's the gist:

> The growing core of Christianity crosses theological lines and includes 707 million born-again people who are increasing by 8% a year. These "core apostolics" are a powerful mix of Charismatics, Pentecostals, and Evangelicals whose main distinction is that they are in expanding, connected, easily countable networks.
>
> The term excludes those groups that are so liberal in theology, so isolated in structure, or so deeply rooted in medieval tradition that they are hardly growing at all.

More Christians Than People?

We rely on God, not statistical trends. Yet it's fascinating to realize that the current core apostolic growth rate would produce a world composed *entirely* of core apostolic Christians by 2032!

Of course, straight-line projections are a fool's game because life never goes in a straight line. There will be pockets of resistance and unforeseen breakthroughs. Still, at the rate we're growing now, to be comically precise, there would be more Christians than people by the autumn of 2032, about 8.2 billion.

In any case, the new realities are massive in scope. The future of your world is being rewritten at this very hour. For instance:

• Up until 1960, Western Evangelicals outnumbered non-Western Evangelicals—mostly Latinos, blacks, and Asians—by two to one. As of 2000, non-Westerners had shot ahead by four to one. By 2010, it will be seven to one![16] (Park this in the back of your brain for the next time you hear someone bad-mouth Christianity as "the white man's religion.")

• If you go through Latin America on a Sunday morning, you will now find more evangelicals than Catholics in church.

• As soon as we produce some church models that are culturally acceptable to Hindus, we could see an additional 70 to 100 million secret Indian Christians go public.

• There are now more missionaries sent from non-Western nations than Western nations.

Are you starting to see the outline of the new world? God writes history, but human eyes have trouble reading His handwriting. It's not that He writes too small, but too big.

Preach It, Bro

If you want to see miracles, the third catalyst is to spread the gospel. Miracles tend to happen when you're presenting Christ to people:

• Sanji Adonga, an Every Home for Christ staff member, was passing out tracts in a sprawling North African city of a million.

One Muslim in his mid-20s got really mad, tore up his tract, threw it in Sanji's face, and threatened to kill him.

The next morning at daybreak, moments after Sanji awoke, someone knocked on his door. It was the same young man, who introduced himself as Abdulai Masa and announced that he now wanted another tract.

"But—how did you find my address?" Sanji asked.

"Last night, a set of hands seized my shoulders and shook me awake violently," Abdulai explained. "I swung my arms, but there was nothing to hit. I turned on the light, sat up shaking, and lit a cigarette. Then a strong voice filled the room. 'YOU HAVE TORN UP THE TRUTH! THE MESSAGE YOU WERE GIVEN WAS GOD'S TRUTH THAT POINTS TO ETERNAL LIFE. IT TOLD OF THE ONLY WAY TO LASTING PEACE AND HAPPINESS, AND YOU HAVE *TORN IT UP!*' Then the voice gave me your address and told me to come at sunrise."

Abdulai took a six-month Bible course and is now a house-to-house evangelist.[17]

• An Egyptian I'll call Rahmad likes to go to remote villages to preach the gospel. At 70, he has his own simple way of speaking directly to people's hearts, and whole families get saved.

In 2000, he was in a village on the banks of the Nile, where twelve men and seven women accepted Christ. But "on the way home," Rahmad relates, "some bearded men approached me, obviously religious fanatics.

"I was suspicious and wanted to avoid them, but they had already started throwing stones at me. I was unprotected and saw my end coming. But as the first stones hit my body, I was surprised that they didn't hurt! Then I saw why: They were turning to dust as they hit me! I thanked God out loud, and my attackers realized that a miracle was happening before their very eyes—so they fled, afraid."[18]

• In the Zhoukou district of China, a rather new Christian began evangelizing on the streets. While he was preaching, a man came up and started swearing at him and beating him with a heavy stick.

The preacher began praying, "Lord, you have to answer my prayer now, or I'm going home!" Then he had a thought. "In Jesus' name, I *bind* you!" he declared.

Immediately, his attacker collapsed into a kneeling position *and was unable to move.*

Soon, five of his relatives came and tried to lift him up—with no success.

The young preacher, now emboldened, warned, "He is bound. If I don't pray for him, the only way you can move him is to hoist him into a truck."

At this, the crowd began shouting, "Please let him free!"

So the preacher relented. "All right, in Jesus' name, get up." The man quickly stood.

Many in that village believed in Jesus because of this wonder.*[19]

Chinese Christians never set out to do miracles. They insist that miracles just happen in the course of evangelizing.**

I believe them. Because of this principle, many Western mass evangelists find themselves running "healing crusades" instead of just gospel crusades.

• A distinguished but modest friend of mine—I'll call him Larry— was invited by German evangelist Reinhard Bonnke to visit his tent crusade in Botswana in 1986.

Seated on the platform with his wife, Mallory, looking out over the audience of 10,000, Larry was amazed to see numerous healings, including eight blind people who came forward and received their sight.

The next day at lunch, Larry got to chat with Bonnke, who said, looking downcast, "Gosh, Larry, I'm sorry you happened to come at such a slow time. We only had eight blind people healed last night."

Sharpen Your Ears

The fourth and final factor in learning to do miracles is learning to listen to the Holy Spirit.

I feel hypocritical in writing to you about this because my own spiritual sensitivity is somewhere just above plankton. But I do have spiritually wired friends whom I can turn to. Take, for instance,

---

* This phenomenon has happened so many times that missionaries have adopted a term to describe it: "getting stuck."
** It's interesting that most of the "evangelism miracles" in China are healings, whereas in India they are more often power confrontations—demonic deliverances or spiritual "turf battles" for a town or neighborhood under Satanic dominance.

Barclay Tait. God tells him all sorts of things about people he meets.

• For one example out of hundreds, in 1999 he was sitting on a bench at the outlet mall in Gatlinburg, Tennessee, when three couples and two children wearing jeans and T-shirts walked by.

Hearing something in his spirit, Barclay stood up and said, "How y'all doin' today! Which one of you is Eddie?" A short man hesitantly raised his hand. "Well, Eddie, God wants you to know that you made the right decision in your ministry. It was hard, but you did what the Lord wanted, and now He's going to bless you. So just ignore the folks who are criticizing you."

Of course that started Eddie crying. It's very touching when you find that God knows your name, knows your worries exactly, and cares enough to send a special messenger to give you a boost.

Over the next few years, the Spirit of God is going to be using such messages more and more as kingdom ministry grows and we need direction and reassurance along the way.*

Sometimes God sends us a message not as guidance, but just so we'll be ready for what's coming.

• Because my friends Kay and Julie Hiramine are well-known Christian leaders, they were invited to the big GCOWE convention in Seoul, Korea, in 1995. At that time, Julie was pregnant with their first child, but she wasn't showing. Yet during the convention, seven women approached her at seven different times with the same three-point message: "You're pregnant. You're going to have a girl. She's going to be a prophetess." These women were from *seven* countries on *four* continents, and none of them knew Julie.

Little Brianna arrived as promised, and sure enough, she has turned out to be a prophetess.** Try to explain away this one!

What the women in Seoul didn't mention was that Brianna was going to be a "Strong-Willed Child"—the crown princess, in fact, of all SWCs. As a two-year-old, she redefined "feisty." She has since mellowed, but without those messages in Seoul, Kay and Julie might have despaired or written off Brianna's prophecies as bratty, show-off behavior ... or worse.

• My friend Wolfgang Simson is an intellectual German, but he recently found himself in a predicament that required him to lay down his intellect and trust God like a child.

---

* In general, most of these messages are a reinforcement of what you already knew or sort of suspected. Much less often, they convey entirely new information. Or rarely, negative reproof.
** Her very first prophecy came at 18 months! As you might imagine, her syntax wasn't too sophisticated. But the message was accurate: It confirmed that a young couple named Paul and Nancy Rivas were to move from California to Colorado Springs for ministry here, to work with Kay and Julie. The message, delivered at a rather high decibel level, was: *PAUL AND NANCY! PAUL AND NANCY! HERE! NOW!!!* (Paul and Nancy came.)

He was scheduled to speak to a houseful of church leaders in Cairo at 5:45 P.M. His contact put him in a cab at 5:00, showed the driver an address, put it back in his pocket, and said farewell.

Half an hour later, the cab pulled up—in the wrong place! And Wolfgang didn't even know what the right address was. Moreover, his Arabic was almost nonexistent. He knew how to count from one to ten, and he knew the words for left, right, and straight ahead, but that was about it. He said a brief prayer for help, and God immediately answered, *Prophesy to the taxi driver!*

"Lord, I-I'm a Lutheran," he stammered in his native German, "and I don't even know which direction it is."

PROPHESY! came the same distinct voice of God again.

So with only fifteen minutes left, Wolfgang obediently began barking orders at the driver: "*Alatuhl!*" (Straight ahead) ... "*El-Shemahl!*" (To the left) ... "*El-Yameen!*" (To the right). Every corner, every alley was a decision, and he strained to feel the Holy Spirit's promptings as the cab bounced through Cairo's chaotic streets in the Egyptian heat. He even took it through shortcuts only a professional driver could have known. It was a high-speed proof-test of Isaiah 30:21: "*Whether you turn to the right or to the left, your ears will hear a voice behind you, saying, 'This is the way; walk in it.'*"

Exactly fifteen minutes later the cab came to a stop right in front of the meeting house. The wide-eyed cabbie, keenly aware of the supernatural nature of the trip, refused to take any fare!

The moral of this story is that **the world has changed, and God wants to speak to you directly, in practical ways, and you need to gear up for this, to learn to listen to Him.**

• Here is the most intricate miracle I've heard of (also from Wolfgang). As editor of the *Friday Fax*, read by seven million readers, he is at the vortex of information on church growth. (See box on page 42 for the Web address.) In 1998 he began to feel God wanted him to leave India and move to a more strategic location. He asked a number of his Christian friends to seek God for guidance on his behalf.

It wasn't long in coming. I'll boil these down:

One of them (Bernard Ankoma of Ghana) said, "You're going to go back to the homeland of your mother."

Another said, "Borders. I see a place surrounded by national borders."

Another said, "I see a nice, clean river. Your place is near a bend in the river."

"Yes, it's hilly country," someone else chimed in, "and I have the name of that river. It's the *Rhine.*"

A YWAM staff member added, "Your home is the middle unit in a triplex. It's got green doors, green window frames, and there's a chimney on one end."

"And don't worry about money," one declared. "I know you don't have any, but God's got it covered for you."

In all, ten friends responded to Wolfgang's request for help. On that basis, he and his wife, Mercy, packed up and went to his mother's homeland, Germany. Arriving there, they went to a town near the Rhine and soon found the triplex with the green windows and doors and the chimney.

(In July, 2000, I stayed with the Simsons, and their home is indeed in a little finger of German territory that juts out into Switzerland near Zurich; there are Swiss borders on three sides within 700 meters.)

The unit was for sale, and he found the owner and introduced himself, "Hello, I'm Wolfgang Simson."

"Oh, yeah," he replied, "the guy who's going to buy my house. God told me someone named Simson was going to buy it. You must be a Christian, too, so here's the keys. Don't worry about money, we'll do the paperwork later. Just give me a down payment when you get it."

THE FROSTING ON THE CAKE: After they got most of their things moved in, Wolfgang decided to clean out the mailbox, as the unit had been vacant for a while. One envelope in the pile was from Switzerland. It was addressed only to the street number. Inside was a letter from a man he'd never heard of, saying, "The Lord has given us this address and impressed upon us that we are to send you fifty thousand Swiss francs. Please send your name and account information so we can wire the money."

Welcome to team Christianity. People with ears, working in teams, will sooner or later outnumber those sitting in rows. Perhaps you can see why.

Intermission Time

OK, let's take time out for a minute and come up for air again.

First, a question: *Why am I telling you all these things?*

Am I trying to impress you? No. I'm trying to reorient you.

Am I trying to get you more excited about what God is doing? Sure, but I'm going for more than an *ooh* or *aah* or *Hallelujah*. I'm hoping you'll join the excitement and become a working part of the miracle scene—and add even more people to the crowds coming to Christ every day. I hope you'll open your eyes, spread your wings, and learn to fly out of whatever cage you may be cooped up in.

Face it, your future changed when you picked up this book. You can't go back to wherever you were. You "know too much," as B-movie mobsters used to say. It may be time for you to disengage from whatever lifestyle you've been living (good or bad) and take on a new identity. (See especially chapter three on "The New Saints.")

If you're like most of us, you've fantasized now and then about getting a fresh start in life. Well, that's what God is offering you right now. He's trashing many of the mindsets and traditions that have held us all back for 17 centuries, and He's setting up networks of strong disciples who know how to hear and take orders from Him directly. This global power shift is giving you an opportunity to leave behind bad habits and sins, deadening relationships, a weak self-image, ignorance, sickly finances, fear, anger, bitterness in your past, or anything else that could slow your sprint to the finish line.

As you're seeing in these pages, we're in a new ball game now. God is using these heart-turning miracles to challenge you to change your outlook and your values. *If you accept this challenge, you'll find yourself doing things you never thought you could do before.*

But for right now, I'll continue with more miracles because until your eyes have seen a number of pieces of the puzzle, your heart may not comprehend the scope of the jigsaw masterpiece He is fitting together.

It's Not About You

Sometimes God does a miracle unrelated to our needs, mostly to show us how wonderful He is. On several occasions, He has brought someone back to life for a few set hours or days—for a specific mission, usually evangelistic.

• In the state of Bihar, India, there is a notoriously anti-Christian tribe called the Malto. When a crew with Campus Crusade's *Jesus* film attempted to schedule a showing there in 1998, they were strongly rebuffed. A few days later, a 16-year-old Malto girl died. But that evening, just as her parents were about to bury her, she came back to life. As an awed crowd gathered around her, she told them that the God of the film crew had sent her back for seven days "to tell as many people as I can that He is real."

The girl and her mother went searching, and the next day, they found the crew in a nearby village and invited them back for a showing. For seven days she told her story in every village they could get to, drawing large crowds for the film. Hundreds of people became Christians and started churches.

After seven days the girl still looked fine, but she collapsed and died once again.[20]

• Two years later and half a world away, a 12-year-old gypsy girl died in Argentina. She had been a Christian for some months, but her attempts to be a witness to the tightly knit gypsy community had been rejected.

In the wee hours of the morning, in the middle of her funeral wake, she suddenly sat up in her casket, causing the people in attendance to jump up, rejoice and dance, and start dismantling the funeral setup.

"Don't take anything down!" the girl warned. "Jesus told me to return just to tell you that He loves you and that you have to accept Him if you want to be saved. That's the only reason I'm here. At ten o'clock, Jesus will come back for me, so leave everything like it is."

At ten A.M., her Lord Jesus came back and took her home.

Her gypsy friends swarmed into the kingdom.[21]

Stop Me If You've Heard This One

Many people, even dedicated Christians, read the miracles in the New Testament with glazed eyes, as if they were reports from a parallel universe.

That should end now. Many of today's incidents are reruns of familiar stories from the Bible:

• In the Punjab state of India, a city called Firozpur lies next to the Pakistan border. Everyone in that town knew a certain man who was so deranged that he had been kept on a chain like a wild animal for eight years.

But in April, 1997, God used an evangelist named Dale* to heal and deliver him. When he later ascended Dale's platform, with a helper carrying the now-useless chain, the crowd broke out in wild cheering.

See photos in photo section.

> *And they came to Jesus, and saw him that was possessed with the devil, and had the legion, sitting, and clothed, and in his right mind: and they were awe-struck.* Mark 5:15

On the last day of the mission in that gospel-hostile region, 50,000 came to hear more and to be healed. The healings included 94 deaf-mutes, 191 polio victims, 35 with tumors, 25 blind people, 12 with kidney stones, and many other illnesses.[22]

• Marilyn Hatfield, a former housekeeper of mine, is a high-energy lady who once put on a Christian camp for teenagers at Wilderness Ranch near St. David, Arizona. She only had about $30, so she prayed earnestly over the choice of food.

Came the first meal on Friday, and extra people showed up. Her two grocery sacks of chicken, rice, beans, oatmeal, powdered milk, and little else suddenly looked pretty small.

---

* I know his last name, but because of the constant persecution he faces, he prefers to use just his first name in public. See the next endnote for details.

22

But she set up a buffet line, said grace, and stood back as the crowd swept through: 20 adults, 16 boys, and two girls—and the teens were voracious eaters, Marilyn emphasizes. They especially swarmed over the chicken, which had all fit neatly into a slightly rounded pile in one medium cake pan.

She kept glancing at the pan nervously, and her eyes began to pop out when she saw that the pile of chicken never went down! The more they ate, the more there was. Perhaps 70 to 90 pieces were taken—much more than she started with. In fact, as Marilyn went to pull out a second piece for herself, she watched the pan intently, and as she yanked her piece from one end of the pile, she was shocked to see the other end jump like popcorn. (She was tempted to play with it by pulling out more, but decided, *Nooo, that might not be such a good idea.*)

The rice, beans, oatmeal, and milk grew apace with the chicken, and by the end of the meal, there was enough food left over to feed the 17 teens and three adults who stayed for the whole next week.[23]

And they did all eat, and were filled: and they took up of the fragments that remained twelve baskets full. Matthew 14:20

Dedivuchi, Russia: *This was the first time she had ever stretched out her hands like this.*

• In the small town of Dedivuchi, near Pskov, Russia, a team of three missionaries came to minister in May, 2000.

After one meeting in a three-room flat, a thin, brown-skinned woman presented her 5-year-old daughter to an American named Eric Olson and asked for prayer. The girl was paralyzed on her right side as a result of being dropped by a careless doctor at birth, and her right hand was curled and tucked in next to her body.

As Olson took her hand and prayed, he began to notice a strange vibration in his right wrist and felt little teardrops on his hand. The longer he prayed, the more openly the girl cried, so finally he gave her back to her mother. But a minute later, she stretched out her arm ... then her fingers ... and then raised her arm straight out in front of her body!

As her mother burst into tears and praised God, Olson got the idea of making

Playtime: *Never was a child so happy to play with soap bubbles.*

some bubbles with a bottle of soap he had. As he waved the wand, the smiling girl reached out and popped bubbles with both hands.[24]

> **Then saith he to the man, Stretch forth thine hand.** Matthew 12:13

• At the 1996 Olympics in Atlanta, Dr. Brad Ihrig was part of the Youth With A Mission team. He started pouring out cups of Gatorade to folks thirsty from the heat and was astounded to discover that his one-gallon (3.8 liter) bottle was staying full no matter how much he poured. After nearly 100 people got a drink, the Gatorade level had fallen about one inch.*[25]

That's an echo of the widow with her bottomless cruse of oil in the time of Elijah:

> *"They brought the jars to her and she kept pouring. When all the jars were full, she said to her son, 'Bring me another one.' But he replied, 'There is not a jar left.' Then the oil stopped flowing."* II Kings 4:6

These days, such events happen continually. Information from more than a million front-line Christian workers now flows daily to the desks of researchers. In the last month, I've had to throw away a stack of reports like these about five inches (13 cm) high. Just too much to catalog.

No Rumors

Yes, I know all this doesn't sound like the picture of the world you get from your local newspaper. But these accounts are *not* urban legends or Internet myths. I try to research and footnote wherever I can, using only reliable resources.**

In most cases, though, verification isn't even an issue for me because of the known integrity of my sources—like my own family:

• In 1995, my brother, Bob, and his wife, Joan, went to New Delhi to help out in a Peter Youngren gospel and healing crusade. Afterward, the cleanup crew had to rent *two* trucks to haul away all the castoff wheelchairs, crutches, and prosthetic devices.

---

* Dr. Ihrig poured from the same bottle the next day, and the Gatorade disappeared as fast as usual.
** If you wish to check out the truth of the latest wild rumor, there are several websites that verify or debunk, such as www.truthminers.com, www.truthorfiction.org, www.snopes.com, www.ship-of-fools.com, and www.urbanlegends.com.

• My nephew Jonathan Rutz was at the Light the Nations conference in Dallas in 1998, along with his wife, Ashley, and their three young children. They got there on faith, with no money.

On the last day, during a time of singing, Ashley felt distressed about dinner (being pregnant and hungry). She prayed, "Lord, we've got *no* food left and *no* money, not even enough for gas to get home to Arkansas. Could you give me some kind of sign that you're still interested in us?"

The Spirit told her, *Just lift up your hands and praise me anyway.* So as she sat there, she lifted her arms and sang along with the rest of the 6,000 people.

After a few moments, she felt something in her left hand. She opened her eyes, and it was money! Looking down at her was a middle-aged lady she'd never seen before, who said, "I don't know why, but God told me to come over and give you this!"

His ravens are not dead yet.*

I could go on with more first-hand stories: my cousin Audrey being cured of cancer; my Aunt Velma being healed of a serious neck injury; my cousin Carol being spectacularly cured of constant, lifelong pain; my athletic nephew Dan, who was born quite pigeon-toed, being given perfectly straight feet, etc.

As you see, this book is heavy on examples from my family and friends. But I'm not trying to wow you with the remarkable people I know. I'm just trying to show you I'm not pushing rumors.

Every 25 Minutes

When I was a kid in Sunday school, I was really impressed that 3,000 people were saved on the Day of Pentecost. I thought, *Wow, that'll never happen again!*

How wrong I was. It now happens around the globe every 25 minutes.

That adds up fast. Be very encouraged: **By tomorrow, there will be 175,000 more Christians than there are today.**** That means, no matter how rotten a day you have today, no matter how many things go haywire, when the sun comes up tomorrow you will have 175,000 new brothers and sisters in Christ in 238 nations around the world!

• One example of how these numbers can happen today: In Lagos, Nigeria, in November, 2000, Reinhard Bonnke held the largest crusade

---

* The reference is to I Kings 17:4, where ravens brought food to Elijah. God actually did use an eagle to feed an Operation Mobilization team one day in Nepal. See the narrative in Friday Fax #9, 1997.
** This is conversions plus births minus deaths. Refers to Christians of any description. The number for core apostolics is 155,000. The other 20,000 come mostly from Catholicism, Orthodoxy, and Mainline Protestantism.

in world history. During the six days and nights, almost six million people came, and 3,400,000 registered decisions for Christ—1,093,745 of them on the last night!

An integral part of the Spirit's move: Hundreds of thousands were healed of every condition imaginable. Many of them were "checked out" by the 1,000 physicians who came nightly for that purpose.

You may ask, "Even with methodical Germans in charge, how on earth did they handle that many new converts?" The answer is, they had 30,000 ushers and spent six months training 200,000 counselors![26]

Campus Crusade for Christ now estimates we'll see a billion new converts in the next ten years. My numbers project a net growth of the

Your Words Have More Power Than You Think

In *The 2 Minute Miracle*, my colleague Lynn Reddick relates a story from a friend of his, gospel singer Candy Hemphill Christmas. It's about a childhood friend of hers named Bobby:

Over the years he became rebellious as anger, bitterness, and resentment took root in his life—against God, his parents, and his church. His life became consumed with drugs as he gradually became shackled with addictions.

One day Bobby disappeared. His brokenhearted parents didn't know if he killed himself with an overdose or was murdered by a drug gang. For two years they didn't hear anything from their son, not one phone call or letter.

He simply vanished.

Bobby's dad felt the crushing grip of months of pent-up frustration and pain while driving on the outskirts of the Arkansas city where he lived. He pulled his car off on the side of the road, got out and walked off some distance from the highway. He pointed his finger towards the north and yelled with all his might, "BOBBY, COME HOME!" Turning to the south, he shouted in the wind, "BOBBY, COME HOME!" To the east and west, same words.

Two days later, this dad heard a knock at the door. There stood Bobby. *Bobby was home.*

It didn't take long before his dad asked, "Son, what brought you home?"

"Dad," Bobby said, "I was sitting on the front porch of an old shack on the edge of the desert in Arizona, stoned out of my mind. A wind started blowing and suddenly grew stronger. Dad, I could have sworn that I heard your voice in the wind, BOBBY, COME HOME! And Dad, I got here just as fast as I could."[27]

Proverbs 18:21: "Life and death are in the power of the tongue."

body of Christ at a billion and a half. But any way you slice it, the kingdom is expanding at a heart-pounding pace. I'm not being triumphalistic or arrogant here, I'm just reporting the numbers. From 1970 to 2000, core apostolics doubled every nine years.

From our vantage point in North America and Europe, where church membership is going nowhere, this sounds like a cooked-up fantasy. But it's true. This is the biggest megashift in history. Can you think of any time when over a billion people eagerly changed their lives and loyalties in one generation?

Within a few years, at current rates, the character of whole nations will be transformed. Majorities will become minorities and vice versa.

As national strongholds of sin are dismantled and pits of misery cleaned up, the true purpose of God for many nations will be revealed. We are in the early stages of a total transformation of our planet.

Victory Shock

You know from thousands of experiences that life is difficult. You've come to expect daily problems. Maybe you've become a pessimist or even a cynic.

But now you're going to have to make an emotional adjustment to handle with humility what I call *victory shock*, the sudden realization that we're winning—that the Holy Spirit is dismantling the foundations of the prince of this world and revealing the Father's glory, which is off-the-scale dazzling.

Once you become an eyewitness to a few miracles—or begin to "assist" in a few yourself—your priorities will get a good shaking up. For example, once you discover you have a gift for healing eye problems or find you can plant a new church every six to eight weeks, your enthusiasm for spending your Saturdays watching the tube or puttering around the house will evaporate.

Pessimism is passé, boredom is obsolete, and defeatism is dead. Adjust to it! Makes no difference if your mental landscape was laid out by John Calvin, Bill Gates, or MTV: If you don't upgrade your head, you're about to become as antiquated as a cuneiform spreadsheet. Don't succumb to pride and conceit, just get with God's program.

The few miracles in this chapter only hint at the big picture, which could fill an encyclopedia. So let's ask the big question: Where do *you* fit into that picture? Could you have a place in this tornado? You bet. Paul hammers on this point in I Corinthians 12. You *do* have a spiritual gift (probably several, in fact). So as they say, use it or lose it.

At long last, there *is* a way to use it—and it's not by wasting away in a pew, counting the dead flies in the fluorescent light fixtures.

There's a new Christianity unfolding before our eyes, and it's bringing enough adventure to fill a Hollywood action movie. I'll unpack it in chapters two through five, but in the meantime, this is what it amounts to: We have streamlined the church by cutting out the middlemen (the pastors, the committees, and the denomination officials) and dealing directly with God. We're helping Him create a new world.

Say Goodbye to Limits

Faith creates new realities.

That's what the Bible means by, "Faith gives substance to things hoped for." (Hebrews 11:1)

Ever feel cramped? Tired of tight limits on your life? Want to double or triple the size of your personal universe? Then Christ-based faith is your answer. Christ is the One who spoke all things into existence. (John 1:3)

"According to your faith be it unto you," He said more than once. And a whole lot of us, especially gen-X types, are pretty motivated to expand our little universes, to escape our limits.

Do you have a Christian background? If so, I hope you love the tradition-encrusted church—with all its faults—as much as I do. But perhaps you're one of those who just can't push themselves to show up on Sunday morning anymore. You love God and believe the Bible, but were disappointed in the church because it didn't meet your needs ...

The Only Known Cure for AIDS

If you have AIDS or are HIV positive, your best bet is a quick trip to Africa, where people are being cured in churches.

For instance, the Synagogue Church of All Nations was founded seven years ago with eight people. Now this church in Lagos, Nigeria, has 250,000, give or take. Their pastor, T.B. Joshua, can't pray for everyone who attends, but he prays for quite a few. So far, over 10,000 have been cured of AIDS, each attested by two medical certificates (before and after). In fact, to belong to their "AIDS Congregation," you must present three certificates, the third one dated three months after your healing.* (Caution: Opinions about Joshua are divided. A number of local leaders claim he is involved with the occult; others defend him in great detail.)

John K. Nduati meets with universal approval. He is currently seeing about 1,000 AIDS victims a week healed at his church in Nairobi. See his story on pages 35-38.

*Source: *Compass Magazine* (England), Summer 2001, pp. 16ff.

or make you feel significant ... or help you rise above the mundane routine of life. There are 23 million in the U.S. who have made a conscious decision at some point to follow the Lord Jesus Christ, yet seldom go to church anymore.[28]

If that's you, then rejoice: There is now a different universe for you to inhabit. Participants in the new Christianity live in a new world where the old, ordinary limits are fading fast. Pushing the envelope of faith is our lifestyle. Chapter three is a showcase of that lifestyle, but to give you a quick example right now, I've thrown together a short list of *some* of the illnesses that are being totally cured in this new universe.

Some of the endnote references are just a mention; some describe the event. I feel awkward citing single cases out of thousands, but I suppose one is better than zero, so here goes:

Alzheimer's[29]
aneurysm[30]
diabetes[31]
epilepsy[32]
lupus[33]
AIDS[34]
Parkinson's[35]
polio[36]
macular
 degeneration[37]
ulcers[38]
goiter[39]
blindness[40]
leprosy[41]
paralysis[42]
deaf-muteness[43]
skin diseases[44]
bleeding wounds[45]
gangrene[46]

shortened limbs[47]
restoration of miss-
 ing body parts[48]
autism[49]
leukemia[50]
severe food
 allergies[51]
lost sense of smell[52]
total memory loss[53]
Down syndrome[54]
Kreuzfeld-Jakob
 ("mad cow")
 disease[55]
ruptured discs[56]
glaucoma[57]
multiple sclerosis[58]
prostatitis[59]
tuberculosis[60]
third-degree burns[61]

cancer[62]
meningitis[63]
malaria, yellow
 fever, and
 typhoid[64]
hydroencephaly[65]
fibromyalgia[66]
cirrhosis and
 rheumatism[67]
hepatitis, migraines,
 scoliosis, arthritis,
 asthma, and
 emphysema[68]
heart disease[69]
kidney disease[70]
ugliness[71]
stroke[72]

That's only a start, of course. In a couple of weekends, you could produce a list just as long ... and just as out of date.

Yet healing miracles are just one dimension of the new universe. The even bigger one is ...

Hundreds of Resurrections

If you needed anything else to persuade you to rethink your life, this is it: God is once again in the business of raising people from the dead.

I'm talking about many hundreds since the mid-'80s, perhaps over a thousand by now. There's a blizzard of reports. And I'm not referring to "near-death experiences" (NDEs), the common phantasm with a tunnel and a light at the end, where Buddhists meet Buddha, Catholics meet Mary, etc.[73] I'm talking about people who were stone dead for up to three days.

Five years ago, I was amazed to hear of resurrection reports from eight countries. Now it's exploded to 52:

Algeria[74]

Argentina[75]

Australia[76]

Bulgaria[77]

Burundi[78]

Cambodia[79]

Canada[80]

China[81]

Congo[82]

Cuba[83]

England[84]

Ethiopia[85]

Fiji[86]

Finland[87]

Germany[88]

Ghana[89]

Guatemala[90]

Haiti[91]

Honduras[92]

India[93]

Indonesia[94]

Iran[95]

Kazakhstan[96]

Kenya[97]

Korea[98]

Malawi[99]

Malaysia[100]

Mexico[101]

Mongolia[102]

Mozambique[103]

Myanmar (Burma)[104]

New Zealand[105]

Nigeria[106]

Pakistan[107]

Panama[108]

Papua New Guinea[109]

Philippines[110]

Romania[111]

Russia[112]

Rwanda[113]

Sierra Leone[114]

Solomon Islands[115]

South Africa[116]

Spain[117]

Sudan[118]

Sri Lanka[119]

Tanzania[120]

Togo[121]

Uganda[122]

Ukraine[123]

United States[124]

Vietnam[125]

Some of the above references give a decent narrative; others just mention that a resurrection happened. Some of these people were dead for less than an hour, some for three days. The causes of death were all over the map.

The process of resurrection ranged from effortless to hours of extreme prayer.* There was no single "method" that worked best. In fact the Holy Spirit seems to be at pains to keep us from imagining that some technique or standard system will "work" at all. The only thing that works is Jesus.

Why the sudden flood of resurrections? In part it's because Christians around the world are starting to realize, *Hey, we can do this!* In part it's because God is calling you and me to a new plane of existence. **Are you ready to move up?**

---

* Here's a helpful exercise for your imagination: Picture yourself praying fervently over a dead body for hours. How does it feel? What keeps you going? Even if you never perform miracles yourself, you *must* learn to understand deeply the volcanic power that God is unleashing in the world today.

Skeptical?

You ought to be! Healthy skepticism is a survival skill these days.

I'm skeptical myself. That's why I took a few trips, made a few hundred phone calls, paid a few thousand dollars in research fees, and rejected a few miracle stories when they turned out to be just . . . stories.

But an overdose of skepticism can poison your life. It can turn into cynicism, which has rightly been called, "the intellectual cripple's substitute for intelligence" and a retreat from life.

When something is true, you harm mainly yourself by rejecting it. For instance, take the resurrections that have recently occurred in 52 countries. Suppose you decided to investigate them yourself, got on a series of airplanes, and flew around the world to check out each and every one. What would you find? Judging from the percentage of wild rumors, urban myths, exaggerated tales, and outright lies I found in my own research, I'd say you might find one or two of the 52 that didn't check out. Maybe.

Is that a good reason to deny them all? I think not—not unless you're willing to commit intellectual hara-kiri for the sake of defending a belief system based upon excluding *massive* evidence. You cannot build towers of truth on the quicksand pools of skepticism.

The Lord Is Not Stingy

A lot of today's miracles cannot be traced to any human efforts—not our faith or obedience or evangelism or sensitive response to the voice of God. They just happen because God saw a need and decided to handle it Himself.

• On Christmas Eve, 1998, a young Hindu named Mohan Kanojia rounded up 25 of his friends to form a hit squad and kill a church planter, 55-year-old Mannu Lal. After a few drinks and sacrifices to evil spirits, they set out on their mission of murder.

They never got close to Lal. On the road, Jesus himself suddenly appeared in great authority, booming out one nerve-shattering command: *ENOUGH!!* The shaken assassin repented and today is planting churches *alongside* Lal among leather workers in Madhya Pradesh state, India.[126]

> *And as he journeyed, he came near Damascus:*
> *and suddenly there shined round about him a*
> *light from heaven: And he fell to the earth,*
> *and heard a voice saying unto him, Saul, Saul,*
> *why persecutest thou me? And he said, Who*

**are thou, Lord? And the Lord said, I am Jesus
whom thou persecutest ...** Acts 9:3-5

• A sweet-tempered Bible college student named Domingos was
caught up in Muslim-Christian riots in Jakarta, Indonesia, in 2000,
which left many dead. Amid the ashes and ruins, police found the body
of Domingos with his head severed nearly altogether. They threw his
body on a truck platform with many others. Domingos found himself
in a big room with a bright light. Deeds were being written down.
Then an angel told him to return to his body because "It is not your
time yet."[127] No one touched him. As best we know, no one prayed for
him. The Lord did it all.

See photo in photo section.

• In Kashmir state, India, a devout Muslim named Jalaluddin had a
dream. A man in a white robe asked him, "Do you want real peace?"
"Oh, yes!" he replied, "But I've been unable to find it."
"Read the holy writings," said the man.
"What are the holy writings? And where can I find them?"
"The holy writings are the Holy Bible, and you can get one from
the India Every Home Crusade, 3 Bishop Rockey Street, Faizabad Road
in Lucknow."
A few days later, the EHC office received a letter, saying, in part, "I
don't know who you people are or whether this address is correct, but I
am writing exactly as I was told in a dream. If you receive this, would you
please immediately send me something that is called a holy Bible?"
Today, Jalaluddin is a church member, happily testifying about the
Christ who speaks to Muslims.[128]

• Athet Pyan Shinthaw Paulu was born in 1958 in the town of
Bogale on the Irrawaddy Delta in southern Burma (now Myanmar).
He became a zealous Buddhist monk and died in 1998, remaining
dead for three days. Then at the end of his funeral, just moments
before his coffin was to be nailed shut and cremated, he sat up in front
of the hundreds of people, shouting:

> It's all a lie! I saw our ancestors burning and being tortured
> in some kind of fire. I also saw Buddha and many other
> Buddhist holy men. They were all in a sea of fire! ... We
> must listen to the Christians. They're the only ones who
> know the truth!

Because Paulu had never read a Bible or even heard of hell, his
vision of hell came as a highly traumatic shock. This account is drawn
from an abbreviated, seven-page transcript of Paulu's widely circulated
cassette tape, and nothing in it contradicts Scripture. Indeed, what he

saw fits the Bible. For example, he saw a man who was "taller than any person I have ever seen." (His description corresponds to about nine feet, four inches.) "He was dressed in military armor. He was also holding a sword and a shield. This man had a wound on his forehead."

He was told, "This man's name is Goliath. He is in hell because he blasphemed the eternal God and His servant David." Paulu says he was "confused because I didn't know who either Goliath or David were."

According to numerous comments from his friends and Christian leaders, Paulu has turned many people to the Lord, including 300 monks.

This oft-validated report is loaded with specifics, from his life story to the gross details of what his coffin looked and smelled like. It is now a serious crime in repressive Myanmar to be caught in possession of Paulu's tape. You'll enjoy reading the edited transcript.[129]

The Most Important Miracles of All

Most miracles simply fill a human need or reveal God's glory. But once in a while they go beyond that. A few of them pack a major lesson:

• In the early '90s, Hawa Ahmed was a Muslim college student in North Africa. One day she received a Christian tract in her dorm room and accepted Christ. Because her father was an emir, a Muslim ruler, she knew he might disown her, but she was completely unprepared for what actually happened.

When she told her family that she had become a Christian and had changed her name to Faith, her father flew into a rage. He and her brothers stripped her naked, then tied her to a chair and put a big metal plate at her back, then wired it for 240 volts of electricity.

Faith begged them to put her Bible in her lap. Her father replied, "If you wish to die with your false teaching, so be it."

A brother added, "This will prove your Christian teachings have no power."

Though her arms were tied, she was able to touch a corner of the Bible, and as she did, she felt a strange peace, as if someone were standing right beside her.

They plugged in the cord—but nothing happened. They fiddled with the wires and tried four times, but the current refused to flow!

Finally, in frustration, the emir beat her severely, screamed, *You are no longer my daughter!* and threw her into the street, still without a stitch of clothing.

Bruised and disheveled, the once-beautiful girl ran through the streets in humiliation and pain. The humid African evening added to her feeling of hot embarrassment, though people did seem to look at her more in curiosity than in shock. Trembling and in tears, she ran all the way to the apartment of a Christian friend named Sarah.

Sarah's jaw dropped when she opened the door to see her naked, panting, wounded friend. She whisked her inside, clothed her, and tended to her needs.

The next day, Sarah was speaking with several neighbors who told her they had seen Faith running up the street.

"Yes," Sarah commented, "how sad that my friend was thrown out of her home and forced to run through the streets unclothed."

"What are you talking about?" asked one of them.

"I'm talking about that young woman who ran naked to my door last night. She ran right past you."

"You must be mistaken. The girl who ran past us last night was wearing a beautiful white gown." The others agreed.

"Yes," added another, "we wondered why someone dressed so nicely was running down the street."[130]

Today, Faith is a full-time evangelist with Every Home for Christ.

> *"... for the marriage day of the Lamb is come, and his bride hath made herself ready. And to her was granted that she should be arrayed in fine linen, clean and white ..."* Revelation 19:7-8

I believe God is telling us here that much of the church (His symbolic bride) is wounded and bleeding. But she should not spend time trying to make herself look good before the world—because if we let Him handle things, He will take care of making His bride appear in great beauty.

• In 1974, 30 children died after eating contaminated food from a street vendor in Seoul, Korea. On that day, David Yonggi Cho, famed pastor of the world's largest church there, was in an elders' meeting when he received an urgent call to go home.

On arrival, he found Samuel, his five-year-old son, dying. Cho later declared, "I simply did not want to accept the death of my son. But after hours of intense prayer and crying, he died anyway.

"I was beside myself. I had to watch him grow cold and stiff, yet I still could not give up. I told God, *I will not leave this room until You give me my son back.*"

Cho prayed and praised God till after midnight. Finally, he stood and thundered, "Samuel!" He clapped his hands loudly. "Samuel! In the name of Jesus Christ of Nazareth, stand up and walk!" The boy sprang to his feet.[131]

There's more: Samuel told his father that he had met Jesus in heaven and that he had seen many deceased Christians from Cho's church there, who shouted, "Look, here comes the pastor's son!"

Then Jesus told the boy, "I cannot keep you here because your father will not let you go. So I'm taking you back to him."

Samuel is now president of a computer company.[132]

> **But Peter made them all leave the room, then he knelt down and prayed; and turning to the body said, Tabitha, arise!** Acts 9:40

I cannot keep you here <u>because your father will not let you go</u>. Let those words burn into your memory. They may tell you more about prayer than the next three books you'll read on the topic. They also cast light onto what kind of prayer it will take to transform your city into a fountainhead of revival, righteousness, and prosperity. Life-changing prayer is not a recitation of words (James 5:16), it's a massive exercise in insistent faith.

I hope these incidents have begun to enlarge your world and make it brighter for you. For diehard cessationists—those who believe that miracles and prophecies ceased in A.D. 95 when the Bible was completed—these are tough days indeed!

"As I call your name, come forward and surrender your gun."

You may be thinking that the above reports are pretty near the fringe. Actually, no. The fringe is what follows. I throw this in to show you how deep the rabbit hole goes:

Just outside Nairobi, the capital of Kenya, there is a church with 12,500 attendees named God's Power Church. The pastor is John K. Nduati.[133]

In the first part of March, 2000, he went to hold a four-day crusade in Eldoret, 160 miles northwest of Nairobi. I take up excerpts from a letter by Joseph Wangigi of Eldoret, reporting to *Joel News International*,[134] with minor edits:

> • The pastor said, "There are forty people in this crusade who are AIDS-HIV positive. Come to the front." He counted 39 as they came; one was missing.
>
> Then the pastor said, "There is a young man back there [pointing] named Philip Ruto. You contracted AIDS from your girlfriend last year, and you have refused to come forward."
>
> I tell you, when his name was called, he *ran* forward. Everybody in the crusade laughed and clapped. The pastor

prayed, and the AIDS was gone [from everyone] immediately ...

• The pastor stood and said, "There are fifty women in this crusade who have no children. Come for prayers." *Sixty* women came forward. Then the man of God said, "Look at me. If you are here and you have no husband, you may go." A few women left. Then he continued, "If you are a second wife, you can go." One woman left. Then he continued, "If in the past you have aborted twice, you may go."

Finally, fifty women were left standing. The pastor then told all of them to move to the right side. Then he said, "If I call your name, move to the left side." To everybody's amazement, as though the pastor had a list [he had never met the women], he started to have a roll call: Njoki, Jane, Chepchumba, ... etc.*[135] As their names were called, they moved to the left and thus were divided into two groups. To one group, he said,

John K. Nduati

"You, tomorrow start shopping for boys' clothes. God is going to give you boys. [And to the other group:] You shop for girls' clothes. God will give you girls." Then he pointed at one of the women and said, "With you, you will have to buy clothes for both a boy and a girl, because you are going to have twins." Then the man of God prayed for them.

When the pastor finished ministering, he asked how many people wanted to receive Jesus as their personal Savior. About eight hundred people came and received Christ ...**

• The man of God said, "There is a woman in the direction I am pointing who does not have a child. The one you have living with you, you bought. Who are you?" The woman refused to lift her hand. Then the man of God

---

* Nduati is not the only person with this gift of names. See, for instance, *Joel News International* #285 for a short report on Theresa D'Souza, a former Catholic nun who prays three to six hours a day. A *Religion Today* reporter commented: "I know of one church where she preached for 15 minutes to a group of 240 people. Even though she had never met them, she called each one of those people by name."

** Cessationists would look at these incidents and say, "Well, it must be Satan who is doing these things." If so, then the devil is one confused dude, performing wonders that draw 800 people to Christ. (Jesus had a scorching comment on that line of reasoning in Matthew 12:22-32.)

called her by her name and said, "I want to pray for you to have your own child. The child you are living with was sold to you by nurses at Eldoret District Hospital. You paid 12,000 shillings. I now want to tell you that the real parents of the kid will come for it next Tuesday at 10:05 A.M."

Two days ago, I [Mr. Wangigi] met a sister who was with the relatives of the woman, and they have confirmed that what Pastor Nduati said did happen... .

• Then the man of God started calling by name those robbers who were in the crusade. He even told when and where they stole, the name of their gang and their gang leader. Many came and received Christ. Pastor Nduati has a licence from the police to collect illegal firearms. Those who surrender and receive Christ in his meetings are never arrested ... .

• Before I conclude, let me tell you one more thing about pastor Nduati. He is a young man, 27 now, and when he wanted to get married, he told God, "Father, I want to get married, but there are so many girls. I don't know what to do." Then God told him, "Get your vehicle and drive to Nyeri [a town about 100 kilometers northeast of Nairobi]. When you reach Nyeri, go to the Nyeri District Hospital. Outside the gate, you will find a woman sitting there. That is your wife." The pastor did that, and outside the gate of the hospital, he saw a woman doctor sitting. He greeted her and said, "I have been told you are to be my wife." The woman (named Dorcas) simply replied, "Yes, there is no problem. I will be your wife." And today, Dorcas is the pastor's wife!

Interesting postscript: As you can imagine, I had a little trouble accepting these incidents. So I asked my brother, Bob, who assisted me in research, to get somebody to go to Nduati's church in Nairobi and check him out. He sent Anthony Timothy Mariano, one of his closest longtime friends. Yesterday I spoke with Dr. Mariano and got his surprising report:

I met with John Nduati on quite a few occasions and hit it off quite well with him.

He speaks on Sundays from 6:00 A.M. to 6:00 P.M. without a break for food, water, or even the toilet! Once when I went with him afterward, he had only one can of soda. He is a very thin, tense, energetic man who doesn't eat much! I would also say that he is a great man, very wise and intelligent. He was first in his high school, but did not attend any kind of college.

In the church, I saw him call out the names of many people and do lots of the healing miracles that have been reported about him. He has had these powers since youth.

I was embarrassed one day at supper when John asked me to speak in his church. I told him I'm a dentist, not a speaker, but he insisted, so the next Sunday, I spoke for about 20 minutes. Even though his meetings are in Kikuyu, I planned to speak in English because I know only a few words of Kikuyu. But when I got up, I started talking in Kikuyu. Such a thing never happened to me before. I didn't know what I was saying, but people starting jumping up and down and yelling, and many fell on their faces before God.

Afterward, my wife, who speaks fluent Kikuyu, came up to me and said, "How did you *do* that?"[136]

With such powerful events popping up around the world, you can see why apostolic Christians are growing by 8% a year. With so many Elijahs and Elishas at work, you can see how the upcoming conversion of the Jews, Muslims, Hindus, and Buddhists is going to spread quickly:

> **The least of you will become a thousand, the smallest a mighty nation. I am Yahweh; in its time I will do this swiftly.** Isaiah 60:22*

But in ancient Israel, Elijah and Elisha were a rarity. Now God is bringing thousands of people like you and me into the middle of things. As He says:

> **And it shall come to pass, that I will pour out my spirit upon all flesh; and your sons and your daughters shall prophesy, your old men shall dream dreams, your young men shall see visions. Even upon the menservants and maidservants in those days will I pour out my spirit.** Joel 2:28-29

Prepare yourself. The endgame of God isn't coming, it's here.

How to Discover the Wrath of God for Yourself

The Lord has a warm place in His heart for folks who believe in Him without seeing any miracles.[137] That's the purest faith.

---

* *Yahweh* is a more accurate rendering of the traditional *Jehovah*.

Yet the precise strategic purpose of miracles is to help us believe and turn to Him.[138] So a miracle-assisted faith is just fine.

However, when God *does* perform a string of miracles and people remain unmoved or unchanged, **look out!** Nothing reveals the wrath of our loving God faster than a rejection of His love as shown in His miracles. In Numbers 13:17-14:35, the people of Israel dismissed all the miracles God had done to get them out of Pharaoh's grasp and said, "We should choose a leader and go back to Egypt."

God's enraged response: *"HOW LONG WILL THESE PEOPLE TREAT ME WITH CONTEMPT? HOW LONG WILL THEY REFUSE TO BELIEVE IN ME, IN SPITE OF ALL THE MIRACULOUS SIGNS I HAVE PERFORMED AMONG THEM? I WILL STRIKE THEM DOWN WITH A PLAGUE AND DESTROY THEM…"*

If Moses had not thrown himself into desperate intercession in a Sinai second, the Judge of Nations would have wiped out four hundred years of work and started all over. When rage like that comes from the lightning-lit throne of the **I AM**, it's pretty scary.

Be an overcomer. And start today.

Now that I've subtly made my point about the importance of paying attention to miracles, here's why I did it. It's because I'm afraid you may be just like me: prone to sluggishness … and very apt to finish this book, put it on the shelf, and say, *Oh, that was nice. I should give a copy to Uncle Wally for Christmas.*

Please, please—don't do that. You're living in the middle of the biggest breakthrough of the last two millennia, and this is your golden chance to grab hold, hang on, and let the momentum force of God's

A Farewell to Fog

The ongoing flood of miracles has a crisp message for the doubters of our day:

• **Armchair Philosophers** who have based their flimsy intellectual superstructure on the snooty premise that miracles obviously cannot exist

• **Blind Dogmatists** who insist—in the face of torrents of irrefutable evidence—that God hasn't done any miracles since the first twelve apostles died. You can keep denying the obvious for only so long.

• **Romantic Optimists** who feel that "it doesn't matter what you believe as long as you're sincere," a position that should have collapsed along with the tragic fall of the World Trade Center. The vague notion that we're all headed toward the same end by different routes has always been baseless, but now looks downright silly. Guesswork is out; reality and truth are in.

kingdom lift you up from whatever treadmill you may be on and place you in a key spot on the battle line where the war for the world is being fought with every tick of the clock. If this sounds like purple prose, reread Revelation, where Jesus makes you the promise:

> *To him who overcomes and does my will to the end, I will give authority over the nations.... To him who overcomes, I will give the right to sit with me on my throne.* Revelation 2:26, 3:31

Are you ready for that?

I hope these miracles and statistics have awakened something deep within you, something that may have been lying dormant since you were a kid, before the world sucked you into its whirlpool and narrowed your concerns mainly to matters of family and finance, coping and career.

For over 3,000 years, your ancestors in the faith prayed and cried and fasted to see what you have seen in these pages. But their time was not right. God gave them only visions and glimpses of the great events to come. Few of His people were ready for them, so He saved this cascade of momentous changes for your day.

Every month now, you have five million more brothers and sisters in Christ around the world. Yet you also lose 14,000 of the family per month, martyrs slain at a point of witness by various persecutors (largely Muslims, I'm afraid).[139] This is the highest drama ever to play

Your Help Welcome

If you have any specific negative information on any of these miracle reports, I would appreciate your help!

I've done what I can to double-check everything, but in future editions of this book I want to make any needed corrections. So if you have inside knowledge about any incident, please send it to me in care of my publisher. If you are the *first* to document an error of fact that substantially undermines the incident, you will receive an editorial help fee.

This is not to be understood as a challenge or dare, but an honest request for help in maintaining a high standard for truthfulness and credibility.

Also, if you have knowledge of an outstanding miraculous event that can be verified without the help of the CIA or a platoon of private detectives, please send it along for inclusion in future editions. Thank you!

Send any comment—along with a means of verification—to Miracle Reports, Open Church Ministries, Portal, Georgia 30450 or miracles@openchurch.com.

on the world's stage. Does it speak to your heart about taking a key role in it?

If you are excited about playing a part in the growth of the new Christianity, I encourage you to read some of the books in the bibliography. To date, the best book in the field is Wolfgang Simson's *Houses That Change the World*. But also read my Appendix Three and take some of the action steps suggested there.

There's Never Been a Time Like This

In 1960, there were 24 nonbelievers for every believer in the world. Now there are only six.

In 1960, even the strongest part of the church was growing as slowly as the rest of the world. Now we're growing almost seven times as fast.

Do you see the picture? Can you feel in your spirit the excitement of what the LORD is doing? Back in the "golden days" of early Christianity, we were outnumbered by 360 pagans for every believer. That's pretty intimidating. Today's 1:6 ratio of born-again believers to everyone else is much less daunting!

The family of Jesus Christ is growing so fast that if our growth simply continues at today's pace, most of us living today may see the fulfillment of Revelation 11:15:

> **Now are the kingdoms of this world become**
> **the kingdom of our Lord and of his Messiah!**
> **And he shall reign for ever and ever.**

Statistically, as I said, we're heading for that grand finale by 2032 or so. But of course, that's just a fragile projection. What's more definite is, you've joined a transformed army that is 707 million strong and adding more every second.

This is the most massive event that will ever touch your life. Don't be a spectator! The Father loves you, so go to Him directly and ask Him:

—"Lord, reveal to me any sins or bad attitudes that might be keeping me from fully functioning as a member of your team."

—"Show me the purposes and immediate plans you have for me."

And as they say in baseball, tell Him, *"Put me in the lineup!"*

In this chapter, I've tried to give you a hint about the tremendous future that awaits you. I know it sounds overwhelming, but you won't have to go unprepared. *For the first time ever, we now have the ways and means to finish quickly the job that Christ gave us to do.*

That's the subject of the next chapter. I think you'll find it encouraging.

Subscribe to These Two
Main Resources

There are dozens of online services that report news about miracles and church growth. The most far-reaching are the *Friday Fax 2* and *Joel News International*.

Friday Fax 2, like its predecessor, *Friday Fax* (whose *Megashift* reports are archived at www.jesus.org.uk/dawn), the new *Friday Fax* is a positive and inspiring Kingdom news service for Christians who need to know where God is going. It has a special focus on mission breakthroughs, strategic and prophetic insights, revivals, the miraculous, church planting, current "apostolic reformation" news, and other exciting stories from around the world.

You may subscribe at www.ffax2.com. Also available in German.

Joel News International, an e-zine on prayer, revival and church growth, has gained a reputation over the years for encouraging and reliable news about what God is doing worldwide. It's for Christians who long for renewal and revival, who want to pray and act. Joel News combines a keen prophetic view with a down-to-earth journalistic treatment of spiritual trends. This regularly leads to innovative articles on the situation of the Body of Christ worldwide. Joel News also gives practical insights in how to grow in strategic prayer, living communities, and the transformation of society.

You may sign up by sending an e-mail to rob@joelnews.org with the subject line, "Subscribe Joel News International." Also available in Dutch, German, Spanish, and Polish.

Please do not query the author or publisher
about e-mail addresses or websites that have changed!
If you can't track them down, we probably can't, either!

---

1. For instance, in the twentieth century, life expectancy jumped 50%, but deaths by war and genocide jumped from seven million (average of the previous 19 centuries) to 133 million. See R.J. Rummel, *Death by Government* (New Brunswick, NJ: Transaction Publishers), 1994.

2. Rodrick Gilbert, Deliverance Church, 3/125-C, Bengali Colony, Mahavir Enclave, New Delhi 110045, India. Phone: (91) 11-25058984. Not all of her resurrections were so difficult. The very first was a year-old boy named Mahesh who had been dead for five hours. Savitri and a small group of friends including the mother were in shock when the cold little body was handed to them, but after ten minutes—which included as much crying as praying—Mahesh came back to life.

3. His e-mail: northgate@adelphia.net.

4. The Sadhu's daughter Lalitah Pillai and her husband Joshua are friends of mine. The report came from Joshua and the *Friday Fax* #36, 9/13/2002.

5. Source: Josef Brueschweiler of the Swiss mission organization, AVC. (Fax: [41] 32-355-4248. Phone: [41] 32-355-4242. E-mail: AVC@swissonline.ch.) Reported in *Friday Fax* #25, 1999.

6. *Joel News International* #271 and *Friday Fax* #12, 1999.

7. Source: Sower's Ministry, Hong Kong. Reported in *Friday Fax* #11, 1997. Also ...

• In China in 1999, the situation was even more desperate. It had not rained in the northern provinces for *five years*. A Chinese pastor was touring the drought area with some visiting Americans and Chinese officials when one of the officials suddenly asked, "Can your God make it rain in the next 20 days?"

Without batting an eye, the Chinese pastor replied, "Yes, of course He can."

"Then pray that it happens," said the official. "If it rains in the next 20 days, we will know that it was your god who did it."

Twelve days later, it rained all across the northern provinces.

(Source: OMF International, Singapore branch. Reported in *Friday Fax* #16, 1999.)

• In Cambodia in 2000, a missionary pastor faced a more difficult task. Residents of one village asked him to pray for a quick rain for their newly planted crops. Residents of a nearby village asked him to pray that it *wouldn't* rain for a week because they hadn't finished sowing.

It rained—but only in the village that had finished sowing. The people of both villages became Christians and were baptized.

(Source: *Advance*, Foursquare Gospel Church. Reported in *Friday Fax* #21, 2000.)

• In the midst of a recent drought in Santiago Atitlan, Guatemala, there was a revival meeting, where a pastor said that God had spoken to him, promising rain, *but only on the farms of believers!* And that night it happened. Nonbelievers (who of course weren't in church) were disappointed to see the storm pouring rain on their neighbors' fields and not their own. But by midnight the word got around, and a crowd of farmers were at the church, banging on the door and demanding to be let in so they could get right with God. As soon as they did, it rained on their farms too.

(Source: Guatemalan church leader Harold Caballeros, speaking on May 1, 2001, in Seattle at the Sentinel Group conference, *Transformations II*.)

• On the opening evening of a crusade in Asbest, Russia, dark clouds began to rain as evangelist David Hathaway stood to speak. Undeterred, he prayed against the rain and then announced to the astonished crowd that the sun would return in five minutes. It did—but the heavy storm continued to lash everything *outside* of the stadium.

(Source: *Prophetic Vision* magazine in U.K., cited in *Friday Fax* #5, 2002.)

8. From a conversation with Phillip Gammill, a staff member with Freedom Ministries, whose U.S. office is in Raymondville, Texas, and main field office in Tampico, Mexico. (956) 347-3802, MWF mornings only. Fax: (956) 347-3430.

9. You can order *Raised from the Dead* for $14.99 from the CfAN Web site, www.cfan.org. It is mostly interviews with Daniel Ekechukwu and his wife, Nneka. But what truly sets it apart is a minute or so of actual footage (less than Hollywood quality) of Ekechukwu starting to come back to life. When he began to breathe, someone ran upstairs and got a videocam. There are also on-site interviews with the doctor, the mortician, a state security officer, and two other pastors who were present and prayed for Ekechukwu.

10. From the autobiography by Cheryl, *A Bright Shining Place: The Story of a Miracle* (Tulsa: Eagle Run Publishing), 1981, p. 256f.

11. Jimmy Crompton, Box 7698, Newton Park, 6055, Republic of South Africa, wof@mweb.co.za, phone: 27 (41) 368-1055.

He is pastor of the Word of Faith Christian Centre in Port Elizabeth, RSA. Cited in *Friday Fax* #9, 1998.

12. K.Y. Geevarghese, IPC-W, Mayur Vihar Phase II, Delhi 91, India, as quoted in *Midnight Herald*, Vol. II, No. 3. Now http://midnightherald.org. Tel: (91) 11-247-1455.

13. Phone conversation with Phillip Gammill of Freedom Ministries staff. The father had been the town drunk, but was dramatically saved and sobered up. Over the next four weeks, his daughter was apparently healed of epilepsy, which had been causing two or three violent seizures every night. So when his daughter suddenly died five months later, the father said, "There's no way God saved me and healed my daughter to let her die!" That's when he sent for prayer support.

14. Except for the last line, the figures are from the U.S. Center for World Mission, www.uscwm.org.

15. I will defend my statistics to the death—or until the numbers change, whichever comes first.

But since the numbers change daily, I doubt I'll have to defend them for any life-threatening span of time. Also, you likely realize the truth of the motto of professional estimators: "Nothing in Life Is Rougher Than an Estimate."

With these two caveats in mind, here is the official basis for the surprising fact that 707 million core apostolics are growing by 8% a year.

First: There are only two statistical surveys of global Christianity in print and current. Patrick Johnstone's huge but readable *Operation World* (Harrisonburg, Virginia: R.R. Donnelley & Sons), 2001, is written for prayer intercessors. David Barrett and Todd Johnson's hernia-inducing, 14-pound, two-volume, $1.1 billion *World Christian Encyclopedia* (New York: Oxford University Press), 2001, is more aimed at scholars and strategists trying to get a grasp on things. Both sets of numbers are conservative.

I have spoken with all three authors and was duly impressed by all, but finally elected to follow Barrett and Johnson's numbers, primarily because their definitions and groupings match mine somewhat better. This is by no means a slight of Johnstone's nugget-laden masterpiece, which every serious intercessor should own.

Second: For the last 100 years, the percentage of the world that is "Christian" has held steady at about 33% to 34%. Not encouraging. But this conceals the fact that:

• some parts of the worldwide church are growing at warp speed

• while other parts are fossilized

• and other parts are thrashing around in the dumper.

My tiny contribution today to church statistics is that I've been able to put a frame around the growing heart of Christianity—a very rough and ruthless frame, but a sensible one:

A. I've placed the entire church on a continuum. On the left side, you have the denominational folks. At the *far* left end, you have a vast pile of tradition-bound, liberal, ancient, highly centralized, and strategically useless organizations that haven't grown much since the 1940s.

On the right side, you have the independents, composed of overlapping groups known by such labels as post-denominational, neo-apostolic, radical, restorationist, free, etc. Barrett and Johnson trace their origins to A.D. 61, starting with the Celts, then flowing onward through the Montanists, Donatists, Monophysites, Arians, Cathari, Bogomils, Waldensians, Lollards, Lutherans, Puritans, Methodists, etc. (*World Christian Trends*, Part 6, p. 293) Eventually, most of them have either turned into denominations or been stomped out of existence by their better-armed brothers in the faith.

At the far right end of the continuum, you have groups that are so independent that they're isolated, weak, strategically useless, and barely keeping up with world growth.

B. I've pinpointed the groups at the growing heart of Christianity. But hold the applause, it was not through a stroke of brilliance by isolating some magical quality that sets the core apostolics apart from everyone else. It was through the far cruder tactic of lopping off the slow-growing groups at both ends of the spectrum *en masse*.

From the left end, I dispensed with 1.238 billion nice folks who comprise the mainline denominations plus the highly overlapping 1.330 billion souls whose only "problem" is that they're capital-E Evangelicals, meaning they are not charismatic or pentecostal. My sincere apologies to my Evangelical friends (now perhaps ex-friends), but my numbers cover 1970 to 2000, and they show that during those 30 years, charismatics and pentecostals grew worldwide at a blistering 8.8% annual rate, while Evangelicals limped along at 1.1%. (This is based on figures graciously supplied to me by Dr. Todd Johnson of *World Christian Trends*, in which he painstakingly calculated the overlap between the groups for me. On page 33 of his book, you will find a startling table that shows the raw data he drew from.)

What is left after eliminating the Evangelicals and mainliners? *A composite of charismatics and pentecostals who are in minor mini-denominations.* There were just 45 million of them in 1970, but 447 million by 2000! Almost a tenfold growth!

From the right end, I dispensed with 96 million perfectly innocent people whose only offense was to be found in independent <u>single</u> congregations, not networked with others of their own persuasion. (As you will see later in this book, I harp on the necessity of house churches to network with one another.)

What is left are the *independent <u>networks</u>, which are a mix of charismatics, pentecostals, and even Evangelicals*. There were just 26 million of them in 1970, but 260 million in 2000. Again, a tenfold increase!

Added together, these two blocs are the core apostolics. From 1970 to 2000, they grew 8% a year, from 71 million to 707 million.

An apostle is someone sent on a mission. So core apostolics are serious about starting new gatherings of believers. In fact, at current rates, half the world would be core apostolics by 2022.

Could I have sliced and diced the numbers differently? Surely. I could have shown a much, much higher growth rate by zooming in on all the house churches in Nepal or the Gen-X meetings in Idaho or something like that. But there's no guarantee that a small local movement will ever catch on worldwide. The 707 million core apostolics are neither small nor local.

I could also have shown a much lower growth rate. Megablocs of conservative Christians have been pegged by various scholars at a 1.2% to 7.3% annual growth since 2000 or so. It all depends on what and how you're counting. In response to a charge of exaggeration, I could list a dozen or two major high-growth groups I *didn't* count among my core apostolics. For instance:

• Plainly, by amputating about 1.3 billion Evangelicals and mainline denominational Christians from my numbers, I have ignored many millions of dedicated believers who are fighting valiantly for the Kingdom with great success and rapid growth.

• Likewise, I have axed 86 million independents who are not networked with other congregations. Obviously, many of those are multiplying.

• Then there's China. I've included only 85 million independents there, mostly in house churches. But I strongly suspect there are really about 130 million. Dr. Todd Johnson, in fact, told me that a nose-by-nose count in China could easily produce 130 million born-agains, but he insists that 10 to 15 million of those noses would be counted twice because so many belong to more than one congregation. That would leave 115 to 120 million—still way more than I've claimed.

China-watching is an art form. For example, try to watch Henan province. In their annual evangelism month, the house churches regularly double (*Friday Fax* #39, 1995). In the Xinyang district in 1995, the number of believers jumped from 1,000 to 10,000 in one month. Who can track that sort of growth with any accuracy?

• Based on 32,000 interviews, the Christian Broadcasting Network estimates that 40 million CBN viewers became Christians in 2000 alone.

• Also in 2000, the *Jesus* film produced 15 million new Christians.

• In April, 1996, a reported 450 million inquirers responded to Billy Graham's global telecast.

Such numbers simply do not find their way into distinguished, scholarly, statistical works. They're too hard to trace down to noses in pews. And in some countries, nine-tenths of them show up on paper as transfers from, say, Catholic to Baptist, rather than as "new" Christians.

• My Indian friends agree that there are perhaps 70-100 million nominal Hindus who secretly believe in Jesus and are awaiting a time when they can come out of the closet. That time will come soon.

• There are millions of secret Christians in Muslim lands.

• The U.S. has about 23 million full-fledged, born-again believers who are church dropouts. In military terminology, they would be *the reserves,* a whole army ready and eager to jump into the fray if they could find a type of fellowship that offers them more than a place in a pew. So they're worth counting, even though I haven't done so.

N.B.: THERE IS NO EXCLUSION BY JUDGMENT HERE. IT'S ALL A MATTER OF NUMBERS AND A QUEST FOR SIMPLICITY. DESPITE MY COLORFUL DESCRIPTIONS, ALL THE CASTOFF GROUPS WERE AXED BECAUSE OF LOW GROWTH. Besides, if I were to include them, you would have a growth rate so high that no one would believe it. Not even me.

16. Patrick Johnstone, *The Church Is Bigger Than You Think*, (Pasadena: Wm. Carey Library) 1998, page 110.

17. For the full story, see Dick Eastman, *op. cit.,* pages 191-195.

18. Source: Swiss mission leader Andrea Xandry, Soz.-Missionarischer Hilfsbund, Zurich. Reported in *Friday Fax* #38, 2000.

19. Source: Open Doors. *Friday Fax* #39, 1995.

20. Letter from Paul Eshleman, Director, the JESUS Film Project, April, 1998. Also, Sentinel Group's *World InSight* magazine, June, 2000, page 3.

21. The Second Call Ministries, www.thesecondcall.org.

22. Source: Brother Dale, World Harvest Ministries, P.O. Box 241, Williamsburg, Virginia 23187. Cited in *Friday Fax* #20, 1997. It is not that unusual to find demonized men chained up by desperate townsfolk.

23. I've chosen a food miracle witnessed by my own housekeeper for the sake of added credibility; we are not dealing in wild rumors here! But I will also reference three others reports: Tani and Dane, volunteers with Operation Mobilization in Albania, recently fed over 200 Kosovo refugees on half a pot of bean soup. It takes four full pots to serve 200. Their O.M. office is in Switzerland, 41 (1) 832-8383. Cited in *Friday Fax* #27, 1999. Also see an incident from Mozambique in *Friday Fax* #7, 2002. Also, see Joan Wester Anderson, *Where Miracles Happen: True Stories of Heavenly Encounters* (Brooklyn: Brett Books) 1994, p. 202f, for a miracle in Ann Arbor of multiplying meat loaf! ... and on p. 207f, multiplying macaroni and cheese!

24. Personal from the late Eric Olson. His widow is at olson.angela@gmail.com.

25. Matthew and Lea Nocas, YWAM project directors, (903) 882-5591, info@ywamtyler.org.

26. *Christianity Today*, Feb. 5, 2001, and eyewitness sources.

27. M. Lynn Reddick, The *2 Minute Miracle* (Portal, GA: Portal Publishing Company), 2003, p. 42.

28. Depending on the degree of former commitment, the number ranges from 7$\frac{1}{2}$ million to 40.7 million. My figure of 23 million is almost halfway between those

numbers. You get the same result by taking top pollster George Barna's estimate of 65 to 70 million unchurched U.S. adults and multiplying that by his estimate that a third of those have made a conscious commitment to Jesus Christ at some time in the past, a decision that is still important to them today. See www.barna.org.

29. C. Peter Wagner and Pablo Deiros, editors, *The Rising Revival* (Ventura, California: Renew Books), 1998, page 157.

30. Jack Deere, *Surprised by the Power of the Holy Spirit*, (Grand Rapids: Zondervan Publishing House) 1993, page 31.

31. *Friday Fax* #46, 1995.

32. Gospel for Asia, India/USA, as reported in *Friday Fax* #33, 1997. Also, during the filming of Mel Gibson's *The Passion of the Christ*, the six-year-old daughter of a crew member stopped having seizures. She had been having up to fifty seizures a day. *Friday Fax* #46, 2003.

33. *Joel News International* #185.

34. An article in *Compass* magazine (U.K.), Summer, 2001, describes the ministry of T.B. Joshua of the Synagogue Church of All Nations in Lagos, Nigeria: "Over 10,000 people have been healed of AIDS, each one confirmed by two medical certificates." Also see www.christian-faith.com/truestories2.html and *Friday Fax* #22, 2001.

35. The Second Call Ministries, www.revivalstudies.org/archive/testimonies/parkinson.htm.

36. During an 18-day gospel crusade in Ferozpur, India, in March, 1997, a total of 520,000 people attended. Of 1,045 testimonies given, 191 people were healed of polio. Source: Spring, 1997, *News* from World Harvest Ministries, P.O. Box 241, Williamsburg, Virginia 23187. Many of these testimonies can be seen on a 24-minute video of this crusade, also available from World Harvest; it also has the testimony of the ex-demoniac who had been chained to a tree.

37. Peter Jacobs, quoted from a report in *Stimme der Stadt* (Voice of the City). Fax: (49) 6109-702958. As reported in *Friday Fax* #41, 1999.

38. *Compass Direct* (Open Doors). Fax: (714) 531-2681. E-mail: info@compass direct.org. Cited in *Friday Fax* #27, 1997.

39. Veronica at the Chaplaincy of Dubai, P.O. Box 7415, Dubai. Cited in *Friday Fax* #1, 1998.

40. Brian Andrews, cited in *Friday Fax* #45, 1999. Marcos Barros, marcos@gona-tions.org and Go to the Nations, www.gonations.org, as reported in *Friday Fax* #14, 1997.

41. Dr. Daniel Sathiaraj, India Mission Association, 48, First Main Road, East Shenoy Nagar, Chennai 600030, India, phone: (91) 44-644-4602, e-mail: jlove@cal.vsnl.net.in, as cited in *Friday Fax* #35, 2000.

42. *Friday Fax* #12, 1999, and *Joel News International* 271. Also see www.mira-clestories.org/miraclehealingtestimony.html or write William Kent at P.O. Box 59, Cascade, Maryland 21719.

43. See http:/www.christian-faith.com/testimonies/India.html. Also *Joel News International* 339 and 459-3.

44. Peter Wenz, Biblische Glaubens gemeinde. Fax: (49) 711-484295. Phone: (49) 711-480400. (Call during office hours.) Cited in *Friday Fax* #11, 1999.

45. Eric Bradshaw, as reported in *Friday Fax* #28, 1999.

46. Greg Fisher, FMI, in *Friday Fax* #32, 1996.

47. See http://www.christian-faith.com/testimonies/taunya.html. Also, *House2 House* magazine, issue 5, page 31.

48. Noted house church leader and therapist Dr. Keith William Smith (keith-smith@castillofuerte.org) told me: "Many times I've prayed and nothing has happened. But in 1977 at Christian Life College in London, a friend and I prayed

for the arm of a fellow student that had been crushed as a child, leaving it as no more than a floppy tube hanging at his side. As we prayed in the chapel service, both my friend and I felt bone moving and growing within the brother's arm. Within a minute his arm was complete. He could move it normally and support weight. This brother went on to plant churches all over London. This was documented on national television."

Also see C. Peter Wagner and Pablo Deiros, *The Rising Revival* (Ventura, California: Renew Books), 1998, page 220. Also, *Joel News International*, #337. And http://www.freshfire.ca/revival_report.asp?ID=Mala001, which describes one of several cases I've found where a complete new eye was formed in an empty socket.

49. Elizabeth Flako, a girl of the Chocoy tribe in Panama, was born autistic and without a voice box. In 2000, when she was five, she had an epileptic-style seizure. After two weeks in this condition, doctors said she would die. Finally, in the night, God awoke a local pastor's wife and told her to "pray for the girl, or she will die tonight." After a hurried search, she found Elizabeth, who was the daughter of a couple who were total strangers to her. She was led to ask for a voice box for the girl. The box formed immediately, and the girl began crying. Then God told the woman to cast out an evil spirit from the girl. As soon as she did, Elizabeth became the normal young girl she is today! Source: 7/1/02 telcon with Jeanne Cook, www.vidaministries.org.

50. Terry Mize, *More Than Conquerors*, (Texarkana: Terry Mize Ministries) 1990, p. 57f.

51. Urvas, Hanikka 47, 02369 Espoo, Finland. Phone: (358) 0-8886045. Cited in *Friday Fax* #28, 1996.

52. *Joel News International*, #266.

53. *Compass Direct* (Open Doors). Fax: 1 (714) 531-2681. E-mail: info@compass direct.org, quoted in *Friday Fax* #27, 1997.

54. 1. During Carlos Annacondia's first televised crusade in Argentina, a mother put her Down's son in front of the TV set, and as Annacondia prayed, she saw him being healed—and his facial features changing—right before her eyes. From one perspective, this is the most astonishing healing on record because Down's is not just a mental condition; God had to change every cell in his body from 47 chromosomes to 46! Source: *Compass* magazine (England), May, 1998. 2. Still healed, Davi Silva, of Londrina, Brazil, now travels in music ministry. E-mail: mzm@mzm.org, telephone (315) 792-4748.

55. A woman was healed of the incurable Kreuzfeld-Jakob disease in Bulgaria in early 2001 through a noted English evangelist of my acquaintance, David Hathaway. Cited in *Friday Fax* 46, 2001.

56. Personal report to me from Dr. Lynn Reddick of Portal, Georgia, president of the Network of Open Church Ministries. E-mail: Reddick_cbi@yahoo.com.

57. Jimmy Crompton, wof@mweb.co.za, 27 (41) 368-1055. Cited in *Friday Fax* #9, 1998.

58. "Amazing Healings" in *News Digest* for August 29, 2000, International Revival Network, www.openheaven.com.

59. San Diego attorney Bill Hitt. The story of his healing is at http://home.san.rr.com/healing/billhitt.htm. E-mail: hitt pink@dslextreme.com.

60. *Compass* magazine (England), May, 1998, p. 10. Also, *Joel News International* #365, June 4, 2001. Also, the March 6, 2003, donor letter from Paul Eshleman for the Jesus Film Project. Also, 52 cases of TB were healed in one crusade with Canadian Todd Bentley (http://www.fresh fire.ca/revival_report.asp?ID=Mala001).

61. A man in Houston, Texas, was burned over 85% of his body and given only a 3% chance to live. He recovered with almost no problems at all. This is an incidental part of a report by Richard Heard, pastor of the Christian Tabernacle of Houston, in

an article printed in *Renewal Journal* in Brisbane, Australia www.pastornet.net .au/renewal/journal10/d-heard.html.

62. In the article cited in the preceding footnote, Richard Heard mentions some cures that accompanied the revival in his church that I detail in chapter five. These included seven cancer cases in just the first week. Significantly, most of them were not "hands-on" events. People would go home, and then a day later phone the church office, saying, "Hey, you'll never guess what happened to my husband's tumor," etc. I have come across hundreds of cancer cures over the years. One heartwarming case is by Sara O'Meara in *Miracles Still Happen*, by Sheri Stone and Therese Marszalek (Tulsa: Harrison House), 2003.

63. *Friday Fax* #25, June 20, 2002.

64. *Joel News International* #266-2.

65. A baby in Malawi: two mentions in http://www.freshfire.ca/revival_report.asp ?ID=Mala001.

66. *Friday Fax* #19, 2001, and #17, 2003.

67. Guillermo Prein, chapter 9 in C. Peter Wagner & Pablo Deiros, *The Rising Revival*, (Ventura, CA: Renew Books), 1998, page 168.

68. You can hear about emphysema and many more healings on the tape series *Eye of the Eagle Prophetic Healing Conference*, Fresh Fire Ministries, P.O. Box 2525, Abbotsford, B.C., Canada V2T6R3 ($25). Toll-free phone: 1 (866) 853-9041.

69. Another direct report from my former housekeeper, Marilyn Hatfield, momzhere @comcast.net:

At age ten, I had rheumatic fever. After that, I often had heart palpitations so severe that you could see my whole body shake. As a cheerleader in high school, I could never do any stunts because I would always pass out. Very embarrassing!

That's the way I lived for the next thirty years. It was bad. At one point, a nurse saw my palpitations and blurted out,

"Oh my God! You're going to die!" (which I didn't think was very professional).

Then in March of 1983, I was at a convention of 2,000 Christian ministers in Little Rock, when the speaker, Ed Dufresne, suddenly stopped and said, "There's somebody here who has a heart problem because of rheumatic fever as a child."

I walked to the front. As I stood facing him about five feet away, I felt a hot fire burning in my chest. He grinned at me and said, "God is healing you!" As he said that, I saw four angels—really *big* angels—standing beside him, two on each side. Then he said, "In fact, angels are doing surgery on your heart right now."

I replied, "Yes, I know!"

After the meeting, I felt great for the first time in my adult life. I went to my doctor, who did some tests and said with astonishment, "What happened to you? You have the heart of a 16-year-old!"

That was 17 years ago. Today, at 65, I can hike in the mountains, I can carry 40-pound boxes up stairs, I can do anything a teenager can.

70. "The ex-pop-star Vanity . . has become a Christian evangelist. Her conversion is the result of experiences in 1994:

Following kidney failure, doctors gave her only three days to live. On her deathbed, she repented and turned her life around.

She was known for her lyrics, sex appeal and appearances in dozens of films. According to her biography ... she was taking $200 worth of cocaine per day before the crisis. 'I wanted to die,' she says. Today, though, she is a full-time preacher in the American free church 'Church of Jesus Christ for All Nations.' 'Not even a million dollars would get me back out there making a mess in the world,' she said ..." Source: Washington Post. See also: www.capitaljournal.com/ stories/030299/fea_relmatthews.shtml.

71. Ted Hagggard (now president of the Nat'l Assn. of Evangelicals) recounts an incident from his youth in Pray Magazine, Sept/Oct 2004, p. 34:

"We were in Dad's [veterinary] office when a man brought in his pet for treatment. As they talked, I noticed that Dad kept focusing not on the animal, but on the owner, who had an unusually large nose and protruding cheekbones.

"Finally, Dad questioned the client about his features. Sheepishly, the man explained that he had looked this way all his life. He had always been taunted for his ugliness. Full of compassion, Dad asked the man's permission to pray for him.

After approval, Dad approached him and put his hand on the man's face, asking God to mold his nose, adjust his cheeks, and make him handsome.

"My life changed as I watched that prayer. When Dad took his hand down, the man was noticeably better-looking. His nose was smaller, his face, had adjusted some, and, oddly enough, his skin tone even seemed to have improved."

72. For 40 years, the creek in Nuku, Naitasiri, Fiji, had been so polluted that the Ministry of Mineral Resources called it "life-threatening." Then in 2004, "After villagers came together for a week of seeking God and asking for His forgiveness for the sins of their forefathers, He heard their cry and He healed their land … . Three days after the atonement, God healed the creek … . Now, people are healed when they drink and wash from the creek. A woman debilitated from a stroke nine months previously was totally healed." "Pattern for Blessing," The Sentinel Group, www.sentinelgroup.org, Dec. 6, 2004.

73. "Six percent of those resuscitated after cardiac arrest reported NDEs." Anita Bartholomew, "After Life: The Scientific Case for the Human Soul," *Reader's Digest*, August, 2003, p. 128.

74. *Friday Fax* #50, 1996.

75. The Second Call Ministries, www.thesecondcall.org, cited in *Joel News International* #337. See also C. Peter Wagner and Pablo Deiros, *The Rising Revival* (Ventura, CA: Renew Books), 1998, p. 168; also, http://hi-venture.org/mis-sions_update.htm, counts nine people as "pronounced dead," then "raised back to life"—by the *children's* ministry of New Life Church in Buenos Aires!

76. Kym Farnik, Marion City Church, 544 Marion Road, South Plymton, SA5038, Australia.

77. Nehemia Info/AVC, www.avc-schweiz.ch in Friday Fax #26, 2005.

78. "In the evening of August 23, 2002, in Burundi, in the up-country town of Ngozi, a 21-month-old boy named Jonathan choked, stopped breathing, and died. His father, Papillon, was attending a seminar with 67 other pastors and leaders at the Ecole Paramedic when a phone call informed him of his son's death. He began to leave for his home nearby, but one of the men, Johnson Nsabimana, immediately got the others to surround him and pray in intense spiritual warfare with tears for the life of Jonathan. Papillon then left for home with Epo Sim, a pastor friend. When the men arrived a few minutes later, the gateman, who was present at Jonathan's death, expressed his condolences. But by the time they walked in the door, the baby's life had been restored, and he was resting in the arms of his mother! He was dead for probably over half an hour, but is doing well now. When the power of God manifested in this place, it touched many in the surrounding area. This is a town where in 1993 hundreds of people were killed. Now this place is a centre of healing and reconciliation between the Tutsis and Hutus." This report is from Mrs. Celia Forsdike of Malvern, Worcestershire, England, Celiaforsdike@aol.com, who was an eyewitness. Also present was the Rev. John Fairbairn, a known and respected English minister on his 14th visit to Africa.

79. Basileia Vineyard Church, Bern, Switzerland. Fax: (41) 31-333-1519. Cited in *Friday Fax* #12, 1996.

80. See the grisly but encouraging incident in *Joel News International* 202, 1997.

50

81. Dennis Balcombe, Revival Christian Church, www.rcchk.org. E-mail: revival@rcchk.org, cited in *Friday Fax* #48, 1996.

82. Mahesh Chavda, *Only Love Can Make a Miracle* (Eastbourne, England: Kingsway Publications), 1999, pp. 11 and 140. Also available at www.glorybarn.com.

83. *Friday Fax* #50, 1997.

84. Richard Edwards, rmhe@jireh.co.uk, cited in *Joel News International* #323.

85. Source: via *United Kingdom & Ireland Revival News*, http://www.openheaven.com, cited in *Friday Fax* #18, 1998. Also see *Friday Fax* #6, 1998 and *Joel News International* #202.

86. New Covenant International, phone (561) 965-3132, fax (561) 965-0373, cited in *Friday Fax* #24, 2000.

87. This resurrection of a young Finnish boy was foretold by William Branham. See www.sendrevival.com/testimonies/categories/deadraised/article_finland_boy.htm.

88. Pastor Le Dinh and Phanh Nguyen, phone (49) 421-235866. Quoted in *Friday Fax* #3, 2001.

89. Dr. Kingsley Fletcher, a noted U.S. pastor from Ghana, has seen eight resurrections. His testimony is on video IS171 from the TV program *It's Supernatural!* produced by Sid Roth, www.sidroth.org.

90. See endnotes 8 and 97 for Mexico. Hogan's work extends to the highlands of Guatemala from his Mexican office in Tampico. Also see George Otis, Jr., *Informed Intercession* (Ventura, California: Renew Books), 1999, page 21.

91. Joel Jeune, a pastor who now oversees 206 churches in Haiti, died as a small boy and was dead for two days. His father, returning from a trip, stopped the procession to the cemetery and prayed for him for 1½ hours. Another 1½ hours later, they heard a sneeze, opened his coffin, unwrapped the body, and found him alive. He has been a major force in the effort to replace Voodoo with Christianity in Haiti. He is now the Haiti coordinator for Gospel Crusade Ministerial Fellowship,www.gcmf.org.

92. This one is unique: the resurrection of an unborn baby who had been dead for several days in its mother's womb! Terry Mize, *More Than Conquerors* (Texarkana: Terry Mize Ministries) 1990, p. 47f.

93. *World InSight*, Sentinel Group, Lynnwood, Washington, www.sentinel group.org, June, 2000. Also, *Friday Fax* #s 7, 20, & 43, 1997; #40 & 48, 1998. And *Friday Fax* #20, 2002, carried an unusual report of Hindu parents who had heard about Jesus, and so prayed for an hour when their four-year-old daughter died. When she came back to life, they became Christians.

94. Suzette Hattingh, Voice in the City, www.grasse.de/voice_in_the_city. Phone: (49) 6109-70295. Fax: (49) 6109-702958. Cited in *Friday Fax* #13, 2000. Also, an American missionary sent out under a well-known but anticharismatic mission board prayed for a baby who had drowned. When the baby came back to life, 80% of the village became Christians. For this, the missionary was fired! Details to be released in a future *Friday Fax*.

95. *Friday Fax* #9, 2003

96. Florian Baertsch, Kingdom Ministries. Fax: (41) 33-437-0016. Cited in *Friday Fax* #41, 1997.

97. A brief mention from a distinguished Christian leader: www.derekprince.com.

98. David Yonggi Cho, Seoul, Korea, cited in *Friday Fax* #16, 1995.

99. Thomas Gegenschatz. Phone: (41) 71-755-1317. Reported in *Friday Fax* #11, 2000.

100. Office of the Diocese, 9 Jalang Tengah, 50-50 Kuala Lumpur, Malaysia. Fax: (60) 214-16460; via Keith Gerner, P.O. Box 1, Newcastle, Co. Down, BT33 OEP, Northern Ireland. Cited in *Friday Fax* #16, 1995.

101. David Hogan, Freedom Ministries (no web site). But see *Renewal Journal #9*, 1997, www.pastornet.net.au/renewal/journal9/9g-hogan.html.

102. Source: HELP International Mongolia, P.O. Box 444, Ulaan Baatar 210 649, phone/fax: (+976) 11/45-46-57, e-mail: him@magicnet.mn. Cited in *Friday Fax #26*, 2001.

103. *Friday Fax #7*, 2002, tells of a team of five who prayed to bring back a decomposing body. Also, *Friday Fax #20*, 2002, gives accounts of two girls, ages three and one, who died of malaria and were resurrected. *Joel News International #409-1* quotes noted missionary Heidi Baker saying, "By now we have had about a dozen resurrections from the dead in our churches." The site for Rolland and Heidi is www.irismin.org. Also see *Friday Fax #38*, 2003.

104. Asia Harvest, P.O. Box 901, Palestine, Texas 75802, www.asiaharvest.org, phone (877) 868-5025, cited in *Friday Fax #9*, 2000. Also see a different incident in *Joel News International #268*.

105. One Purpose: www.aog.org.uk/News/aognews1.htm

106. Seven resurrections are mentioned in Pete Greig, *Awakening Cry* (London: Silver Fish Publishing), 1998, p. 88. **Most impressive:** the report from *Joel News International* you can get by sending an email to lyris@xc.org with the subject line blank and this exact message: get joel-news-international ekechukwu-raised-from-death.

107. See Gulshan Esther *The Torn Veil*, (CLC Publications, P.O. Box 1449, Ft. Washington, PA 19034) 2001, pages 101-109, for a powerfully moving account of a resurrection against incredible odds.

108. In 1995, a group of 16 Choco Indians from Raemae in Darien province were on a three-day ocean trip via canoe when they suddenly encountered four-foot waves. One particularly bad wave swept a five-month-old girl overboard. Her mother briefly asked God for help, then dived into the murky, shark-infested waters. Swimming down into total blackness, she felt her lungs nearly exploding. She flashed a prayer for help, then flung out her hands for one last grope into the vast darkness—and grasped the hand of her baby! But once back in the boat, she found the child was dead. She prayed for her for $3^1/_2$ to 4 hours without result. Then suddenly, the girl came back to life and coughed up large quantities of water! Today the child, Betsy Barcoriso, is a healthy second-grader with no signs of any brain damage whatsoever.

There have been seven recent resurrections in Panama, two of them directly involving Dennis and Jeanne Cook, Vida Ministries, P.O. Box 2243, Kokomo, Indiana 46904-2243 (www.vidaministries.com, email: vidaministries@aol.com, phone: 765/628-0177). Panama phone: (507) 226-2317. Jeanne gave me this report.

109. Article by Min Tobitt in Outreach magazine, March 12, 1997, cited in *Joel News International 202*.

110. For documentation and pictures of Anthony Arellano, a 4?-year-old boy raised from the dead on September 4, 2000, see www.plantanotherchurch.com/risen.htm.

111. Paul van der Hagen, Lyon, France. See also, Richard M. Riss, "How to Raise the Dead," at www.etpv.org/1998/hrd.html.

112. Larry Walker, managing editor, Destiny Image Publishers. See "How to Raise the Dead" at www.etpv.org/1998/hrd.html.

113. This is the only case I've found in which the person was dead more than three days. Emanuel Tuwagirairmana, who is now a pastor in Kenya, died in the Rwanda civil war in 1994 and was dead for seven days. See photos at a non-Christian website, www.near-death.com/forum/nde/000/45.html.

114. March 17, 2004, letter from Russ

Tatro, International Missions Corp., Box 471890, Tulsa, OK 74147, imc@mission-ary.net, www.missionary.net.

115. Dick Eastman, *op. cit.*, p. 1ff.

116. Jimmy Crompton, wof@mweb.co.za. Cited in *Friday Fax #9*, 1998.

117. AMIGOS, phone: (49) 2681-941256. Mobile: (49) 179-120-8232. Fax (49) 2618-941100. E-mail: wardein@stalker.es. Cited in *Friday Fax #50*, 1997.

118. A report written by George Canty about the Reinhard Bonnke crusade in Khartoum, Sudan in April, 2000, www.cfan.org: "A woman whose baby had died in her womb and was to be removed the next Monday wept with joy as her child suddenly jerked to life—it will be born soon."

119. When a factory girl named Vasanthy fell ill, Dan, her boss, was called to her home. But moments after his arrival, she died. *The Cutting Edge*, September 1998, page 9, quotes Dan: "There were about forty to fifty people gathered in the house [all Buddhists].... Then, the Lord told me that this was not a natural event, but that it was a demon taking her life. He told me, 'Command this girl to come back to life, in the name of Jesus... .' At once, I commanded the demon of death to come out ... This girl came back to life within four minutes.... The first thing she said was, 'Mother, what is my boss doing in our house?' About forty Buddhists surrendered their lives to Jesus as a result." (Cutting Edge Ministries, Box 1788, Medford, OR 97501)

120. From a well-known 1961 prophecy by Rick Hicks in *How to Heal the Sick* by Charles and Frances Hunter (Hunter Books, City of Light, 201 McClellan Rd., Kingwood, Texas 77339), pp. 8-16. Also at http://crash.ihug.co.nz/~revival/index2.html.

121. Markus Moser, mjmoser@v-c-b.ch, and Cosmos Touleassi, cosmospeace@hot-mail.com, cited in *Friday Fax #10*, 2004, tell of the resurrection of a four-year-old

boy that caused the conversion of 150 people, mostly Muslims. *Friday Fax #38*, 2001, cites a two-year-old boy being resurrected out of desperation because the parents couldn't afford the morgue fee!

122. George Otis, Jr., and *The Christian Science Monitor*, (617) 450-2000; cited in *Friday Fax #44*, 1997.

123. The resurrection of Boris Pilipchuk, a senior police lieutenant living near Khmelnitsky, is about as spectacular as they get. He was dead for 2½ hours after a massive brain hemorrhage. My contacts in Ukraine have talked with several of his friends and an involved doctor, and they all agree the story is true. Read an abridged version of the story on our site, www.megashift.com, or a full version on the website of the largest church in Europe, http://old.godembassy.org/2002/obschenie/svidetelstva/svid-e/svid2.htm. You can make inquiries to their church at mail@godembassy.org.

124. Personal to me from Michael Zdorov. Also see four instances in *Joel News International* #202. Plus two resurrections in Richard E. Eby, D.O., *Caught Up Into Paradise* (Grand Rapids: Spire/Revell), 1997. And Terry Mize, *More Than Conquerors*, p. 62f. An interesting first-hand report from Troy Stone is in *Miracles Still Happen* by Sheri Stone and Therese Marszalek (Tulsa: Harrison House) 2003. Two interesting cases are on pages 167 and 173 of Jane Rumph, *Signs and Wonders in America Today* (Ann Arbor: Servant Publications) 2003. And Prof. Richard M. Riss has compiled a number of U.S. and foreign resurrections at www.etpv.org/1998/hrd.html.

125. *Joel News International* #277.

126. E-mail from Florian Baertsch, Kingdom Ministries, Switzerland, fbaertsch@gmx.ch.

127. Suzette Hattingh, an evangelist with Voice in the City, commented, "I am a trained nurse, and I know that nobody who had lost so much blood through such a serious wound could survive. This young man did not survive: he died and

returned to life. Today, he is alive and well." *Friday Fax* #13, 2000

128. Dick Eastman, president of Every Home for Christ, in *Beyond Imagination* (Grand Rapids: Chosen Books, 1997), page 200f.

129. You can access the seven-page transcript I've quoted from by sending an e-mail to lyris@xc.org. Leave the subject line blank and type precisely this, and only this, as the body of the message: get joel-news-international buddhist-monk-story. (Watch the hyphens.) You can also access the *Friday Fax* condensation of the report by going to www.jesus.org.uk/dawn/2000/dawn0015.html.

130. Dick Eastman, *op. cit.*, page 213ff.

131. Nell L. Kennedy, *Dream Your Way to Success* (Logos Int'l) 1980, quoted in David Pytches, *Spiritual Gifts in the Local Church* (Minneapolis: Bethany House), p. 237.

132. David Yonggi Cho, speaking at a church growth seminar in Salem Church, Helsinki, Finland, 1995. Reported in *Friday Fax* #16, 1995, by editor Wolfgang Simson, who was in attendance there. Samuel Cho was 26 years old in 1995.

133. *San Diego Union-Tribune*, April 1, 2001, article by Ian Fisher.

134. Joseph Wangigi has been a correspondent to Joel News for 18 years. You may download the full report by addressing lyris@xc.org and typing in: get joel-news-international wangigi-multitude-of-revelations in the body of your message. Leave the subject line blank. Watch those hyphens.

135. It's very motivating to know that God has your name ... and not just "on file." He also has your phone number. In 1990 I spoke with Ken Gaub, now 66, a pastor who was once on vacation in a motor home. He and his family stopped for food on Route 741 south of Dayton, Ohio, and he took a short walk to get a Coke and stretch his legs. Strolling past a gas station, he noticed the phone ringing incessantly in a booth in front of the station. Out of curiosity, he answered it. The operator said, "Long distance call for Ken Gaub." He almost choked on a chunk of ice from the Coke. The call was from Millie in Harrisburg, Pennsyvania, a woman who had heard him speak on TV. Sobbing profusely, she told Ken that she felt he was the only one in the world who could help her. She was writing a suicide note when God gave her the phone booth number. You can read the rest of the story in *God's Got Your Number* (Green Forest, AR: New Leaf Press, 1998). Ken directs Youth Outreach Unlimited, Box 1, Yakima, Washington 98907. Phone: (509) 575-1965.

136. This is an interesting example of the so-called "new journalism," in which the presence of the reporter changes the dimensions of the story.

British visitors recently made a short film about Nduati's work. You may contact Dr. Mariano about it at P.O. Box 40593, Nairobi, Kenya. His dental office phone: (254) 20 222306. As a favor, he may also be willing to help with contact with Nduati if you wish to have him speak outside Africa.

137. John 4:48, 20:29.

138. John 10:38, 14:11, 20:30-31.

139. Source: World Evangelical Alliance and the Evangelical Alliance U.K. Cited in Friday Fax #41, 1998.

> Why has the world changed so radically? What has been moving the hand of God to produce such miracles and kingdom growth? He has been pleased to pour His power through believers by ten "new" strategies.

2

The New Engines of Change
Ten Rediscovered Forces Behind It All

"Verily, verily, I say unto you, He that believeth on me, the works that I do shall he do also; and greater works than these shall he do; because I go unto my Father." John 14:12

Did you have trouble envisioning yourself doing the miracles in chapter one? If so, hang on tight because we're going to go above and beyond them. You're about to learn the secrets that are now transforming the entire globe.

Chances are, you'll be touring unfamiliar territory rather than the familiar roadways of tradition. But that's good because you'll be forced to rely on God directly. As Doc Brown, the wild-eyed scientist of the sci-fi comedy Back to the Future, *says at the end of the film as his nuclear-powered DeLorean heads for the sky: "Roads? Where we're going, we don't <u>need</u> roads."*

In 1999, three Bushmen from the Kalahari Desert changed history. And they weren't movers and shakers of society, but penniless illiterates who lace strips of leather to the bottoms of their feet whenever they need "shoes." However, they stood out from the crowd in three major ways:

• They knew God, and they knew how to move His hand, to convince Him to transform Africa.
• They had discovered, through conversations with readers and researchers, how Africa came to be known as the *Dark Continent*, the home of the poorest nations on earth.
• Thinking in sync with the Spirit of God, they determined that the continent had had enough of misery, and it was high time to take a stand and reverse the curse.

Indeed, it was curses that they found to lie at the root of the problem. Archeologists and anthropologists have lately pieced together——through ancient pottery shards, cave art, etc.—a coherent picture of how Africa was settled and encultured. Long ago, the original settlers came down very slowly from the North through the Rift Valley, a geological crack that runs from the Dead Sea down toward South Africa. Wherever they set up communities, they made pacts with the local

The Rift Valley

gods—actually demons—putting themselves under the thumb of these evil powers. The results have been massive and ghastly.

But the Bushmen knew what to do. They organized a prayer expedition to conduct...

Spiritual Warfare

Calling together a team of experienced prayer intercessors, including some westerners, they journeyed north 5000 miles for three months, starting in July at Cape Agulhas, the southernmost tip of Africa, and stopping at numerous old sites, mostly along the Rift Valley, to renounce and break the original deals and curses.

Every prayer session at every stop was what we call a **power confrontation**. By far the biggest came in Zimbabwe. After a very long, rough ride in jeeps, the team arrived at Mount Injalele (in-ja-*lay*-lee) in the Motobo Hills, two thousand square kilometers of reddish granite, and home to the black eagle.

Though remote, the region was a popular destination for pilgrims, many of them presidents, kings, or tribal chiefs. For many years they had come to Injalele to seek advice and guidance. There, an "oracle" supposedly spoke to them out of a large crack on the back side of the mountain.

You can safely assume that any advice coming from the crack was of extremely poor quality. Yet over the years it had become such a busy shrine that the witch doctor network across Southern Africa had built four temples around the edges of the crack.

So the team prayed.

They worshipped God.

They repented for the sins of their people in worshipping demonic gods.

They vociferously decreed the downfall of the evil powers and declared the ownership of the land transferred to the kingdom of Christ.

Then they left for the next stop.

Shortly afterward, God hit, and hit hard. *All four* of the temples were struck by lightning and totally incinerated! As you can imagine, it was all over the region's newspapers and on everyone's lips. (See this endnote for further examples of temples destroyed by God after prayer.)[1]

MORE: Within two days, the most respected witch doctor in the whole of Southern Africa arrived to assess the damage and see what could be done to restore the site. Though it was a cloudless day, *he was struck by lightning and killed on the spot.*

MORE: Then came the storm. You may have seen the damage reports on CNN World News. The most torrential rains in memory lashed a wide region, washing away whole villages and especially devastating the occult sites and witchcraft training centers, which were numerous there.

But in the western areas, the same storm system made the Kalahari blossom like a garden. There, where many Christians live, the land was transformed into a greenhouse of trees, lush grass, blooming plants, flowing streams, and wild game—virtually unseen for at least a century. The locals are awestruck, and the fear of the Lord has fallen on the whole territory.

MORE (maybe): The plot is still unfolding, but as I understand it now, we are tracking the fortunes of the last 19 or 20 top leaders to visit Injalele. Except for Robert Mugabe, president of Zimbabwe, they all died not long after the intercessors came through.

Say Hello to the Continent of Light

Since that prayer journey, things have started to change. There's a long way to go, but up and down the Rift Valley, spiritual breakthroughs are popping out here and there.

For instance, you already read about the world record response to the gospel in Lagos, with 1,097,000 signing decision cards in one evening. But the most visible transformation has come in Uganda. Once the most wretched place in Africa (thanks to dictators Idi Amin and Milton Obote, in whose reigns even children were tortured), Uganda has made a roaring comeback recently. On New Year's Eve, 1999, the largest stadium in the country was filled with Ugandans—including President Yoweri Museveni—repenting for the nation's past, especially its ties to ancestral religion and Islam.[2]

Now, 64 of Uganda's 240 members of Parliament have become believers. Inflation has fallen from 380% to 6-8%, the GDP is climbing at a healthy 6% a year, and the morale of the people has changed from hopelessness to optimism. But the most remarkable reversal has been in their health: The AIDS rate, once 33%, the highest in the world, has fallen to 5%, while everywhere else in Africa it is skyrocketing, with 26.5 million now living with AIDS and about 15 million more already dead.

Kampala, the capital, has 1.8 million people, 95% of whom may be Christians within eight to ten years.[3] Nationwide, Islam has collapsed from nearly 40% of the population to less than 10%.

You Just Saw Two of Our "Tools of Victory," Prayer Warfare and Spiritual Mapping

As you can see, prayer ain't what it used to be.

When I was a kid, the last thing you ever wanted to get roped into was a prayer meeting. They were always dull as dust, predictable as the sunset, and fun as a funeral.

Worse, they seldom yielded major results. The first person to pray was usually the one with the biggest mouth. The second-biggest mouth would go next, and so on. Each would cover several pet topics, droning on in evangelical jargon without focusing on anything in particular—which yielded results commensurate with the pale effort.

I'll stomp on dead prayers some more in chapter five, where I reveal our new prayer styles, but for right now, let's just say we've made some stupendous improvements. Today, in many of our "strategic intercession" gatherings, prayer is *war*—intelligent, all-out, take-no-prisoners war.*

Spiritual warfare through intercessory prayer is typically focused on one goal—or at least one at a time. Often, the united prayers of a large number of people in an area are aimed at what we perceive to be the main fountainhead of evil there. Normally this is not a person, but:

• a spiritual force (such as a spirit of violence, control, crime, lust, alcoholism, idolatry, revenge, pride, etc.) or

• a demonic presence (such as a Jezebel spirit of rebellion, a stronghold of witchcraft or other evils, a nexus of occult attachments, or some kind of territorial spirit that keeps a city or region in long-term turmoil or ruin). For instance, the adventures of Ana Méndez and her team in taking spiritual control over certain pagan temples, demon-infested sites, and whole geographical regions has gotten her into hair-raising encounters equal to the special effects of any Hollywood sci-fi thriller ever made. For Señora Méndez, as for others, such takeovers have become routine (if you can speak of such electric events as routine). Reading her unique book, *Shaking the Heavens*, will add greatly to your confidence.

For reasons of space, I'll just give you a tame example of how some saints in Mexico have been gobbling up Satan's territory like a giant Pac-Man. This will give you the flavor:

> Several of us once engaged in territorial warfare by attacking the major temple of idolatry in Mexico City.... We completely surrounded the place, pouring out oil as we went and anointing each altar in the name of Jesus. We decreed that this place, where all kinds of witchcraft and idolatry had been performed, would be robbed of its power.
>
> After this spiritual battle, God blessed us with a tremendous earthquake as a sign of victory! Within two weeks, the main priest of the temple appeared on television saying that a sudden crack in the building could not be explained. Engineers came from various countries, and they all concluded that the building would inevitably fall. From this date, the basements that had been places of terrible acts of high magic have remained closed.[4]

---

* If you've never been in on one of these affairs, you have quite an experience coming. You kind of expect men to be loud and insistent when something big is at stake, as it usually is in strategic prayer meetings. But what always shocks me is to see quiet, modest women of God suddenly transmute into flaming prayer warriors, fighting like tigresses protecting their cubs or like Jacob wrestling with God. (See Genesis 32) Makes my hair stand on end! They cast a spotlight onto Galatians 3:28, which says that in Christ Jesus "there is neither ... male nor female."

Note that spiritual warfare is *not* against individuals—except in rare cases of people consciously dedicated to evil aims. The West doesn't currently have any Stalins, Hitlers, or Maos, and we have few Howard Sterns or Marilyn Mansons (active opponents of Biblical values). So when you think of strategic level spiritual warfare, don't envision a circle of crazed believers sticking pins in a voodoo doll of the mayor.

We do, however, pray for people a lot. We pray for their salvation, healing, success, divine guidance, freedom from problems, etc.

Homework First, Fun Afterward

The next engine of change I'll touch on is SPIRITUAL MAPPING—which in three-fourths of cases doesn't have anything to do with maps. It's simply hard, plodding, basic research aimed at discovering the spiritual history of a town, region, or nation.* It tries to answer the central questions:

"How did this place come to have all its problems?"
"Exactly how is the enemy messing us up today?"
"What can we do about it?"[5]

Too often in the past, we Christians have gone off half-cocked. We've jumped on problems before we knew what really caused them. The bell rang, and we came out swinging in five directions. Not cool.

The Rift Valley prayer team was wiser than that. They did their homework first. They tracked down the ultimate origins of the poverty, disease, and ignorance that have plagued Africa since day one. *Then* they moved—and God moved with them. Smart. Effective. Efficient.

We in North America now have thousands of communities in the early stages of transformation. United, persistent, focused prayer and spiritual mapping are the starting point. And closely related is warfare prayer.

Of course, nobody *has* to do spiritual mapping. You can just go out and "do something" and ask God to bless it. But today we're trying to avoid haphazard activity. Life is too short to spend half of it spinning our wheels.

---

* So why does everybody call it spiritual mapping? Because *research* sounds so blah.

The #1 Log Jam and How to Break It

The most dangerous place in the U.S.A. used to be the Soboba Indian Reservation in Southern California. It averaged one murder a month—tough to do with a population of only 150!

Then in August of 1990, a tiny band of Christian activists stopped the bloodshed in one day.

Now, if you don't believe in "territorial spirits" (the bad kind), the Soboba story will give you pause. It all started one day about 350 years ago when the Soboba men were out working their fields. Warriors from the neighboring Pachanga tribe attacked and slaughtered them, then chased most of their women and children into a box canyon now called "Massacre Canyon" and hacked them to death even as they begged for mercy.

The resulting spirit of anger and revenge spawned centuries of violence—and an atmosphere quite resistant to the good news of Christ. But then Bob Beckett, pastor of *The Dwelling Place Family Church* in nearby Hemet, called for a meeting at Massacre Canyon. At the meeting, a Christian from the Pachanga tribe asked forgiveness of four Christians from the Sobobas. They tearfully forgave, took communion together, made a little memorial pile of rocks, and poured the remainder of the wine over the rocks. Then they got in their cars and drove two miles east to the Pachangan reservation, where they made another pile of rocks and did the same thing. Finally, they proclaimed to the spirits and their principalities that their power over the land was broken by Christ's blood and the old wounds all were healed.

There was not another murder for the next five years—and that one was done by an outsider. Instead, there were Christian meetings marked by healings and other signs and wonders. Perhaps one-third of the Sobobas, including the shaman-chief, have made a commitment to Christ, and the revival has spread to many other reservations.[6]

Revivals must often start with an apology. God will not work strongly where His people are divided. Rapid spiritual growth will never come in a community with lingering resentment or bitterness between Christian blacks and whites, charismatics and evangelicals, Euro-Americans and native Americans, Anglos and latinos, etc. That's why we need the third engine of change, RECONCILIATION.

We've staged many hundreds of reconciliation meetings around the world where representatives of one group publicly apologize to representatives of another group (and vice versa) for past offenses. Such meetings almost always create high emotions but tremendous healing and unity.

I think it's thrilling that one of our prime weapons of war is the bond of peace. The world religions are not bringing peace.* Christian activists are the exception. As Jesus said in Matthew 5:9, "Blessed are the peacemakers: for they shall be called the children of God."

Identificational Repentance

These days, as you saw in the Soboba story, you occasionally have to apologize for stuff you didn't do.

Is that fair? No. But often it's the only way to break the cycle of regional violence. Or the only way to shatter a familial, multi-generational pattern of inherited misery, like alcoholism, poverty, wife-beating, emotional deadness, multiple divorces, crime, etc., that trickle down unto the third and fourth generation.

We call it IDENTIFICATIONAL REPENTANCE (or I.R. for the lip lazy), and it's powerful. At first blush, it looks like a silly exercise in play-acting for people with a guilt complex. It's not. I.R. is like a hydrogen bomb in reverse, rapidly undoing heavy damage of a hundred kinds.

I.R. is not for the weak. It's for those whose self-image is strong and secure enough to handle the humbling experience of asking forgiveness for sins committed by others—often by ancestors you can't even name.

If you think I.R. isn't Biblical, you might take a look at the Scripture references in this endnote, which shows that I.R. was indeed practiced in the Old Testament by some real heavyweights.[7] Or if you think you should never have to take the blame for sins you didn't do, you might take another look at the cross. For which of His sins was Jesus crucified?

We've only just begun to tap God's power to heal through I.R. But already we feel that it can solve global problems which otherwise might involve whole divisions of troops and weaponry.

How to Pray Without Words

Want to triple or quadruple the power of your prayers? Have a huge need or problem that you're desperate about? By all means, try FASTING.

Jesus didn't say, "If you fast ..." He said, "When you fast ..." Fasting was commonplace then, and it's becoming commonplace now as part of the powerful new Christian lifestyle you'll read about in the

---

* More often, they trigger war. Last time I checked, there were 28 wars going on, 20 of which involved Muslims as aggressors.

next chapter. I just spoke with Ruth Ruibal, the widow of martyred pastor Julio Ruibal, whose death was the catalyst for the ongoing transformation in Cali, Colombia, seen in the famous *Transformations* video.[8] She told me that out of the 250 members of her church, Ekklesia Centro Cristiano Colombia, there is *always* some group that's fasting—"because their lives are on the line." Such high-powered fasting is becoming more common in North America.

For many, fasting means juices or tea. For others, it means just water.* (It never means just air!) In 1990, fewer than 1,000 people in the world had done water fasts for 40 days; now several hundred thousand have.[9]

Besides making you feel terrific by giving your body a much-needed chance to clean itself out deeply, fasting clears your mind and puts you in closer touch with God.

But it's not just a devotional exercise. It's a *tool* that strengthens you for greater things than you've ever done before. Jesus didn't fast for 40 days in the desert to make himself weak, but to prepare for the heavy tasks of ministry. And when His disciples complained that they couldn't cast out one especially recalcitrant demon, Jesus said (according to some versions), "This kind doesn't come out except by prayer and fasting." (Matt. 17:21)

Besides all that, think of the fun you'll have shopping for a whole new wardrobe.

How Is Satan Going to Stop 707,000,000 Missionaries?

VERY SHORT STORY: An elderly man in India got saved, then started 42 churches—in his first year.[10]

The moral of the story:

1. It's never too late to start planting churches.

2. You can move real fast if you don't have to build buildings.

3. You can move even faster if you don't have to hire pastors to do all the work. (Just let the people do the work. What a concept!)

4. You don't need an M.Div. (master of divinity), special ordination, or even a year of Bible study to start telling people about the new life in Christ. It's basically simple. A famous German theologian was once asked if he could summarize his theology briefly. He replied with the classic children's song:[11]

---

* I prefer the water option. Right off, it lets your stomach know who's boss.

Jesus loves me, this I know,
for the Bible tells me so.

5. It's easy to start an open, family-like church that meets in a house. That elderly Indian was sharp, but not a world-beater. He wasn't even very far ahead of the pack. For example, in 2001 I gave the contents of this book as a 2-day seminar in India, Kyrgyzstan, Ukraine, and one country where I have to go undercover. Total attendance was about 2,000 (90% laymen). At the end, I polled them, asking, "How many open churches/house churches do you now expect to plant in the next three years?" They promised over 35,000. And that wasn't hot air; they're already doing it.

What does this tell you? It tells you that EMPOWERMENT of what used to be called "the laity" is the greatest paradigm-shattering event since the rise of the priesthood class in the second century. **What we are seeing today is the greatest megashift in the history of the church: a transfer of momentum from the steady hands of the leaders to the fleet feet of the followers.** Which is to say, we amateurs are finally starting to take the ball and run with it.

Southern Baptist strategist David Garrison, in his short but exciting landmark book, *Church Planting Movements*, mentions a field report he received from a refugee resettlement camp worker in the Netherlands:

> All of our cell churches have lay pastors/leaders because we turn over the work so fast that the missionary seldom leads as many as two or three Bible studies before God raises at least one leader.
>
> The new leader seems to be both saved and called to lead at the same time, so we baptize him and give him a Bible. After the new believers/leaders are baptized, they are so on fire that we simply cannot hold them back. They fan out all over the country starting Bible studies, and a few weeks later we begin to get word back how many have started.
>
> It's the craziest thing we ever saw! We did not start it, and we couldn't stop it if we tried.[12]

Empowerment of non-professional Christians is behind most of the miracles we see today. Paid leaders are realizing (with great relief) that their job is not to do all the ministry work, but to equip others to do it (which is exactly what Ephesians 4:12 says).

In total contrast, a poll of several traditional U.S. churches asked members about the direction in which empowerment flows:

In your expression of the body of Christ, is it your experience that the resources are expected to flow ...

A. From you to the leaders, so that they might fulfill their ministries and visions?

B. From them to you, so that you might fulfill yours?

Answer A was nearly unanimous.[13] That is why so many churches are switching to team Christianity, where ...

Small Groups Rule!

The Holy Spirit is rapidly revising Christianity.

He is putting at the core of His new church small groups that are interactive, informal, exciting, and geared to rapid multiplication.

This is the beginning of the end for Spectator Christianity. Suddenly, it's out of style to be a pew potato, doing little for the kingdom except sitting in a row on Sundays, looking at the back of someone's head, and wondering if your team will win the afternoon game on TV.

For centuries, the main way to express your Christian identity has been by "going to church." There, a lone, overworked pastor exhorted you to be holy, love your neighbor, be salt and light, and do great stuff for God.

But before you got a chance to actually *do* any of that, you got a benediction and a hearty handshake at the door ... after which you were supposed to go home and improvise your own lifestyle of state-of-the-art sainthood. And a week later, there you were in the pew again, looking at the back of someone's head.

The 100× Church Hits the Field Running

Both laymen and pastors are starting to figure out what was wrong in that routine: It was like having the hockey team listen to the coach's pep talk for an hour, and calling that "the game."

So now we're changing the whole shebang. Around the world, we're rapidly drafting Christians into ministry teams—and the players are loving it. The bleachers are beginning to empty as 707 million action-oriented Christians start to pour out onto the playing field and discover the joy and challenge of every-member ministry.

The church's "fighting force" is thus being multiplied—up to 100 times—as God redeploys large, passive audiences into small, power-filled teams where *every* person has an important function—plus a

chance to widen his or her ministry by reaching out to help more and more people while pursuing the higher gifts.

Instead of one pastor doing the heavy lifting while 100 laymen watch (and often criticize), you may now have 100 "team Christians" sharing the work of ministry while various people with pastoral gifts coach and equip from the sidelines. This megashift to EMPOWERMENT is at the core of the new Christianity.

The Fatal Flaw of the Pastoral System

Don't Be a Baby

Being part of a small group takes effort. It requires thinking, whether you're in a house church or cell church meeting—or some other group with a name like microchurch, heart church, Alpha group, metachurch mouse cell, organic church, Serendipity team, simple church, life transformation group, community of care, jacuzzi fellowship, or just a plain old open church meeting in a pub.

But it's worth the work. Whereas traditional churches tend to produce spiritual babies, small groups tend to produce *maturity*. (BABIES is my acronym for Born Again But Is Enjoying Siesta.)

Nobody snoozes in small groups. The body life of the group will buff up your character, soothe your sorrows, sprout your gifts, heal your wounds, lift your spirit, teach your mind, disciple your soul, and bring you face to face with God again and again. I'll camp on this in chapter four, but for right now, you should understand that if you're serious, an open fellowship looms large in your future.

Other Avenues of Growth

The Lord has many other ways to accelerate your growth and empowerment. Here are three of the more popular ones:

• **Tentmaking** is doing secular work overseas as a way of supporting yourself as an evangelist, missionary, apostle, etc. (The name comes from the apostle Paul, who made tents for a living while he started churches.) Frequently the country is one that doesn't give missionary visas. Some of them, like Saudi Arabia and North Korea, will boot you out in a heartbeat if they find you "proselytizing" their citizenry, so after a while, you get good at tiptoe evangelism. Guaranteed to raise your testosterone level, even if you're a woman! Over four million jobs are available for Americans right now.[14]

• **Short-Term Missions** (two to ten weeks abroad) have been booming in popularity for 20 years. The immediate results aren't too impressive, but every year over one million North Americans (mostly the 16-25 set) have gotten a first-hand look at needy fields and acquired a taste for the adventure of mission work. It has also greatly raised the commitment level of Western churches to mission involvement.[15]

• **Training Near Home** for church planting has been a breakthrough, especially in poor nations where young Christians can't afford to go to a Bible school for even one year. By correspondence, you can now train at home under the guidance of an experienced church planter. Formally called **Theological Education by Extension (TEE)**, it has been broadened by a number of missionary statesmen. Professor George Patterson, for instance, has added a strong element of personal discipling and "lab work," the lab being a new house church that the student is charged with developing and multiplying.[16]

Those are just three avenues of empowerment. The Master Mentor has a thousand more. The bottom line to all of them is creating a new class of disciples who have the experience and the power to change the world. You're invited to join.

Rabbit Teams

Kamla Bai was a Christian, but that didn't seem to be doing her much good.* For a long time, her two children had been slowly dying of two different diseases.

Then in 1997 she had a dream. She saw a small group of westerners coming to visit her city in Madhya Pradesh state of central India.

---

* Her first name is Kamla. *Bai* is a title given to married women in India.

An overweight man came up to her and said that God was going to make her a prophetess, and as a sign that this was of God, he would pray for her children, and God would heal them.

The next morning, she awoke to find both children perfectly well.

Ironically, neither she nor her pastor, Dinesh Patel, believed in prophecy. In fact, Patel was sure she had gone off the deep end.

But two months later, a mission team from Kingdom Ministries in Switzerland came through the area, and Kamla immediately recognized one of them, Erich Reber, as the man in her dream. As he spoke that evening, the Lord did indeed give her the gift of prophecy.

Ever since then, she has been a key person in a **rabbit team** that goes from town to town, starting churches that are geared to multiplying quickly, like rabbits (my own "pet" term).

Her *modus operandi*: When her little team enters a village, they ask God to show them the house of a "man of peace." (That's a person of either sex who is hospitable, fairly prosperous, modestly influential, and open to the gospel. In Luke 10, Jesus ordered His disciples to build their work in each town on such people rather than going door to door.) In every village, as they pray, the Holy Spirit points out to Kamla a certain house—and reveals unknowable things about the occupants, such as hidden sins, special needs, or the presence of occult objects. Then they just knock on the door. Most of the people are so touched that they quickly accept Jesus Christ as their Lord and become the hub of a new house church.

She and her band of rapid rabbits plant about fifty churches a year.[17] Of course, these home churches are smaller than traditional congregations (in India, about 6-20 instead of 75 or so). But Curtis Sergeant has brilliantly dramatized the advantage of smallness. He sketches the potential of locking two elephants—or two rabbits—in a closet for three years. Ignoring all practical problems and calculating the mere mathematics of gestation periods, litter size, etc., you would have three elephants—or 476 million rabbits.

MORAL: To think really big, think small.[18]

Five Secrets of Success

Why are rabbit teams starting to multiply so fast? Because God is on the move—and because we've learned a few things:

1. We no longer try to get converts; we're trying to make disciples. Major difference.

2. We often work in teams to reach *families* and *groups* of disciples to form an instant church. This greatly speeds things up and also

reduces the friction that can result when only one person in a family turns to Christ.

3. We're not just planting scattered churches here and there; we're trying to saturate whole areas and regions.

4. We don't just plant a church and say, "Well, that's done." (Simple addition.) We're planting church-planting *movements*. (Multiplication.) Every new church is an independent ring of activity and growth, not just a sub-unit of the rabbit team. (This new freedom appeals especially to men.)

5. We're no longer asking ourselves, "How can we expand our existing networks?" Our thinking has changed. We're into starting our planning with the end goal. We're using "outside in" thinking, where the big question is, "What's it going to take to finish the job, to reach our whole city/region/country?" Then we do "whatever it takes" to plant *movements* aimed at saturating a whole city or nation.

Yes, the church has hundreds of thousands of fine "mercy ministries" worldwide that reach out to help the disadvantaged, the fallen, and the ill. I support a number of them. But today we're not just nibbling at the edges of society. We're going for its heart.

For example, in 2001 I was at a buffet dinner in Raipur, India, chatting with a laid-back, thirty-something lady named Rajani.

Now, in India it's still controversial for a woman to do any ministry at all. And Rajani admitted to being controversial—for leading other women to the Lord and baptizing them.

So I asked her, "Well, just how many have you baptized?"

"Five hundred," she said. "And another two hundred are waiting to be baptized."

Suddenly I felt very small and wimpy. A red neon sign began flashing in my head. It said, *Jim, you pipsqueak, it's time to get serious about life.*

After a sudden illness, Rajani went to be with the Lord in 2003. But the impact she had on the kingdom in half a lifetime will continue to multiply exponentially.

An Example of the Group-by-Group Approach

A Vietnamese pastor named Ai was in jail for being a Christian. There he met a young man I'll call Duc from the "Tai Dang" tribe and led him to Christ.

After their releases, Ai started Duc in a Bible training course for remote church planters. It's a four-level course. In the first level, the student has one month to lead five others to the Lord.

After that month, Ai was surprised to get a phone call from Duc, asking if he would journey to the Tai Dang area to baptize his converts. His answer, in brief, was, "Why should I travel all that way just to baptize five people?" (I would have added, "Baptize your own converts!")

Duc replied, "I haven't won five people, but five villages. It's 753 people."[19]

BIGGER EXAMPLE of group-by-group: In 1999, a Chinese man led an underground six-day Evangelism Explosion seminar in China. Near the end, he gave his students a vague assignment: "For the next 16 weeks, do just what you've been doing here for the last six days."

One of his students took him literally. For 16 weeks, he trained his church in Evangelism Explosion techniques seven days a week. As a result of this error, over 30,000 people heard the gospel, and about 20,000 of them decided to become Christians![20]

Oh well, mistakes happen.

Now, lest you get the impression that God works only in the outer boondocks, let me mention Goiânia, Brazil (pop. 1,200,000), the busy capital of Goiás state.

Back in 1989, a housewife and mother named Elizabeth Cornelio became concerned about Goiânia because it was a major center of spiritism—among other problems. So she began meeting for prayer with four women from other churches.

Then in 1993, she invited Christians all over the city to unite and pray. When 850 showed up, her pastor kicked her out of the church, saying, "Members of other churches are not spiritual brothers and sisters; they are at most spiritual cousins." (A good example of the thinking you *won't* find in today's open fellowships.)

Currently, almost 200,000 women pray for the city every day, linked by her radio program. When the program had to go off the air from March through May of 1999, the crime rate quickly ballooned by 50%. The city sent a delegation including the mayor and police chief, beseeching her to get back on the air. (She did, and the crime rate sank.)

Goiânia does have rabbit teams, which on a typical weekend will start one new church (altogether). But every believer in town gets into the act in his or her own way: Christian midwives anoint newborns with oil, dedicating them to Jesus; Christians walk the aisles in supermarkets, praying for people; a few preach in bars, to great effect; and some even get up at 4:00 a.m. to walk through the empty streetcars, praying that God will bless each rider that day.

The result? *In seven years, evangelicals in Goiânia went from 7% of the population to 45%.*[21]

As Sherlock Holmes once exclaimed, "Come, Watson, come! The game is afoot."[22]

Prayers on Wheels

The new church has broken out of the box. To borrow a phrase from the movies, we now go on *location*. Here is an example of the eighth change engine, ON-SITE PRAYER.

Another former housekeeper of mine (who declines to be named) joined a prayer expedition of 24 people and climbed Mount Everest.

Well, not all the way to the top. Most of them weren't athletes, but they went through a lot of physical conditioning. So they got beyond the lodge and the base camp to their target area.

They were there because of persistent reports from many prophets that the strongest territorial spirit in the world, an evil power usually referred to as "The Queen of Heaven," was solidly entrenched in the Everest area. The damage it was doing was of course impossible to estimate in any scientific way, but the reports agreed that its destructive power extended far beyond Nepal to include most of Southeast Asia.

So in September of 1997, the *Operation Ice Castle* team of veteran intercessors and prayer warriors converged from various countries upon Everest. While thirteen of them stayed to pray at the rustic lodge at 13,000 feet, eleven trekked up to the first base camp, a flattish location chosen for its safety. Secular groups from Korea, Italy, France, and Spain shared the camp site.

Leaving the base camp, they climbed through the "Ice Fall," the most dangerous part of Everest (with no guide but angels!) and were approaching the exact center of the spirit's seat of power when a huge avalanche sent megatons of ice and snow racing toward them. By God's grace, they were just below a large crevasse which consumed the avalanche, leaving them only to cope for ten minutes with a life-threatening cloud of ice particles burning their lungs. They were able to continue on to confront and pray against the spirit's controlling power over many of the false religions of the world. Then they returned to the base camp.

Just before daylight the next morning, the Holy Spirit awoke Ana Méndez of Mexico, the team leader, and said, "Go out from this mountain before 11:00 A.M." So as soon as it was light enough to see, they scrambled to pack up and head downhill by 10:30. Señora Méndez described the event: "When the last of our 36 beasts of burden (yaks) had come out, not one, but all three mountain slopes which surrounded Base Camp—Everest, Loh-La, and Nuptse—simultaneously collapsed in one of the greatest avalanches ever seen on Everest."[23]

CNN News carried the story, but without video footage. Méndez, however, made a video of the avalanche, which I have seen.

Inside of two weeks, a number of startling setbacks hit major religious systems that are heavily influenced by this "Queen of Heaven."[24]

Disciplined Christians are the apprentice owners of the world, and intercessors who hear from God are its unseen regents.

WARNING: A major power confrontation like this is *not* an exercise for your Sunday school class. And never, never try it on your own; you will return home in a basket.*

Prayer Was Never Like This

ON-SITE PRAYER is a change engine with many forms:

• *Prayer journeys* (such as the Rift Valley expedition) may cover a lot of territory. The most ambitious journey to date was the Reconciliation Walk, which began in 1996 in Cologne, Germany (starting point of the medieval Crusades), and finished in 1999 in Jerusalem. For three years, a total of 2,500 Christians from 43 nations walked the roads through Greece, Turkey, Lebanon, Syria, and Israel, apologizing everywhere to Muslims who lined the streets in awed appreciation, asking forgiveness for the cruel excesses of the Crusades. (The walkers even wore T-shirts proclaiming in Arabic or Turkish, *I Apologize*.) In many places, astonished Muslim citizens and officials were deeply moved. Often they cried as they applauded wildly—and invited the Christians into their homes for meals. Such things are unheard of in the bitter Mideast. For the first time, many Muslims are starting to rethink *their* sins against Christians and Jews.[25]

• *Prayer battles* may be defensive or offensive:

Christians had an offensive confrontation on August 12, 2000, in Czestehowa, Poland, the home of the shrine of the Black Madonna (yet another image of the Queen of Heaven). A team of 56 intercessors went to her site at the Jasna Gora Temple, where one million pilgrims were expected to come revere her three days later. There they repented of the idolatry of the past, and they followed that with worship, prayer, and proclamations. People all across Poland were amazed when only 250,000 visitors showed up.

---

* God protects His people in many ways:

Another incident involved "men in white cloaks" standing around a church building, intimidating the Stasi, the East German police, in 1986 (reported in *Friday Fax* #45, 1995). When the Stasi arrested the pastor and questioned him about the men, he "laughed until it hurt."

In 1995, a gang of punks planned a raid to destroy a Christian coffee house in Switzerland. It was foiled when they barged in and discovered a big, tough bouncer in every corner of the place. "We wouldn't have had a chance," they lamented afterward. As you might guess, the punks were the only ones who could see the bouncers. (Source: Gebet fur die Schweiz, cited in *Friday Fax* #41, 1995)

And in 2000 we received a report (*Friday Fax* #36, 2000) of an attempt by ten men to ambush a Christian Chamula family in Chiapas state, Mexico. It backfired when a long line of "people with guns" suddenly appeared, aiming at the ten men. The attackers freaked out and cut their feet and tore their chamarras in panicked flight. To date, 60 Chamulas have been martyred, but their blood has brought 1.3 million Chamulas to faith in Christ—about 40% of the population of Chiapas!

A defensive confrontation took place in October, 1996, in Ramtek, Madhya Pradesh, India, where elaborate preparations were made to host 70,000 Hindu militants at a national convention where they planned to take an oath to destroy every Christian and Muslim in the country. The alarmed Christians rounded up prayer support from near and far, about 30,000 intercessors. On the opening day, as my friend Mrs. Bindu Choudrie wrote, "Sure enough, as we approached the area, a storm began to build up, the wind howled, and it rained heavily ... Everything was in the mud. It became chilly and cold. Instead of 70,000 people, there were not more than 700. (And when the time came to take the oath, *nobody* showed up.) A newspaper called the event a 'megaflop.' "[26]

• *Covering-prayer stations* are places where intercessors go and sit behind the scenes to give prayer support, or "covering" for some event or project. Many top evangelists are unwilling to preach to large crowds without a team of seasoned prayer warriors in a nearby room. And 18 governors of Philippine provinces now have intercessors on site, praying for practical matters of state.[27]

• *Prayer walks* are usually very casual and low-key, with perhaps two to three people strolling through a neighborhood while praying quietly for residents in each home. I know it doesn't sound too impressive, but the results are frequently powerful. Or they may pray while circling around a target area or town several times in a *Joshua Walk*, reminiscent of Joshua's seven loops around Jericho.

TWO SMALL EXAMPLES: Ram Gopal, an evangelist in India, recently walked into a village and started handing out tracts. He was stopped by the headman, who scattered his tracts to the four winds, made serious threats on his life, and ordered him to leave. A week later Gopal came back—after circling the village several times, praying. But this time the headman warmly invited him into his home, where he now hosts a house church.

Also in India, "a group of intercessors prayer-walked a block of flats (apartments) daily for several days and left the neighboring block alone. Later, when contacted, over 70% of the prayer-walked block welcomed the intercessors while 90% of the unwalked block rejected them."*[28]

---

* The typical process among up-to-date teams in India is: 1. Spiritual mapping—to find out what the target people are like. 2. Prayer walking—to discern what the predominant territorial spirits or spiritual strongholds of evil are. (Indians tell me that God is unfailing in revealing them.) 3. "Binding the strongman" (Matthew 12:29), breaking down the spiritual powers of evil that prevail there. (Indians stress that if you don't do this first, you may be beating your head against a wall for a long time.) 4. Entering the village or neighborhood and inquiring for the "man of peace." (Lately, he or she often approaches the team before they even have a chance to look around!) 5. Ministering to the man of peace and his family. 6. Discipling them and witnessing to them—simultaneously! 7. Baptizing them. 8. Working through them rather exclusively, and not going door to door, so that all additional believers are baptized and nurtured by the household of the man of peace. See Luke 10.

Two heavy examples: In September, 2001, in Chhindwara, Madhya Pradesh, India, I interviewed a beautiful, dignified lady of about 30 who had been active in ministry for two years and had baptized 50 women and planted 16 house churches. Her name is Poonam Jadhav, and she is a model of politeness and decorum. A mother of two, she is a quiet, obedient woman with finely chiseled features.

The previous May she was just starting a seminar for Chhindwara women when the Hindu temple next door began blaring loud music with its sound system and creating other havoc. They all went out and began walking around the temple, praying and binding the powers of the shrines and idols there, anointing them with oil. The priest, a man named Rahminen, came out to hassle them, so they bound his powers, too, and finished circling the temple *70 times*.

Result: At that point, the temple sound system broke down, and they were able to finish the seminar in peace.

Three days later, as it ended, they were leaving the building when they noticed a crowd in the street next door. They went over to check it out and were shocked to see Rahminen lying in their midst, dead. A heart attack, someone said.

The previous July, Poonam was trying to lead some evangelism work in a slum area. It was tough, and they were getting nowhere, so she asked her team what the problem was. They said the area's spiritual atmosphere was plagued by three witches. (Forget pointy hats and broomsticks; we're talking *real* witches here.) Their big thing was casting spells on all the new babies. About 30 babies had died or been stillborn, just in that little area of about fifty families.

So they went to work. Eight women went prayer-walking, circling the entire area *250 times!* (Me, I would have done seven laps and called it a day.) They prayed intensely and anointed houses with oil. They urged the witches to repent and stop killing babies, but with no success.

Result: Six days later, all three of the witches had died terrible deaths. The community was shot through with the fear of God and today has a thriving open fellowship.

Large examples: The heaviest prayer-walking in recent memory was in East Germany in 1989, where groups of ten or twelve were meeting in homes on Monday nights to pray for peace—some 50,000 people by October. After that, they quietly moved into churches and the streets. News reports said their numbers swelled to 300,000, and on November 9, the Berlin Wall fell.

In India, Christians and "untouchable" dalits had suffered persecution and caste-based suppression for centuries. But as the 2004 election drew near, about five million Christians around the world united in prayer and fasting against the Hindu nationalists who controlled the government. Polls all said that the anti-Christian BJP party had an unbreakable lock on the nation. Everyone was stunned on May 13 when the BJP was swept from power and firmly replaced by the Christian-friendly Congress Party.

In the late '90s, millions of Christians took part in their local March for Jesus in cities around the world. On May 2, 2004, over 20 million gathered in 56 nations of Africa, resulting in miracle after miracle.[29] My own guesstimate is that over 50 million of us are now praying tirelessly for world revival.

What I'm asking you to join is no clever fad. It is rapidly becoming the biggest force the world has ever seen, and at its heart is the overwhelming love of God.

Evangelism Through Technology and the Media

A 30-year-old farmer we call Noah lives in a flat part of China—which is good because he can see the police coming a long way away. This gives him plenty of time to lose his cell phone and take his prayer list off the wall.

I talked recently with an American who went to visit him one afternoon last year. When he arrived, he noticed that Mrs. Noah was kind of sunburned because she had put in long hours in the fields that day. A typical, hard-working farm family ... except for that cell phone.

Over dinner with other guests, the visitor asked Noah, in his beginner's Chinese, "How many Christian workers do you have?"

He got an answer that sounded to him like thirty thousand.

"No," he objected. "I said, 'How many full-time missionaries do you have in your church network?' "

He got the same answer. So he waved at his interpreter. "Hey, I'm trying to ask this guy how many church planters he's responsible for."

The interpreter queried Noah, then replied, "He says thirty thousand—in a radius of 500 kilometers."

The American couldn't quite handle that. So he asked, "Well—how many total members does that make in his whole network?"

The answer funneled its way back: *eight million.*

The American told me that he suddenly felt extremely humble to be sitting with a young farmer who looks after the welfare of 8,000,000 people with one lousy cell phone. In his spare time.

Later in the same trip, he was smacked by an even larger wave of humility when he met another leader responsible for ten million.

After that, he met "Big John," a thirty-something man much respected across China who leads twelve million. At that point, he said he felt inexpressibly tiny.

He probably would have felt downright invisible if he had met "The Heavenly Man." That's the pet name of Brother Yun, a much-loved gentleman who provides leadership for China's largest network of house churches, totaling 60 million.* I recently heard through the grapevine that his movement is planning on winning 45 million more to Christ this year.

Again, I'm not trying to wow you or make you feel bad. Nor am I plugging cell phones as the answer to our prayers. I'm trying to acquaint you with a new stage of Christianity in which freshly empowered disciples are turning basic tools into engines of change that are creating a whole new reality.

Our Biggest Guns

The media picture is bright as gold. Some highlights:

• **Radio**. Right now, 4,857,000,000 people, 81% of the world, can tune in to hear the gospel in their native tongue. Perhaps 90% can understand the broadcasts. Live radio is warm, and it works. For instance, there are now thousands of "radio churches" across North Africa and the Middle East.[30]

• **Film**. The last time I checked www.jesusfilm.org, it said the biographical film Jesus has now been dubbed in 712 languages and seen by 4.6 billion people. That's three-fourths of the world! So far, 176 million have given their lives to the Jesus they've met in the movie.

• **Television**. Appearing on *The 700 Club* in 1993 gave me a look behind the scenes at CBN and left me with great respect for their painstaking methods. Based on 32,000 interviews in 51 cities, they estimate that in 2000, 40 million people (mostly outside the U.S.) made a decision to follow the Lord Jesus Christ through their broadcasts. I don't doubt them.

CBN's retention rate seems to be sky-high too. For example, out of 25 million who responded to the gospel in Nigeria through CBN in 2001, 22 million have joined a church.

In 1996, Billy Graham put on a worldwide simulcast that was seen by 2 billion viewers. Dr. Graham is quite reluctant to toot his own horn, but my sources state that the 450 million follow-up packets they printed for new converts were mostly snatched up within a few hours.

---

* How do they escape being caught? They don't. Without exception, every top Christian leader in China has done hard time in prison—at least three years, usually 20 years or more. It goes with the territory. A Chinese believer won't ask you if you have a theological degree. He'll typically ask just three things: How many people have you led to the Lord? How many churches have you started? How many years have you spent in prison for Jesus?

• **The Internet**. In the spring of 1995, the Adventist Medical Clinic in Moscow was threatened repeatedly and strongly by the Russian Mafia. They called with threats of violence if the clinic didn't start making high monthly payments. When the clinic leader appealed for worldwide prayer via the Internet, he got over 10,000 letters, faxes, and e-mails of support, quite a few of which were duly posted in front of the clinic. The Mafia backed off. Christian solidarity works.[31]

If you wish to dip your toe into this ocean, you will find some of the better house church websites listed in the bibliography. Read it fast because it will be out of date in about two seconds! The Christian presence on this new Tower of Babble is huge and growing.

Christian Cooperation Is Not an Oxymoron Any More

It sounds odd to say that LEADERSHIP TEAMWORK is a *new* engine of change, but it really is.

Let me illustrate the point at three levels:

• **Local**. Until recent decades, relations between pastors of competing churches in America seldom rose much above *polite*. And it was worse overseas.

In the U.S., the quarterly luncheon of any town's ministerial union usually produced a level of fellowship and unity about one notch above the *gemutlichkeit* among passengers on Continental 3578 between Philly and Newark. Overseas, pastors of Evangelical, Charismatic, and Pentecostal churches traded brickbats with one another, while rank-and-file churchmen yielded to suspicion and kept to their own kind.

Praise God, that's ending fast. As tens of thousands of pastors have come together humbly, repenting for past attitudes, they have broken the chains of spiritual darkness in their cities. Regions mired in ecclesiastical quicksand for centuries are starting to see revival and growth.[32]

Even more encouraging, we are just beginning to discover how we can re-create entire cities and regions by providing an unelected, broad leadership combining pastors with widely respected elders, keen-eared prophets, and modern-day apostles (highly gifted missionaries and accomplished church planters).[33]

• **National** (U.S.) Denominationalism is dead.* Denominations, however, are another story.

---

* Today, none but the cultist or culturally challenged diehard thinks that his is the one true church and fount of all truth.

While some are still the same hidebound packs of apparatchiks and control freaks they always were, many have reformed themselves into exciting models of servant-hearted humility and dynamic outreach. Despite the rumors you've heard, denominations are alive and kicking. Many denominations today are providing needed help to their congregations and are doing a fine job in the right ways.

But ever since World War II, servant ("parachurch") ministries have fared far better than denominations. (Examples: Campus Crusade for Christ, World Vision, Focus on the Family, Christian Broadcasting Network, Billy Graham Evangelistic Association.) By their free, entrepreneurial nature, they create more excitement, draw in more money (and waste less), inspire more devotion, and attract higher quality leaders than denominations, most of which, alas, are a network of miniature hierarchies enmeshed in outdated traditions.

I especially want to commend those servant associations whose purpose is to network Christian groups and individuals in synergistic ways, such as the giant umbrella Mission America (with 80+ denominations and 350+ servant ministries). They are beginning to turn the North American church around.

• **Worldwide.** International cooperative bodies like the World Evangelical Alliance, Lausanne Committee for World Evangelization, and International Charismatic Congress on World Evangelization have performed myriad services for Christians everywhere. They have created a global forum for all of us without resorting to command-and-control structures.

I also want to salute Dawn Ministries, which has revolutionized evangelism and united the churches into action in 156 nations worldwide. Their goal is to stimulate and help guide the creation of as many as 20 million more house churches worldwide, and so far, they've been meeting or beating their goals in nation after nation.[34]

Summary

In somewhat clearer order, the ten engines of change are:
1. **Intercessory Prayer**
    A. Prayer Warfare (Strategic-Level Intercession)
    B. Prayer Evangelism
2. **Empowerment**
3. **Reconciliation**
4. **Identificational Repentance**
5. **Spiritual Mapping**
6. **Rabbit Teams** (Saturation Church Planting Movements)
7. **On-Site Prayer**

8. **Fasting**
9. **Leadership Teamwork**
    A. Area (apostolic spearheading and coordination)
    B. National servant ministries
    C. Worldwide servant ministries
10. **Media Evangelism**

Engine 11:
You'd never guess this one

Often, God doesn't wait for us to get our engines running. He just goes ahead and does things on His own. So my humble nomination for the eleventh engine of change is God himself!

If that sounds a bit loopy, consider what He is doing in Islamic areas. He has appeared directly in visions and night dreams to *millions* of Muslims in the last decade.[35] In roughly 70% of cases, they see Jesus, and He declares to them some variant of John 14:6, "I am the way, the truth, and the life. No one comes to the Father except by me."[36] And for reasons I don't fully understand, He almost always appears as a white man dressed in a white robe.

South African church growth specialist Karel Sanders reported in 1998 that 42% of the new Muslim converts are coming to Christ because of these "visions, dreams, angelic appearances, and hearing God's voice."[37] Combined with gospel radio, this phenomenon is producing a tidal wave of interest in Jesus Christ. For instance, the Campus Crusade for Christ Communication Center for North Africa and the Middle East is struggling to cope with a flood of 3,000 inquiry letters a day, most asking for Bibles and literature.[38]

But the Lord's direct interventions in history go far beyond Muslim areas. For instance:

• In 1996, in the village of Dadar-Gaon in the Dindori district of Madhya Pradesh (central India), God brought a 16-year-old girl named Bhagavathi back to life after another 16-year-old girl prayed for her for about 12 hours!

News of this reached a 38-year-old Hindu who had been severely crippled all his life. He had never even stood up. But when he heard about the girl, God gave him faith. He convinced a young boy to walk alongside him and guide him all the way to Dadar-Gaon. He kept saying to himself, *If only I can reach that village where God is, I will be healed.*

They started at dawn, and the man crawled nonstop till dusk, his face to the ground, inching along the road with increasing difficulty.

When they finally neared Dadar-Gaon, the boy announced, "There is the village," and pointed uphill at some lights 500 yards away. The exhausted man lifted his head. Then he stood up—*and ran all the way to the village!*

Today he is an elder in his church and an evangelist with Gospel for Asia.[39]

• John Paul Jackson reports a startling occurrence in Switzerland in 1990.[40]

I was on a 21-day ministry trip through Europe, but after speaking in Geneva, I doubled over in pain from what doctors later told me was pancreatitis.

Lying on my bed in excruciating pain that night, I told God that if He didn't heal me, I would cancel the rest of my trip and check into a hospital.

Around 2:30 a.m., I sensed someone standing beside my bed. To my right was an elderly man with weathered skin and thick, knotted fingers. First, I thought I was hallucinating; then I thought it was an angel. As the old man reached out his hand toward me, he said, "I have come to pray for you." Placing his hand on top of mine, which rested on my stomach, he began to pray. I felt heat leave his hands and enter into mine. It felt thick like honey and was glowing hot. Heat unrolled like a scroll— down my legs and out my feet and up my abdomen and out my head. As it steadily unrolled, the searing pain left my body. Then we looked at each other, and he disappeared before my eyes.

I jumped out of bed and began dancing around the room, thanking God for healing me and sending His angel. That's when He said it wasn't an angel. Nor was it the devil. A vision occurred to me of a man with outstretched hands and tears running down his face, telling God, *"I just want to be used by you, but I'm an old man in a small village. People think I'm crazy. Can you use me?"*

And God said to me, "I took him from an obscure village in Mexico, used him, and sent him back."

With Facts Like These,
Who Needs Theories?

The ten engines of change are not just clever experiments. God has been using them to expand His family quite rapidly. A few typical infobites of evidence:

• Kazakhstan went from 100 evangelicals in 1990 to 6,000 in 2000.[41]

• Between 1990 and 2004, Christians in Cambodia grew from 200 to 400,000.[42]

• Until about 1990, the death rate from unnatural causes in Colombia's Bellavista Prison was 600 a year—all murders! It quickly sank to one a year when prisoners began receiving Christ in large numbers. The atmosphere of violence has been erased.[43]

• Guatemala is now 44% born-again Christians.[44] Neighboring El Salvador is at 53.6%.[45]

• In 1981 Rio de Janeiro had 30 spiritist centers for each evangelical church. By 1996, that had flip-flopped to 40 evangelical churches for each spiritist center.[46]

• About 25,000 house churches were started in India in 2002. The more well-informed networks are growing at over 100% a year.

• In beleaguered Kurdistan, there were no believers in 1992. Today, there are churches in every major city.[47]

• "In Mongolia the 500 believers have suddenly jumped to 50,000."[48]

• A confidential survey in India (about 1995) showed that 25% of the people would like to become Christians if they could stay in their family groupings![49]

• In the Fugou area of China's Henan province, over 90% of the people are Christians now.[50]

• Swedish radio mission IBRA estimates, "In the Middle East, there are perhaps millions of isolated 'radio Christians' who have become Christians through hearing evangelistic transmissions ..."[51]

• More Muslims have turned to Christ in the last ten years than in the previous 1,000 years.

• You probably remember the bumper sticker that said, **Illiterate? Write For Help**. This is even funnier: More than 100,000 members of the Hmong tribe in northern Vietnam have

(continued on next page)

turned to the Lord after listening to Christian radio programs. (No missionaries involved.) This was discovered by accident because none of them were literate enough to write the station and report their massive response.[52]

• Nagaland and Mizoram states in India now claim to be 100% Christian.[53]

• Eight out of ten humans now have access to the entire Bible in their own language.[54]

• As of 1970, Nepal had 5,200 Christians. As of 2000, it's 543,340.[55]

• In Hainan province, China, a revival sparked in part by an American friend of mine grew from zero to 255,000 new converts in eight years. During the annual "month of evangelism" there, they now expect each believer to try to bring at least one other person to faith in Christ.[56]

• The church in Laos grew from 32,000 to 80,000 in three years. To combat government oppression, believers turned to fasting, some eating only on weekends.[57]

• From 1992 to 1997, Christians among the Pygmies in the Congo grew from about zero to 300,000.[58]

• Zimbabwe added 6000 new churches from 1992 to 1998. That comes to 2,240,000 new Christians.[59]

• As noted before, China has the largest church in the world, with 115 to 120 million true Christians, mostly in house churches. They have about one million active church planters.[60]

You could burn out your TV and go broke subscribing to magazines, yet still see hardly a glimpse of this grand picture. It's not that the major media are corrupt or incompetent, it's just that they are at the periphery of real life. The epicenter, the "still point of the turning world," is the quiet room where a nameless prayer warrior is interceding for the souls of nations, fervently turning the mighty hand of God.

David Garrison's booklet *Church Planting Movements* concludes that "Every region of the world now pulsates with some kind of Church Planting Movement."[61] *Every region!* These are tough times for a pessimist.

1. I heard John Robb of World Vision describing in Seattle on 11/19/97 how a temple in Bali, Indonesia, was struck by lightning and burned, with a loss of over $100,000. Two large trees fell on another temple there, causing a fire that destroyed the head of a statue that was planned to be 400 feet high. It was a head of the Hindu god Vishnu, *and it was made of bronze!*

A report from Dennis Balcombe and N. Anderson of Hong Kong in 1997 related events leading up to the handover of Hong Kong to the Chinese. A 24-hour Christian prayer meeting ended at 6:00 p.m. on July 1. About five o'clock the next morning, after a rain, a landslide destroyed much of the "Ten Thousand Buddhas Temple" in Shatin. It holds 13,000 Buddhist statues, some of which were in pieces and others knocked over. A Chinese paper, *Ming Pao*, printed photographs of the landslide and the area's largest Buddha statue under the headline, "He can't even help himself!" Further landslides ruined the foundations, and the whole area became unusable. (From Dennis Balcombe, revival@rcchk.org, reported in *Friday Fax* #32, 1997.)

Recently, a team of intercessors went to Bhutan and marched around one of the most well-known Buddhist temples, Joshua-style. That night, the world-famous, 1,200-year-old Tiger's Lair Convent burned to the ground. (From the International Prayer Leaders' Consultation, Cape Town, reported in *Friday Fax* #47, 2002.)

2. Among other sources, John Mulinde, "Learning Prayer the Hard Way," in a 10/30/03 e-letter from the Sentinel Group of Lynnwood, WA.

3. Sources: 1. World Trumpet Mission, P.O. Box 8085, Kampala, Uganda. Phone: (256) 41-232813, fax: (256) 41-271862, email: ebmaster@trumpetmission.org.uk, www.trumpetmission.org.uk. Reported in *Friday Fax* #49, 1999. 2. John Mulinde, reported in *Friday Fax* #33, 2000. 3. Los Angeles Times, July 12, 2003. 4. See statistics at http://hivinsite.ucsf.edu/global?page=cr09-00-00 and www.prcdc.org/summaries/aidsinafrica/aidsinafrica.html. 5. Jackson Senyonga, "We Want It Quick, Big, and Cheap," *Pray* magazine, July/August, 2003, p. 36f.

4. Ana Méndez, *Shaking the Heavens* (Ventura, California: Renew Books), 2000, page 166.

5. For further orientation and involvement with spiritual mapping, go to www.sentinelgroup.org or e-mail info@sentinelgroup.org. An excellent book on spiritual mapping is George Otis's *Informed Intercession* (Ventura, California: Renew Books), 1999—especially chapter three.

6. Bob Beckett, *Commitment to Conquer* (Grand Rapids: Chosen Books) 1997, pages 134-137. Also other sources.

7. Check out Exodus 34:9, Leviticus 26:40-42, Ezra 9:1-15, Nehemiah 1:4-7 and 9:1-2, Psalm 106:6, Jeremiah 3:25 and 32:18, Ezekiel 4:4-7, Daniel 9:3-11. A balance is provided by Ezekiel 18:20 and Jeremiah 31:29-30.

8. Available from The Sentinel Group, P.O. Box 6334, Lynnwood, Washington 98036. Phone: (800) 668-5657 with credit card. E-mail: info@sentinelgroup.org. Website: www.sentinelgroup.org.

9. Cited in *Friday Fax* #47, 2002, quoting from a document produced during the International Prayer Leaders' Consultation in Cape Town November 12-17, 2002. It also notes a related growth spurt: "At the start of the 1990s, there were fewer than 100 known prayer chains around the world; today, there are more than 4,000 places in which people pray around the clock. At the start of the 1980s, there were no national prayer movements; today, two decades later, more than half of all nations have a national prayer movement in some form." *PERSONAL OPINION*: The deepest root cause of the miracles and church growth in the world today is our army of intercessors pouring out their hearts in

impassioned prayer hour after hour, day after day, year after year.

10. David Garrison, *Church Planting Movements* (Richmond, VA: International Mission Board of the Southern Baptist Convention), 1999, page 38. The man is from the Bhojpuri tribal group. Also available online at www.imb.org/CPM/default.htm.

11. Mark Water, compiler, quoting Karl Barth in *The New Encyclopedia of Christian Quotations*, (Grand Rapids: Baker Books), 2000, page 1056.

12. Garrison, *op.cit.*, page 4.

13. Doug Morrell, *Christian Outfitters*, 301 Hunterview Dr., Granbury, TX 76048. Text is at www.christianoutfitters.com/fathhart.html.

14. For information on tentmaking, contact Global Opportunities, 1600 East Elizabeth, Pasadena, California 91104. Phone: (626) 398-2393, fax (626) 398-2396. On the Web: www.globalopps.org.

15. David Bryant, *The Hope at Hand* (Grand Rapids: Baker Books), 1996, page 223. Also, Ken Walker, "Agencies Announce Short-Term Mission Standards" in Christianity Today, Oct., 2003, p. 30.

16. Contact Dr. Patterson at Community Vision International, 5511 S.E. Hawthorne Boulevard, Portland, Oregon 97215. Phone: (503) 517-1895, fax: (503) 239-4216. Or contact U.S. Center for World Mission, 1605 East Elizabeth, Pasadena, California 91104. Phone: (626) 797-1111.

17. Source: Kingdom Ministries, fax: (41) 33-437-0016, e-mail: fbaertsch@gmx.ch. Reported in *Friday Fax* #28, 2000.

18. See www.newwway.org/cpm/cpm_insights.htm (note the 6 w's). Also, Simson, *op. cit.*, page 106.

19. Source: Pastor Ai, Vietnam, Offene Grenzen. Reported in *Friday Fax* #28, 1995.

20. Source: *Evangelism Explosion*, P.O. Box 23820, Fort Lauderdale, Florida 33307. Fax: 1 (954) 771-2256. Cited in *Friday Fax* #23, 1999.

21. Sources: Elizabeth Cornelio, Brian Mills of *Interprayer*, and Hildegard Schneider of Bad Nauheim. Reported in *Friday Fax* #9, 26, and 37, 1999.

22. *The Return of Sherlock Holmes*, 1904. The Adventure of the Abbey Grange.

23. For Anna Mendez's own account, see www.jesus.org.uk/dawn/2000/dawn27.html.

24. For example, an earthquake destroyed the Basilica of Assisi in Italy, the place where the Pope had called a meeting to unify all world religions, which evangelicals assumed would create a powerful monstrosity. Also, Hurricane Paulina destroyed the infamous Temple of Baal-Christ in Acapulco, Mexico. And Indonesia, the largest Christian-persecuting Muslim nation in the world, was struck by a series of horrendous fires. Then three months later, the largest regular religious festival in the world, the Hindu's Kumbh Mela in India, suffered an amazing setback when the expected crowds of 16 million simply failed to show up; fewer than a million came.

25. Sources: Lynn Green and Carl Heatley, *The Reconciliation Walk*, P.O. Box 61, Harpenden, Herts AL5 4JJ, England. Reported in *Friday Fax* #18, 40, and 45, 1996, plus #33, 1999.

26. Pages 24-25 of an unpublished manuscript by Bindu Choudhrie.

27. In September, 2000, Ed and Ruth Silvoso had dinner with the wife of the president of the Philippines and some officials. This is from their prayer letter dated October 28, 2000.

28. Victor Choudhrie, *The Prayer Warrior: Church Planters' Daily Prayer Guide*, page 25. Available from the author at Padhar 460005, Betul District, Madhya Pradesh, India, US $5.00.

29. "A Continent Prays," Explorer Report, July 7, 2004, The Sentinel Group (www.sentinelgroup.org).

30. Arnold Remtema, International Radio Resource Office, World by Radio, Box 62577, Colorado Springs, Colorado 80962. E-mail: aremtema@wbradio.org. Website: www.wbradio.org. Phone: (719) 548-7490.

31. Source: APD. Cited in *Friday Fax* #32, 1995.

32. See, for instance, Jack Dennison's *City Reaching* (Pasadena: William Carey Library), 1999.

33. The major figure in this move is C. Peter Wagner, author/editor of 50 books and chancellor of the Wagner Leadership Institute in Colorado Springs, Colorado. See his book *Churchquake: How the New Apostolic Reformation Is Shaking Up the Church As We Know It* (Ventura, CA: Regal Books), 1999.

34. Their first nation was the Philippines, where in 1974, the 5,000 churches made a goal of becoming 50,000 churches by 2000. As of mid-2001, they were at 60,000.

35. The estimate of millions comes from various missions researchers. It is one of those numbers that is difficult to pin down with any precision at all.

36. The estimate of 70% is from Wolfgang Simson, whose desk is flooded with such reports.

37. Karel Sanders, AFMIN, USA, P.O. Box 25983, Colorado Springs, Colorado 80936, (719) 380-8792, e-mail: info@ afmin.com. Reported in *Friday Fax* #5, 1998.

38. Circular letter from Bill Bright, *Campus Crusade for Christ*, 100 Lake Hart Drive, Orlando, Florida 32832, November, 2000.

39. Personal to the author from Joshua Pillai, September, 2001, and January, 2002.

40. Jackson's address is c/o Streams Ministries, P.O. Box 550, North Sutton, New Hampshire 03260, phone: (603) 927-4224, fax: (603) 927-4883, e-mail info@streamsministries.com, website: www.streamsministries.com.

41. Joel News International #325.

42. Sam Hoffman, "Prayer for the Nations" in *Agape Voice*, March, 2004, p.2. Also refer to *Friday Fax* #33, 2001.

43. Semaille et Moisson Nr. 107. Cited in *Friday Fax* #20, 1995. Also, Compass Direct, July 19, 2002, page 8.

44. Harold Caballeros, pastor of El Shaddai in Guatemala, speaking May 2, 2001, at the Transformations II Conference in Seattle.

45. *Friday Fax* #33, 1995.

46. *Friday Fax* #17, 1996.

47. Letter from Douglas Layton, Servant Group Int'l, 506 Tanksley Avenue, Nashville, Tennessee 37211, Feb. 15, 2001. Phone: 1 (615) 832-2282. Fax: (615) 832-0373.

48. C. Peter Wagner in his Global Prayer News, January-March, 2005, page 10.

49. David Bryant, *The Hope at Hand*, Grand Rapids: Baker Books), 1995, page 224.

50. C. Peter Wagner, speaking at Living Way Christian Fellowship, Greensboro, North Carolina, April 25, 1997. Cited by Doug Demick at www.etpv.org/1998/hrd.html.

51. *Friday Fax* #14, 1996.

52. Source: *Advance*, August, 1995. Cited in *Friday Fax* #31, 1995.

53. Bryant, *op.cit.*, p. 224.

54. Mission Frontiers, June, 2000, p.15.

55. David Barrett, *World Christian Encyclopedia* (New York: Oxford University Press), 2001, p. 527.

56. *Friday Fax* #39, 1995.

57. Bryant, *op.cit.*, p. 224.

58. Dick Eastman, quoted in *Friday Fax* #25, 1997.

59. *Friday Fax* #35, 1998.

60. *Joel News International* #335, October 11, 2000.

61. Garrison, *op.cit.*, p. 4.

3

The New Saints

Seven Signs of Today's Overcomers

> "... where the Spirit of the Lord is, there is freedom. And we all, with no veils on our faces, are reflecting like mirrors the glory of the Lord and being transformed into his own image, from one degree of splendor to the next." II Corinthians 3:17-18

Pew warmers are passé. They're stuck at half past yesterday and simply are not ready for the high demands of the current explosion.

Two generations ago, eminent Christian spokesman A.W. Tozer thundered, "The fact is that we are not producing saints. We are making converts to an effete type of Christianity that bears little resemblance to that of the New Testament. The average so-called Bible Christian in our times is but a wretched parody of true sainthood. Yet we put millions of dollars behind movements to perpetuate this degenerate form of religion and attack the man who dares to challenge the wisdom of it."[1]

In 1994, George Verwer, the gutsy founder of Operation Mobilisation, distilled Tozer's point, declaring, "Most people in the church in America are wimps."[2]

True enough on both counts, I suppose. And yet, and yet ... the times, they are a-changin'.

There I was in Raipur, standing in a crowd of 150 Indians, holding a paper plate of chapatis and curried chicken, when my host introduced yet another church planter who came to attend my seminar: Gas Ram Barwe.

Now, Gas is a regular guy: 34, 5'5", and a bit on the quiet side. Has a wife, Chandrika, and a son, Ram Jeet.

When I prompted him for a short version of his life story, he recounted that when he was six, his father went crazy because of his chronic poverty. So with no more family income, his mother had to pull him out of school after two months of his first year. Thus, Gas never learned to read.

But then at 22, he got saved—and really, *really* wanted to learn to read the Bible. Couldn't afford lessons, though.

So one day, he sat down with a Hindi Bible, opened it, pointed to a word, and said, "OK, Lord, what does *this* mean?" And God spoke to him, telling him what it said.*

He scanned for another interesting-looking word. "OK, Lord, now what does *that* mean?" And again, God told him what it meant.

Incredibly, he continued on word by word, and in two weeks, he was reading fluently!**

He has suffered heavy persecution, including being fed poison—which God miraculously saved him from. (His poisoners became Christians.) He has become bold in communicating the gospel. At last report, he has planted 212 house churches.

About February 20, 2001, he and his pastor, Harish Pattel, led prayer walks around the temples in Girodhpuri, Chhattisgarh, where 700,000 Satnamis come for a yearly religious fair. Within three days, the main temple sank and partially collapsed, the holy bath pond dried up, and the priestess died.

A few moments after my conversation with Gas, I spoke quietly with another attendee, and commented, "Wow! That guy over there actually learned how to read without going to school!"

Her answer: "Oh, yeah. Gas is one of those people that God has taught directly, without—"

---

* About 99% of the time, when I (or most other folks) say "the Lord spoke," we're not implying an audible voice. God can speak quietly to our spirits with great clarity.

** About three months later, this "untouchable" former day laborer was lecturing on Jesus Christ to a roomful of medical students, mostly Brahmins and other high-caste Hindus.

"Hold it!" I said. "*One* of those?"

"Yes, yes. There are a number of people around here God has taught to read."

I glanced at the sky. *Yep, still blue. I'm still on Planet Earth.*[3]

The New Empowerment

Look, this isn't easy for me, either—even though I've been there, seen it for myself, and heard it from a hundred horses' mouths, even talking with people who have come back from the dead.

I was raised to believe that miracles faded away long ago. So every time I come across a high-octane disciple like Gas, my barely adequate brain has to reset itself to zero and start all over again: *OK, Jim, we just stepped into a new reality, and we're at square one. Five minutes ago was a past life. Now we've got a new game, and the old rules no longer apply.*

The new saints seem to have a motto designed to keep me permanently off balance: **NO LIMITS.** When the situation demands it, they know how to operate in the power of God, to do the impossible. It sort of crumbles your static little universe when you meet people who not only do miracles, but do types of miracles that aren't even mentioned in the Bible. Clearly, we are in the endgame described by the prophets of old (like Joel 2:28-30 quoted above). We are no longer standing on tiptoe at the perimeter of the kingdom of God, peering over its wall. We are in the thick of it. We are fulfilling Jesus' words about his miracles, *"Greater works than these shall ye do ..."*

The Catholic, Orthodox, and old-line Protestant churches tend to parcel out empowerment rather sparingly. They are all run from the top down, with leadership mainly by position rather than by example or gifting. Typically, to even get started as a pastor or priest, you have to earn a three-year seminary degree. Authority and power don't just flow straight from God's throne to you. This limitation puts members of the more traditional churches at a great disadvantage in adjusting to the string of a million and one emergencies that we call life.

In the new, more open churches, you don't have to wait for someone to give you permission for every little thing. You just do it. For one example, take the case of ...

William Lerrick: A Man Without Limits

He is Indonesian, one of the leaders of the '60s revival in his country. As his ministry flourished, he began to make trips to speak abroad. By 1973 that grew to include Germany, where he spoke

The Farewell Sermon

It was evening, and the beloved pastor looked out over the pulpit at his flock for the final time as he read his last sermon to them before they set sail the following morning on an adventure that would change all their lives. He spoke slowly:

We are now ere long to part asunder, and the Lord knoweth whether we shall see each other's faces again. But whether the Lord hath appointed it or not, I charge you before God and His blessed angels that you follow me no further than you have seen me follow the Lord Jesus Christ. If God reveals anything to you by any other instrument of His, be as ready to receive it as you were to receive any truth of my ministry, for I am verily persuaded the Lord hath more truth yet to break forth out of His holy Word.

For my part, I cannot sufficiently bewail the condition of those reformed churches which are come to a period [a full stop] in religion, and will go, at present, no further than the instrument of their reformation. The Lutherans cannot be drawn to go beyond what Luther saw; whatever part of His will our God has revealed to Calvin, they will rather die than embrace it; and the Calvinists, you see, stick fast where they were left by that great man of God, who yet saw not all things.

This is a misery to be much lamented, for though they were burning lights in their times, yet they penetrated not into the whole counsel of God, but were they now living, would be as willing to embrace further light as that which they first received, for it is not possible the Christian world should come so lately out of such thick anti-Christian darkness and that perfection of knowledge should break forth all at once.

The pastor was John Robinson. The place was the Pieterskerk in Delfshaven, Holland. The date was July 31, 1620, and his listeners were the 120 brave pilgrims who founded America.

As heirs of their adventurous faith, new saints in the U.S. still seek to "embrace further light."

through interpreters.

March 27, 1977, was the most memorable occasion of his life. On that evening, Lerrick went to speak to a roomful of 100 Germans at the Heidelberg YMCA. But when he rose to speak, he saw no interpreter. His hosts had assumed he spoke German!

What a dilemma. In the old days, they would have drafted another speaker or just gone home. But this is the era of God's new empowerment. Lerrick bowed his head and prayed, *Lord Jesus, what do you have in mind? Help me, Lord!*

After a minute that seemed an eternity, the Lord brought to his mind some words he had never heard before: He admitted slowly in

German, "Forgive me. I've never learned how to speak German. I understand some words in your language, but it's very hard to pronounce." (Languages come hard for Lerrick.)

He bowed his head again and said, *Lord, how can I go on? Help me!* Suddenly, Philippians 4:13 (the *only* verse he knew in German) popped into his head. So he spoke it out—and kept on going!—for 15 minutes straight, with full tonal inflection.

Young people stared at him with wide eyes and open mouths. He knew what he was saying, yet he didn't know he was speaking German. But when he saw some elderly ladies with tears running down their cheeks, he knew it was German.*

William Lerrick

Lerrick told me, "From that very moment on, the Lord transformed my mind so that I can read the German Bible and preach from it. I even understand a lot of German, Austrian, and Swiss dialects—and know what area people come from."[4]

Twenty-five years later, he is still lecturing in German, not with an Indonesian accent, but an English-Dutch-Swedish accent!

It's a new day. I'm calling you to a new, empowered life with virtually unlimited options. I'm not implying that God will be in your pocket. He's the Boss. But if you stay clean and usable, you'll be in *His* pocket. And in that place, "Nothing will be impossible for you." (Matthew 17:21)

The New Freedom

Your new empowerment will depend on your willingness to accept your new freedom and run with it. Like the Pilgrims, like William Lerrick and Ana Méndez and Faith Ahmed and the noble Kalahari bushmen, you have to be willing to step out in faith and *use* your freedom, often at some risk, even if mere embarrassment:

In a village about 45 miles (70 kilometers) outside Hefei, capital of China's Anhui province, house church people reach out to help by going to the hospital and finding patients whom the doctors have given up on.

"You have to take risks for God," says one believer. "We prayed for 20 days for one patient, and he was only healed at the very last."

---

* You are likely familiar with the usual "speaking in tongues" that is common in pentecostal and charismatic churches. It sounds mostly like English-language phonemes, but scrambled. Unless there is an "interpreter," as the New Testament requires, it is unintelligible. Those who have this gift value it simply as direct communication to God—something beyond words. On rare occasions, however, a message in tongues is just that: a word from God in a known foreign language.

A friend added, "We were sweating, because the family was telling us to go away because we were angering the gods. They were beginning to threaten violence against us."

In one year they prayed for 20 terminal cases, and all were healed, mostly of cancer. The church grew from zero to 200 members.[5]

In China, they have little political freedom, but great spiritual freedom, and they use every drop of it.

In the West, it's been the other way around. Here, centuries ago, we imprisoned ourselves in a system that confined us mostly to spectator roles, while dumping on our pastoral staff all the heavy responsibilities. But as I said, all that is changing fast.

Freedom dissolves before your eyes if you don't use it. Unused freedom rots and turns into bondage. Paul summed it up precisely in Galatians 5:1: "For freedom Christ has set us free. Stand fast, therefore, and do not submit again to a yoke of slavery."

A majority of North Americans live like a ping-pong ball tossed on the ocean waves. To a great extent, they

Lily and Zhang

From Open Doors' Pierre Tschanz comes a charming report that will make you delighted or embarrassed or both:

One of our workers took some Bibles to a house church in central China and gave them to two new believers, Lily and Zhang, sisters who had been saved that day in the house church.

Around two years later, another member of our staff was in the same town and met Lily and Zhang. He wanted to know what they had done since becoming Christians.

Ashamed, the two girls blushed and bowed their heads, as though it were an exam. "We planted churches," they said.

"How many?"

The girls looked at each other cautiously. "Only 29."

Astonished, the representative asked how many members the churches had.

"In the smallest, only 300 come for prayer," they said humbly. "And in the largest, no more than 5,000."[6]

bounce through life as slaves of circumstance. I want you to rise above that and be free. And this is where it starts, with ...

Your New Identity

Noted author Neil Anderson told me last year that he had done some counting in his Bible.

He found 330 places where unsaved people are called *sinners*.

He found 240 places where saved people are called *saints*.

But he found exactly *zero* places where saved people are called *sinners*.

Now, that stands in wild contrast to the 16-centuries-long effort to make all Christians think they're still sinners. How many condemnatory sermons have you suffered through? Two hundred too many?

We do sin, it's true, and we need to confess, repent, and make amends whenever we do. But "sinner" is not our main identity anymore, and you need to reverse your self-image and free yourself from this crippling distortion.[7]

The apostle Paul had no problem with this. Did he ever address a letter to the "sinners" in Rome or Ephesus or Philippi? If the Bible calls you a saint, why would you demean yourself by denying it? The Lord Jesus paid a steep price to make you a saint, so smile and accept it and get on with a higher life.

This is not just semantics. It's a practical matter. Ask yourself this: *Just how many shining deeds should we ever expect from dirty, low-down, no-good sinners?* See the problem? The SINNER label becomes a self-fulfilling prophecy. If you've made a genuine, 100% commitment to the Lord Jesus Christ, you're just as much a saint as Peter or Paul.

Awhile back I went to a novelty shop and blew five bucks on a silvery magic wand set with big jewels. (Go for quality, I always say.) So now in my seminars I walk down the aisle and canonize folks, touching them on the head and saying, "I pronounce thee, Saint Kevin; I pronounce thee, Saint Heather," etc. Instant sainthood! My ritual may not be as impressive as the full-on Vatican treatment, but it has the advantages of no dying and no waiting.

As you can see, I'm willing to go to extremes and parody myself if it will get people to lift their faces out of the mud, throw their shoulders back, and walk confidently with the Father.

My aim is simple. I want to put a song in your heart and show you how to *enjoy* being a true son or daughter of the living Lord. You don't have to be a worker of miracles, but you do have to know who you are.

The New Sense of Responsibility

At 8:46 a.m. on January 26, 2001, I was eating breakfast with retired surgeon Dr. Victor Choudhrie in a hotel in Ujjain, Madhya Pradesh, when the biggest earthquake in 50 years hit India.

While Dr. Choudhrie jumped up and went outside to "assess the damage," I calmly continued eating. Having lived most of my life in shaky Southern California, I knew that the gentle rolling motion meant the epicenter was at least 200 miles away. And it was: Bhuj, Gujarat. About 13,000 died. You likely recall the news reports.

God's fingerprints were all over this:

- It was *Republic Day*, their big day of national pride—perhaps a bit more pride than is justified for a country that still harbors a caste system that makes apartheid look like heaven on earth.
- It was at the time of the *Kumbh Mela*, the quadrennial festival of Hinduism, when tens of millions flock to the Ganges River to bathe.
- Most of all, Gujarat was the most anti-Christian state in India, the center of vigorous persecution of both Christians and Muslims.

All that makes it very easy to fold one's arms and say, "Well, they had it coming." And a smug attitude would be simple to support: Less than two years before, when Hindu fanatics burned to death Australian missionary Graham Staines and his two sons in their car in Orissa state, a hurricane quickly struck almost the exact spot of the murders. God is apparently not happy when His children are persecuted or killed.

But is that the whole story? Not anymore. Not these days. Mercy Simson, an Indian prophetess living in Germany, saw a deeper problem behind the quake. She wisely observed:

> Christians cannot afford to stand safe and proud at one side, continuing their purely spiritual battles and boasting that this earthquake shows God to be on their side. All of God's people in India are called to bow down under the nation's sin, bringing India's need united before God.
>
> They must also ask forgiveness of Gujarat: **"We are guilty, in that we did not pray more for you, were poor representatives of God, and did not represent you before God enough."**[8]

Do you see the megashift in attitude here?

"I looked for a man ... but I found no one."

When you pray for something big, and you pound on the door of heaven day after day, you begin to see God as aloof and uncaring, while you are the good-hearted, needy petitioner.

Surprise: God sees it differently. For example, about 593 B.C., He is explaining to Ezekiel why He is soon going to destroy the nation, deporting them to Babylon as captives. He catalogs their callousness and evil, then gives this shocking revelation:

When I looked among them for a man who would build up
the wall, and stand in the gap before me in defense of the
land, to prevent my destroying it, I found <u>no one</u>. So I will
pour out my wrath upon them... Ezekiel 22:30-31

If that isn't a tragedy, I don't know what is. In the whole nation of
Judah, the all-seeing YAHWEH couldn't find even one intercessor with
the backbone to stand up to Him and say, *No, Lord! Spare your people!*
This must not be!

Yes, the Lord actually adores fighters who will take Him on,
wrestling tenaciously like Jacob with the Angel of the Lord. (Genesis
32:22-30) The new saints understand God's highest desires, and they're
willing to fight tooth and nail, with fiery passion, to make sure He
doesn't settle for anything less.

It's like painting your kitchen. You want to do it, but you also want
to spend the weekend goofing off. (That's where a skillful spouse can
appeal to your higher purposes without making you angry.) Now, God
is as complex as you are. He has conflicts that He wants us to help
resolve, like destroying Judah versus not. He wants you to speak in His
ear and remind Him about why He should be compassionate and
patient instead of giving us what we well deserve. In extreme cases, He
wants you to engage Him in something analogous to hand-to-hand
combat if that's what it takes.*

God wants you to take joint responsibility for what happens in this
perilous world. He doesn't want you to mumble a polite prayer, shrug
your shoulders, and say, "Well, it's out of my hands now." Remember
Jesus' words in heaven to Samuel Cho as his father prayed in desperation over the boy's corpse: *"I cannot keep you here because your*
father will not let you go."

Small Things Now, Big Things Later

What's fairly new here is what we call **the ownership mentality** or
responsible stewardship.

Like the committed environmentalists, the new saints are beginning to understand that God wants us to take really good care of His
creation, which for us includes not only the earth's ecosystems, but
people's social systems and their very souls.

It's something you have to learn. You don't start off with a challenge like Operation Ice Castle on Mt. Everest. You start with maybe

---

* This helps to explain why we're now seeing so much fasting and so many all-night prayer vigils
around the world.

picking up trash on the street or helping your neighbor fix his roof. Then much later you may hear Jesus say, "Well done, my good servant. Because you have been faithful in a very small matter, I am going to put you in charge of ten cities." (Luke 19:17)

Taking responsibility for the welfare of others is tricky. Often, the Spirit of God will prompt you to do something, but so quietly that you suspect it's not God, just your own thoughts rattling around in your head. George Otis, Jr., tells the story of his dad's response to the Spirit's gentle prompting about a former boss—in this case, William Lear, the genius behind the Lear Executive Jet:[9]

> My father had worked for Lear in the late 1950s as his corporate general manager. Despite the latter's reputation as a hard-living eccentric, my father retained a fondness for him. Years after leaving Lear's employ, my father was prompted by the Lord to call Bill. Although the two had not spoken for many years, he still knew how to reach his home in Reno, Nevada.
>
> Bill Lear answered the phone.
>
> "Bill, this is George Otis. I know this may sound odd, but the Lord placed you on my heart this morning. I just had to call and find out what's happening in your life. God's thinking about you, Bill."
>
> There was a long silence on the other end of the line.
>
> "It's good to hear from you," Lear said tersely. "But could you call back in ten or fifteen minutes?"
>
> The second time Bill's voice sounded brighter.
>
> "I need to share something with you, George. Something amazing. When you called a few minutes ago, I was sitting at my desk preparing to take my own life. I haven't been well, and I thought my revolver was the answer."

Lear invited Otis to fly to Reno. With Otis's help, he found Jesus Christ as his Savior and Lord.

He died shortly afterward, at peace, a son of the King.

The New Understanding of the Gospel

If Disney were to do a movie on the modern church, they could call it, "Honey, I Shrunk the Gospel."

We've downsized the gospel in two ways:

1. It used to be good news about a Person, the risen Christ. Now it's often presented as a set of doctrinal truths. PROBLEM: You cannot get to heaven by just believing a set of facts.

2. In the first century, the awe-inspiring part of the gospel news was Christ's resurrection. Today, the only life-changing element in it is the cross. PROBLEM: The resurrection is not a tack-on to the "good news of the cross." Even without the resurrection, the cross is good news; by itself, the cross perhaps means that God isn't mad at us anymore. *But we're all still dead!* "If Christ be not raised, your faith is futile, you are yet in your sins." (I Corinthians 15:17)

What's the basic problem of human beings? **They all die!** As I wrote in *The Open Church,* "Within thirty years of Christ's ascension, the gospel was being preached in every outpost of the Roman Empire."[10]

What was that gospel that spread so quickly? That **in Christ the death problem has been solved!** Just look at this summary of the gospel in Romans 10:9: "... if you confess with your mouth the Lord Jesus and believe in your heart that God has raised Him from the dead, you will be saved." Where are the cross and atonement here? No place. Neither are they in the summaries of the gospel in John 1:12, 3:18, 36, 11:25-27, 20:31; Acts 4:1-2, 4:33, 8:37, 17:18; Romans 1:1-5; I Peter 1:3-5; and I John 5:1, among others.

But let me hasten to add that any *full* presentation of the Christian gospel must contain a careful explanation of Christ's cross and atonement for forgiveness of sins. In fact, if you're a theologian instead of an evangelist, you might well focus on the cross as the central event of world history—because it was at the cross that the powers of sin and death were defeated. *So please don't spread rumors that I'm trying to downplay the cross.* Here is the understanding you should strive to communicate: The death and resurrection of Christ are two parts of the same event, two sides of the same coin. And only in the light of Easter morning does the cross shine brightly.

The key book on this topic is James E. Leuschen's *Gospel of Victory: The Revolutionary Keys of the Early Church Gospel.* In it he reveals the eye-opening fact that "there is no major early Christian work [before the fourth century] devoted to the meaning or significance of the cross." Instead, "The early Christians ... vigorously preached the Resurrection of the crucified Christ as the core of their message ... They wrote book after book to defend the Christian doctrine of the resurrection ... *The early church fathers paid more attention to the theme of resurrection than almost any other single subject.*" (emphasis in original)[11] Every major religion of that time had, I suppose, some system of sacrifice for sins. What they didn't have was a back-from-the-dead Savior.

Today, the new saints understand that the true gospel is Jesus Christ himself, and He offers a future in heaven *plus* a victorious life here on earth. In stark contrast, the church of the early to medieval times devised a gospel in which the resurrection was divorced from the cross and de-emphasized. That's because after about 325, the church hierarchy simply had less and less use for an ocean of liberated believers running around loose, enjoying a superabundant life, advancing the kingdom, exercising their own ministry, and doing their own thing. To maintain their primacy and power, the guys with the funny hats devised a state-backed, force-fed religion in which the Christian life was a matter of adherence to rituals, the gospel was only about getting into heaven, and they were the keepers of its keys.

The New Lifestyle of Victory

In the last chapter you met Rajani, the Indian evangelist. Her widower is a church network planter named Haroon Jonathan, a pleasant, 30-something guy whom I also spoke with in Raipur.

He told me they lived about two miles from the village of Mundee, where a 45-year-old woman named Kulawati became demonized three years ago. Her friends and family tried gurus, psychiatrists, witch doctors—no one could help her in the least.

After two or three months of this, she got worse. She started crawling on all fours, eating nothing but grass, hay, and weeds—by the basketful. After six days of watching her crawl around, they got really tired of it, and somebody in this all-Hindu village had the novel idea, "Hey, there's a Christian evangelist just up the road. Why don't we send for him?" So they did.

When he arrived in Mundee, Kulawati charged at him like a bull and had to be held back by several men! The startled Haroon took stock of the situation and said, "Uh ... I'll be back in three days." (He was familiar with snake demons, fear demons, and plain vanilla demons, but this was a bizarre throwback to the time of Nebuchadnezzar.) So he went home and prayed and fasted for three days.

When he returned, the entire village came to watch. He quickly cast out the cow demon. Immediately, Kulawati stood up and said, "Boy, I'm hungry. You guys got anything to eat?"

The village turned to Christ that day.

Christians in Diapers

Most people who are called Christians are spiritual babies. They can't even feed themselves. They have to be spoon-fed weekly by sitting passively in a church service. Trouble is, this only makes the problem worse.

That's why improved sermons, bigger churches, and better-trained pastors can't help. Quaker statesman Elton Trueblood once gave me a copy of his book *The Company of the Committed*, in which he lamented dumping all religious affairs onto the clergy, thus secularizing everybody else: "The basic trouble [with the traditional church] is that the proposed cure has such a striking similarity to the disease."[12]

It takes many steps to reach spiritual maturity. The biggest is when you become self-feeding. That means you are able to receive your strength directly from God (especially through the Bible) instead of depending solely on second-hand resources.

Take Haroon, for instance. At first, he just wasn't up to the challenge of a demon-powered housewife who wanted to gore him to death. So he went home. Now, Haroon lives, in precise geographic terms, clear out in the heck and gone. He doesn't have a matched set of Christian advisors in his back yard to draw upon. Thus he simply had to fast and wait on God. After three days of focusing on the Lord of Glory, the exorcism was a cakewalk. He is truly one of the new saints—and an overcomer.

How to Become an Overcomer

When you're a self-feeder, you can grow like Jack's beanstalk. You'll never have to worry about where your next spiritual meal is coming from, and you'll always have the strength to overcome the bad stuff life throws at you.

So don't just cope. Overcome!

I can't offer you a guaranteed formula for gliding through every minefield of spiritual warfare, but I can promise you that these ten guidelines can bring you into the presence of Christ as a complete, mature person, ready to share His throne.

1. Delight yourself in the Lord, and so **learn to enjoy life**. Find your joy in Him, as He does in you.*

When life gets rough, it can drag you down, so make God your primary relationship. Everything in life begins and ends with Him.

This means you must **learn to enjoy your "quiet time" with the Lord every day**. It's sort of OK if you maintain a special time with God by iron self-discipline. That will get you through the spiritually dry spells. But really, the trouble doesn't start when you miss or chop your time of prayer; the trouble starts when you don't eagerly *want* to be with Him. So center on Him. Use your spirit, not just your mind.

---

* Do you know what motivated Jesus to keep going during the last hours before His crucifixion? It was His joy at the thought of meeting *you* in heaven! (See Hebrews 12:2. Also Nehemiah 8:10.)

2. **Get prayer support.** You need, of course, to be part of a ring of people who pray together. But beyond that, you need to find pray-ers who will commit to reminding God about you and protecting you from evil by His power.

HEADS-UP NOTE: Lots of people will say "I'll pray for you." But unless you find strong-hearted, loyal people who will commit to do so, that support will fizzle away to nothing.

3. **Study the Bible.** The average person's mind is a randomly acquired patchwork of contradictory slogans, clichés, catch-phrases, and myths, all of which work together at Pentium-chip speed along logic lines that Rube Goldberg could never have dreamed of. You cannot become a mature Christian disciple unless your mind is transformed, and much of that transformation will come as you study Scripture. Read, mark, and reflect on the Word—then act on it. You aren't just trying to learn the Bible, but to know God *through* the Bible—and become like Him.

4. **Take steps of faith**—every day if you can. When you get up, say, "Lord, give me a chance today to show in some new way that I love you. Help me to do (or endure) something I've never done before." That's one prayer God will be sure to answer!

A variation is the prayer of Jabez: "Oh, that you would bless me indeed and enlarge my territory! May your hand be with me and keep me from harm, that I might not cause pain." (I Chronicles 4:10)

Pray such a prayer daily until it's a part of you. Then move on to another, such as Luke 11:9, John 15:7, Psalm 103:1-5, Hebrews 10:38, Psalm 23, Job 11:13-18, Isaiah 40:27-31, Romans 8:28, Luke 17:6, Deuteronomy 4:29, II Chronicles 7:14, I Corinthians 10:13, Isaiah 41:10, Joshua 1:7-9, Numbers 6:24-26, or Psalm 91:15-16.

SUGGESTION: Make up your own! Take an hour and compose your own "lifetime prayer." Think: What are the deepest desires of your heart? Write that down, keep it in your pocket or purse, maybe even do it in calligraphy and hang it on the wall.

5. **Get used to the growth cycle.** Over and over, the Holy Spirit will put you through the process of CONVICTION, REPENTANCE, OBEDIENCE, JOY. Just when you start to think your heart is spotless, when you're feeling like Hercules after cleaning up the Aegean stables—bam! The Spirit taps you on the shoulder, and there's another sin you kind of forgot about.

Going through this process is not fun (until the end of each cycle), but it's crucial that you learn to adjust to it as one of the rhythms of life. If you dig in your heels and keep refusing to repent of some particular thing the Spirit shows you, He eventually gives up and lets you live with that sin. As a result, your growth and ministry hit a sharply defined limit. *This is why over 90% of Christians reach a certain level and stop.* You may even wind up with a stiff neck and a prideful heart that eventually turns to stone.

You've noticed this book doesn't harp on sin. That's because I want to maintain a positive focus here. I want you to feel the excitement of what God is doing around the world. But mark this well: *Until you come to see the horror of sin as God does, you will never grow spiritually.*

6. **Keep your commitments.** If you don't honor your word, your integrity eventually turns into a hollow shell.

For a prime instance, take your marriage vows. How do you love your wife when she acts unlovable or obey your husband when he becomes unrespectable? You remember that your vows were taken before God, and ultimately you answer to Him.

Those who stand by their pledges at any cost stand close to God. As Psalm 15 puts it, "Yahweh, who shall be a guest in your tent? ... One who swears to his own harm, and does not change."

You can't become spiritually mature by sitting in a pew for fifty years. Nothing happens until you take action. So set your course and stay true to it.

7. **Read!** Most people grow only in certain narrow fields. Big mistake. Read widely. Read to stretch. Let books and magazines written by gifted saints of the present and past expand your mind, your heart, your gifting, your universe.

Mature Christians can recall the turning points in their lives, points at which they jumped ahead. Sometimes it was an event, but quite often it was a book or speech. One well-timed book can save you a decade of headaches. If you learn a certain lesson on paper, the Lord won't have to teach it to you the hard way. Trust me on this: *It's much easier to spend ten hours reading a book than to suffer ten years of disasters caused by your own ignorance.*

8. **Join or start an open fellowship—a ring, a team, a house church.** Unless you have a horse named Silver and a faithful Indian companion named Tonto, you're going to need some good, spiritual friendships to get anywhere as a Christian. I've never met an exception.

As one of the new saints, you need the advanced, high-powered, personalized support and encouragement that can only be found in a small-group setting, where you can be part of the action instead of part of the scenery. In a participatory atmosphere, you'll learn to use your gifts and grow much faster.

Groups with such "body life" interaction are greater than the sum of their parts. They include the Holy Spirit—as Master of Ceremonies, not just Guest of Honor. That makes team Christianity wildly different from being a pew potato in a program-based church. Once you've been in open meetings where the Lord orchestrates each contribution and lives are changed every time, nothing else will be good enough for you!

9. **Be a giant.** Yes, enjoying body life will do wonders for you. So will meditation, reading, and prayer. Yet you'll never generate weapons-grade spiritual power until you begin to grow through your gifts and the great disciplines.

I repeat: You reach the higher levels only when you use your spiritual gifts heavily and adopt some of the classic disciplines of the faith.

A. *Gifts.* There are thousands of gifts.* They include being an apostle, teacher, donor, encourager, administrator, miracle worker, healer, helper, or someone who receives insights about specific situations or people directly from the Spirit of God. Use such gifts to help others, but also as a growth track for yourself.

For example, the Bible urges us to nurture an absolute mania for the highest gifts, especially the gift of prophecy. (I Corinthians 12:31 and 14:1) Paul adds in 14:31, "... you may all prophesy one by one, so that *all* may learn and *all* may be encouraged." If you've succumbed to the idea that "I'm just not the prophet type," you may be fighting Scripture. Very likely, you can grow into prophethood, and that will in turn open up to you vast new avenues of growth. For a start, I highly recommend you get Steve Thompson's *You May All Prophesy* (Charlotte: MorningStar Publications), 2000. It's an example-rich, super-practical primer on how to learn to prophesy.

B. *Disciplines.* The great disciplines are for everyone. They include:

- fasting (if you're not diabetic or something)
- prayer (especially including praise and confession)
- Bible memorization
- a regular time with God—in worship, prayer, singing, and simply listening ("waiting on the Lord").

These are not grim duties, but exciting steps that can catapult you rapidly upward.

10. **Focus outward.** A psycholinguist once surveyed the writings (ramblings, actually) of patients in a mental hospital. When he asked them to simply write their thoughts on any topic, he found, as I recall, that about one word out of six was "I." Sad! And yet many Christians are stuck at a level not far from that. Appallingly self-centered, they

---

* Most are unnamed variations on the standard ones found in Romans 12, I Corinthians 12, and Ephesians 4. For instance, I have a gift of teaching, but it's mostly a writing gift, which isn't mentioned specifically on these lists.

are doomed to live out their unhappy lives as spiritual dwarfs, unable to focus on much except their own problems and frustrated desires. (And wow, can they be boring!)

World-class Christians are quite the opposite. It's a joy to be around them because they *focus outward*. They're here to serve *you* and reach out to you in love. They endlessly tell others about their friend, the Lord Jesus Christ. And when they're with other Christians, they take every opportunity to disciple them and help them grow.

How do you gain an outward focus? You start by centering on the LORD. And when you pray, try to spend more time praying for others than for yourself.

Summary

Here are the signs that will mark you as an overcomer:

1. A new **identity**: a saint, not a sinner

2. A new kind of **empowerment** that supersedes your old self-image of limited gifting and ability ... leading to **victory** as a lifestyle

3. A broader sense of **responsibility**, with a new "ownership" mentality

4. A new **freedom**, *responsible* freedom that liberates you from both your own past and the false burdens of centuries of heavy, oppressive, restrictive rule and customs ... all without going overboard into license or causing disorder in the church

5. The **new understanding of the gospel** in which Christ's resurrection is not an afterthought or bonus, but an essential

6. A far higher level of **support**: knowing how to live as a member of a team, with strong backup instead of going it alone

7. A new **maturity**, measurable in the eight stages found in II Peter 1:5-7.

Are You a Team Player?

I'm worried. Maybe I've given you the impression that Christianity is a self-improvement project.

It's not. Team Christianity is for team players, not solo performers. God prizes *unity*.

People may say you're a perfect "10" in maturity. You may live on the narrow edge of martyrdom. You may perform miracles in your sleep. But if you don't pull together in unity with your brothers and sisters, your value to the kingdom is sharply limited.

How important is unity to the Lord? He spoke dramatically to this point in 1997. I got the following report directly from a highly placed U.S. leader in world missions.

The true (non-government) church in China now has seven main strands, or families, each led by a man who has done hard time in prison for his faith, typically about 20 years. They meet twice a year, and this U.S. leader has met with them on several such occasions.

The Most Important Resurrection Since Christ

One of those seven leaders is Wang Xin Cai, a tough-as-nails, highly outspoken man about 5'3".

Wang spent 13 years in prison loading rocks onto trucks by hand. His daily quota was a staggering 20 tons. By 1996, his health was broken and he was near death. The government didn't want the embarrassment of a top religious leader dying in prison, so they sent him home to die with his family.

SURPRISE: God healed him.

The next year, he and his wife had a second child, another girl. (The first was three years old at his arrest. He returned to find she was a 16-year-old traveling evangelist.)

Though things were going well for him, Wang was quite distressed by a major problem: At that time, there were just four major strands of the Chinese church that had ever cooperated with one another, and even they had unraveled from each other because of some minor differences. Suspicion and condemnation reigned all across the land.

He saw this as a major threat to the future of the church in China, so in December he called for a summit meeting in his city in Henan province.

On the morning the other three leaders were arriving, Wang's daughter was hanging out clothes on a clothesline attached to their fourth-floor apartment. She had the baby in a baby pack, but as she leaned out, the baby twisted unexpectedly and fell out, plunging three floors to instant death, her head split wide open.

In a state of shock, Wang gathered up the remains, put the body on a blanket, and laid it on the couch in his living room. Then he prayed loudly, "Lord, if this unity meeting is of You, then You have to heal my daughter. If you don't, I'm finished serving you because I just can't take it anymore. And I'll know that this unity vision is not of You." He then left his heart behind and staggered off to the meeting—to struggle earnestly for unity in the church.

I can't imagine any American—myself included—willing to look so foolish.

After a hard day of prayer and negotiation, Wang returned home and looked at the couch. The baby was still dead, but amazingly, her head was together again, in one piece! In faith, Wang gave thanks.

The next morning there was no change, but instead of staying to pray, he left for another day of conference.

That evening, he returned home to find the baby breathing! But she was in a deep coma. Again he gave thanks.

The third morning, he put his feelings behind him as best he could and went to the meeting again. That was a day of salvation for the church of China. In a breakthrough of immense importance, the four brothers resolved their differences and found ways to work together as the body of Christ. The largest church on earth was saved from perhaps decades of fragmentation and destructive conflict.

Returning home that evening, Wang Xin Cai found his daughter awake, alert, eating happily, and perfectly whole in every way. Today she is a bouncy seven-year-old who reflects the joy of the Father when He sees His children living in unity.

Why didn't God bring back Wang's baby in one moment? Why did He take three days? Because of *you*. He wanted to make you stop and think about how important it is to Him to have unity in His family.

This resurrection is one of the foremost object lessons in all history, and in the simplest terms, the lesson is this: A split in the church is like a split head. To be healed, we must have unity.

I hope this chapter has inspired you to be an overcomer. But if it leaves you feeling as though you are standing on the outside of the Kingdom looking in, your problem may be exactly that. If so, please let me offer you more help. I wrote Appendix One, "Invitation to Life," especially for those who are not 100% sure they are truly a son or daughter of God with their names written in heaven. The topic is the most important matter in your life, and it cries out for a careful look.

1. Quoted in *Reality*, April, 1997 (P.O. Box 50, Washington, DC 20044).

2. And he said it in public! (At Village Seven Presbyterian Church, Colorado Springs, Colorado, on November 27, 1994.)

3. On a later trip (2003), I discovered that there are probably, at a guess, 350 Christians in India whom God has directly taught to read.

4. I will list William Lerrick's e-mail address for you, but please do *not* ask him for language information or for his prayers that God will grant you the sudden ability to speak a foreign language. Lerrick does not do that. His address for all reasonable correspondence

is wimler@t-online.de. Ana Méndez, for one, has also had identical experiences—instantly speaking English, French, and Portuguese; see *Friday Fax* #27, 2002.

5. *Compass Direct* (P.O. Box 27250, Santa Ana, California 92799), February 18, 2000.

6. *Friday Fax* #29, 2002, quoting Pierre Tschanz, *Open Doors*, Postfach 267, 1008 Prilly, Switzerland.

7. See, for instance, the first ten verses of I John chapter 3.

8. Cited in *Friday Fax* #8, 2001.

9. George Otis, Jr., *God's Trademarks* (Grand Rapids: Chosen Books), 2000, p. 80.

10. James H. Rutz, *The Open Church* (Portal, Georgia: Open Church Ministries), 1993, page 8.

11. Leuschen, *op.cit.*, page 8. Available for $5.00 + $1.50 shipping through Restoration of Hope Ministries, 3617 N. Normandie, Spokane, Washington 99205, or jleuschen@asaccess.com.

12. Elton Trueblood, *The Company of the Committed* (New York: Harper & Row), 1961, page 10.

4

The New Church

Thirty Hallmarks of Emerging, Scripture-Based Fellowships

"And he is the head of the body, the church ... so that in all things he alone may be supreme." Colossians 1:18

"And God has placed all things under his feet and set him up as head over everything for the church." Ephesians 1:22

When the report came in from India, we were jolted.

Those of us who sift through stacks of reports of miracles are used to eyebrow-raising stories, but this was overwhelming, even for us. Some of us implored our Indian contact to double-check the details. In fact, we begged him to send out a research team with a trustworthy leader and a camera.

He graciously complied, but it wasn't easy. His team had to travel 400 kilometers into what they call the jungle, right into the midst of hostile anti-Christian territory seething with Naxalites, militant Hindu vigilantes who will stop you, search your gear, confiscate cameras, and beat you to a pulp if they find out why you're there.

But on September 14, 2000, they completed their mission and sent back a final report with photographs (snapshots, really, because no professional photographer would brave such a trip).

After I read the report, I had to spend weeks reevaluating my life. Perhaps you will too.

On the night of September 1, 1999, in the remote tribal village of Sukropath, Madhya Pradesh, a Christian woman of 25 named Sukhwari Bai gave birth to a baby girl. Her husband was Dashru, and the delivery was assisted by three local women: Nanhi, Dashri, and Sumatra.*

It was not a happy event. It was a tragedy.

The baby had two heads. It was not even a Siamese-twin type of problem, but a case where a second head was growing out of the top of the first. Also, it had only one real eye; the other three places that ought to have been eyes were just lumps of flesh.

Sukhwari, Dashru, and the midwives were of course horrified. They said the baby looked like "the devil incarnate," and they felt they should just put the thing in a clay pot and throw it out into the jungle for the animals to eat.

But finally they decided, *No, we're Christians now, so we shouldn't do that. We should pray for this baby.*

A Night of Gut-Wrenching Prayers

It's hard to think positively when you're praying over something that a supermarket tabloid wouldn't touch, and it's your own flesh and blood. But in pure faith they went ahead.

At that time there were just 15 or 16 Christians in Sukropath. Four men—Dashru, Adru, Shadru, and Labhu—joined the women to pray. They prayed fervently for healing, unaware of the standard Western postulate that God just doesn't do such things.

---

* Last names are uncommon there.

108

As they poured their hearts out in intercessory prayer, the Lord was moved, and the girl's face began to change. They prayed all night, and by morning, she was a beautiful infant girl, normal in every way, with one head and two normal eyes! A new day dawned in Sukropath—and the rest of the world.

That morning two evangelists, Kalam and I. Sybet, came to the house, prayed with them, and named the baby Esther. (In Jewish tradition, Queen Esther was the most beautiful woman in the Hebrew Scriptures. She appeared at a crucial moment in Israel's history, and by her bravery was able to save the nation from annihilation. To encourage her, her uncle spoke the now-famous words of advice, "Who knows but you were born for such a time as this?")

See photos in photo section.

Can You Read This Sign?

The facts of this event leave no basis for debate. We simply have too many eyewitnesses—plus some photos, as you see. The research team was led by Earnest Singh, a trusted senior pastor, whose supervisor, Amos Singh, I met in Raipur in January of 2001. The facts have been further endorsed by Prof. Alex Abraham, a widely noted Indian Christian leader, and my friend, Dr. Victor Choudrie of Betul, who sent Earnest out. Dr. Choudhrie is a nationally known surgeon, now retired.

The facts about the little Indian Esther are quite impressive, but their meaning roars like thunder. When I realized the meaning, it shook me to the core. It came this way: Word of Esther's healing quickly reached Erich Reber, perhaps the most respected prophet in Switzerland. Even before he received the final proof of the case, he said, "God spoke to me very clearly" about it.

What God told Reber reveals that Esther's healing is the most significant healing event of our time, an object lesson that no Christian can afford to ignore. In brief:

> For too long the church has been a two-headed monster. The Lord Jesus Christ is the only rightful head, but men have set themselves up as heads *above* Christ, saying, "No, *we* will run the church."
>
> This is quite confusing to the world. People look at the church and say, "Sure, we understand that system. The guy on top calls the shots. It's just like our governments." The world will not see Christ clearly in the church until we restore Him as the supreme and only head.

ALSO: The Father is today preparing a bride for Christ: His church. She will be a perfect and spotless bride without flaw. It is time for Christians everywhere to stop putting up with the deformities of the church, the structural and procedural traditions that have brought the continued weakness and stagnation of this ecclesiastical monstrosity which we have evolved over 20 centuries.

Perfect Timing

Little Esther was indeed born for such a time as this.

A thousand years ago—or a hundred—no one would have responded to her plight. Even twenty years ago, her parents and their friends would not have bothered to pray for her. Today's core apostolics are perhaps the first generation to take so seriously Christ's words, "Whoever perseveres in believing in me will be able to do what I do; and greater things than these shall he do because I am going to my Father." (John 14:12)

Even if Esther had been born <u>and</u> healed twenty years ago, the significance of it would not have been perceived by a prophet, relayed to me and others by the *Friday Fax*, and published around the world.

At this writing, Esther is five. But already she speaks eloquently to you and me and all of us. I believe the little lady is saying:

> *I am a sign for the nations. My message is that none of us are without blemish, yet all can be healed. If He has done such a great wonder for me, what can He do for you?*
>
> *Let us turn to God with our whole hearts and become a perfect body, witnesses together to His love and care. Christ is our head. Let us be the perfect bride He longs for, beautiful and strong.*

The New Church: Everything You Always Wanted, But Were Afraid to Ask For

What's new about the new church?

Plenty! New freedom, new excitement, new empowerment, new growth, a new relationship to God, new kinds of people, new open meetings, new spontaneity, new close relationships, a new flow of authority, new depth in sharing, new servant-leadership, new kinds of prayer, a new use of gifts, new training, new teamwork, new communal righteousness, new ministry focus, new regional cooperation, new flexibility, new low expenses, new wider outreach, new variety of activities, new higher goals, new unity in love, and lots of new surprises!

In the table below I've tried to capture all this on one page. Please pardon the clipped phrases and sweeping generalizations. The rest of the chapter adds some detail.

The Gulf Between Old and New

The Traditional Church	The Open Church: Team Christianity
1. 5% participation in meetings	100% (open worship/sharing/ministry)
2. Meetings programmed	Meetings open, spontaneous
3. Meet in building, sit in rows	Meet in homes, offices, dorms, etc.
4. Meeting format boring	Every meeting different
5. Pastor-centered	Christ-centered, Spirit-driven
6. Clergy and laity divided	People united
7. Based on tradition	Based on Scripture
8. Emasculating	Empowering for ever-wider ministry
9. Two-thirds women	Slightly more men than women
10. Most decisions by decree	Most decisions by consensus
11. Led by one pastor or board	Led by elders and 5-fold ministry
12. People passive	People proactive
13. People controlled	People free
14. Inquirers must visit church	Members go to outsiders
15. Expensive	Cheap
16. Emphasis on large meeting	Emphasis on small groups
17. Denominational oversight	Apostolic oversight
18. Building a private empire	Building the Kingdom
19. Doctrine is flag, battle cry	Doctrine is anchor, foundation
20. Isolation, loneliness	Teamwork, closeness
21. Jesus as guest of honor	Jesus as host, emcee
22. Hidden sin often lingers	Communal righteousness
23. Self-image: sinners	Self-image: saints
24. Goal: perseverance, stability	Goal: overcoming, victory
25. Immaturity, growth plateau	Spiritual maturity
26. Leadership limits expansion	Leaders created continuously
27. Churches isolated and weak	Area teamwork and city "elders"
28. Fossilizes over time	Always reforming, learning, growing
29. Institutional hierarchy	Family-type relationships
30. Your presence irrelevant	You are needed, loved, important.

If you think this 30-line table is nitpicky, check out Dr. David Barrett's 280-line masterpiece in *World Christian Trends*.[1]

A Friendly Little Preamble

By the time you finish this chapter, you may have the impression that I hate traditional churches.

Not so. I've dozed peacefully through countless worship services and have been greatly refreshed. I've also taught Sunday school, sung solos, prayed, tithed, organized, and set up a gazillion folding chairs. I'm on excellent terms with hundreds of top leaders of the traditional church and count myself lucky to work with them in many ways.

The traditional institutional church is not the enemy—except in the comic sense captured so well by cartoonist Walt Kelly. Surveying a trash-littered part of his native swamp, Kelly's little hero, Pogo the Possum, uttered the famous conclusion, "We have met the enemy, and he is us."*

Our real enemies are the world, the flesh, and the devil.[2] So the copious flak I'm about to fling should be thought of as a mere rap on the knuckles for a dear friend or brother—or indeed for myself since I'm part of the same family of God they are. My main excuse for the tone of ecclesiastical hatchetry is that it's just darned hard to be diplomatic and tactful while pointing out flaws that can be seen from orbiting spacecraft, especially when those flaws are destroying thousands of lives daily and inoculating people against the church.

1. PARTICIPATION: When you're a nobody all your life, it hurts.

Let's say you've just had your greatest week ever. You landed a new job at twice the salary, your brother-in-law got saved, and you finally gathered the gumption to have your computer encased in concrete and dumped 100 miles off Guam. Life is a rhapsody.

You come bouncing into your traditional church, eager to share your joy with the whole congregation. But alas, there is no time allotted for unscheduled interruptions, so you just have to suck it in.

---

* A neat takeoff on Captain Oliver Perry's 1813 victory report from Lake Erie, "We have met the enemy, and they are ours."

You're not really part of the service, you're part of the decor. And the budget.

Or let's say you've just had your *worst* week ever. You've gone broke, your spouse has left you, and you've been diagnosed with mad chipmunk disease.

You come crawling into church, desperate for prayer, helping hands, or just a sympathetic ear. But no, you're not part of the program. (If you think you are, take a look at the bulletin. See your name in there anywhere?) The prevailing sentiment is, *If you have a problem, make an appointment with the pastor. That's what he's here for.*

Face it. No matter how high the joy or how deep the sorrow, you will not be allowed to share your heart, your inner life, with your fellow members. And the same goes for any song you've written, any lesson you've learned, any message burning in your soul. While the pastor is forced to produce 45 minutes of fresh material every Sunday, you are prohibited from sharing 45 seconds of anything. Ever. Lifelong attendance in a closed church can be emotionally and spiritually crippling.

If your church is better than this, count yourself blessed.

Open Churches. In an open fellowship, you are not only *allowed* to share, but prodded, coaxed, and *trained* to share. A Spirit-driven meeting is an unscripted drama that unfolds before your eyes, and the team players are there to play.

Note: Lions don't grow in small cages.

2. MEETINGS: Open or Programmed?

Open worship, open sharing, open ministry. These are the heartbeat of your house church, the touchstone of your team, the very breath of body life.

Programming is a way of maintaining order, but at a steep price.* Yes, the God of Grace can and will operate through programs run by dedicated people. In the future, as in the past, millions of people will come to Christ and be built up at programmed events. But He is limited to what He can do through 2% to 5% of the people with their limited gifts.

In open meetings He can draw from 100% of the people, who together have a very wide range of gifts. Home church pioneer Doris Funck calls them ESP meetings: Every Saint Participation. When you have ESP, you have a season ticket to the world's greatest symphony, where the Maestro will freely conduct a full orchestra. And the name of the composition is *LIFE*.

---

* As house church coach John White says, "Programming is what you do when you don't know how to listen to God."

KEY QUESTION TO BEAR IN MIND: *If God wants to speak strongly to your church next week through Joe Nobody, will He be able to do it? Can He put a burning message in the heart of Jane Nobody for faithful delivery to your fellowship?* If not, then you've slapped handcuffs onto the Holy Spirit. You've blocked Him from using 95% of His resources. Your church has usurped His authority and "put a covering" over the head of Christ.*

Humans are creatures of habit. Even in the best of open groups, customs may turn into unwritten liturgies before you can blink. If Gaseous Gary has taken it upon himself to start your last 19 meetings by jumping up and leading a peppy song, then Shy-Heart Cherie is going to have a whale of a struggle starting off the next meeting with, "I think the Lord would have us begin today with a few minutes of silence before Him." As one of the leaders, your job is to keep everyone's options open. (Start by telling Gary nobody appointed him the Grand Boojum of Music.)

3. MEETING PLACE: It's the menu, not the venue.

Some house-church types have sofamania. A couch, doorbell, and back yard are their non-negotiables for a happy happening.

I softly demur. Sure, there are advantages to meeting in homes: comfort, economy, warmth, infinite expandability, and more. For family warmth, there's no place like home. But *what* is happening is way more important than *where* it's happening.

Location, location, and location are the keys in real estate. But in the family of God, it's *participation* (which creates inspiration, affirmation, information, celebration, and transformation). So whether you meet in a house, barn, office, dorm, bar, catacomb, Starbucks, forest glen, nursing home, or hot tub, you're expected to jump in with both feet and do your part. That's what makes open gatherings so great.

There are, however, *poor* places to meet. My nomination for the booby prize is a church with theater seats. (Pews at least allow you to slide around and look back at a speaker without doing permanent damage to your neck.) Screwed-in seats make everyone face forward and behave like an audience—Faceless Freddies and Anonymous Annies. Rows of noses do not a church make.

In fact, most church buildings are poor places to meet simply because the pews or chairs all face forward, meaning that all talking is

---

* The reference to a covering means a woman's scarf as a symbol of submission. See I Corinthians 11. In some matters *outside of* the meeting, elders are needed to lead us. But when the church gathers, there must be no one taking authority over Christ. *Exception:* Some unusual situation, such as misbehavior or bad teaching.

Harvard, Hollywood, IBM, and Wal-Mart

Let's suppose your open church rents Don Corleone's Pizza Emporium on Sunday mornings. (Nobody wants pizza on Sunday morning, so you got a sweet deal on the empty restaurant.)

But right across the street from Don Corleone's is Old First Church, the town's biggest, with 4,000 members, ivy-covered walls, 12 buses, and a pipe organ that could shake loose every filling in your teeth. Now, which one is the *real* church?

Most people would say that the big church looks more like the real McCoy. But is it? Chances are, it's a blend of four unbiblical models:

• **Harvard**, where the professor is a preacher, the lectern is a pulpit, and the students are parishioners. Trouble is, they can sit and take notes for forty years, but they'll never graduate, never get a degree, and never ever become professors themselves.

• **Hollywood**, with its stage, entertainers, polished performances, costumed singers, applauding audiences, etc. All the church needs is popcorn.

• **IBM**, where a board of directors runs everything from the top down, where permission to do things is denied or granted by the CEO and committees, where finances are the overriding factor behind policies, and where the institution competes with other churches for market share.

• **Wal-Mart**, whose aisles and aisles of tempting merchandise offer something for everybody. Seeker-sensitive megachurches, with their array of 100+ programs, mirror beautifully the "consumer heaven" ideal of Wal-Mart.

But even if Old First Church were an ingenious blend of the very best of Harvard, Hollywood, IBM, and Wal-Mart, it still might not comprise a real church in God's eyes. It could fall far short of a true church in which the Holy Spirit lives and directs each and every heart. The moral is, "Don't feel bad if you don't have stained-glass windows with the sun shining through. If the Son shines through your members' eyes, *your* church is the genuine article."

Is there a perfect word to describe the true church? Several are good: bride, family, body, army, team, flock, fellowship, royal priesthood, network, partnership, circle of power, etc. But under a microscope, all metaphors show flaws. So this chapter answers the tough questions: *What does a true church look like? What are the hallmarks of a real New Testament church today? What distinguishes a Biblical church from a Nicolaitan church with a facelift?*

supposed to be done by the one person at the front. This audience layout creates irresponsibility, trivializes membership, and robs the congregation of its voice. The architecture almost dictates a closed church, and the closing of the church was the worst mistake of the past two thousand years.

4. FORMAT: Bored for the Lord?

The Snowflake Effect is more than a catchphrase. It's a stunning reality for those of us who have been in hundreds of Spirit-driven meetings without seeing two alike. The more we let Jesus run the show, the more different it will

'My theme for today is effective communication...'

Thanks to Tony Collins of Monarch Books, East Sussex, England, publishers of *101 Things to Do with a Dull Church*. Illustrator: Simon Jenkins.

be. When He orchestrates the band, the variety is endless, and no one gets bored.

The Protestant meeting format, the hymn sandwich, was passed down to us from John Chrysostom about 386 through Gregory the Great in 500 to Martin Luther and John Calvin in the 1500s. Like any one-size-fits-all mandate, it's terribly Procrustean and tends to produce cookie-cutter Christians. But the worst thing is, it shuts the Lord Jesus out of the design/planning loop. If He wants to have any input into a traditional service, He'd better give it to the pastor before the bulletin is printed Friday night, or He's out of luck.

> "I didn't realize how boring church was until I sat at the back."
> —Dr. Martyn Lloyd-Jones, the famous pastor of Westminster Chapel in London, after retiring and visiting other churches*

I often remember the old Baptist deacon from the South who prayed, "Lord, please make something happen today that ain't in the bulletin." If he'd been in a good open church, his prayer would have been answered in spades, diamonds, hearts, and clubs. When God calls the shots, touching one person after another, prompting a firecracker string of actions and responses, the results are as surprising as a whale at a pool party.

---

* Gerald Coates, *Non-Religious Christianity*, (Shippensburg, Pennsylvania: Revival Press) 1998, p. 87.

5. THE HUB: Pastor or Savior?

Any modern pastor worth his salt wants to see Christ honored and praised as the very center of His church.

Reality fights that. The dynamics of the meeting, the architecture, P.A. system, and historical customs all combine to produce a pastor-centered church. Despite the best intentions, everything tends to revolve around the visible hub of activity, the "preacher."*

In a typical church, the pastor and his staff have to do about 70% of the total ministry. That's counting evangelism, church services, everything. Why such a lopsided work load? Because the "laymen" like it that way.** They like dropping their typical $27 in the offering plate,[3] going home, and watching the game on TV.

That's inexpensive, but not efficient. Barrett and Johnson calculate that it costs the U.S. institutional church $1,551,466 to baptize each new member. While this is not quite as bad as the $2 million+ in Northern Europe, it makes us look like Diamond Jim Brady next to Mozambique's $1,366 (and others).[4] And from what I know of *home church* movements in poor countries, I'd guess it's closer to $25-40. But even in the U.S., home churches are dog-cheap. Like, how much does it cost to sit on your neighbor's porch and tell him about a new life in Christ? Especially when you're drinking *his* beer?

I've found that at least 10% of Christians worldwide have a pastoral gift. In a typical Christocentric open church, the Lord enables them to do their thing, and it doesn't cost the church a cent.***

6. The Clergy-Laity Schism

Jamie Buckingham, who was a gray eminence among U.S. Christians, once nailed a major point:

> The New Testament teaches the priesthood of all believers, not just those who are ordained as "men of the cloth." Therefore, unless we want to widen the rift between believers in the Body of Christ, I strongly recommend we forever omit any title—Reverend, Pastor, Father, etc.—that tends to describe one man as holier than another or even better than another.[5]

---

* In the New Testament, *preaching* is always to non-Christians. Calling a pastor a "preacher" is another of our semantic distortions. That's why we're so short on personal evangelists: The "preacher" is supposed to do our preaching.

** And who can blame them? Laymen don't even have to visit the sick in the hospital anymore. Just let the pastor do it.

*** However, we do need to pay well any full-time traveling workers, such as apostles, prophets, and high-level teachers. And there's the irony: In the church of the future, pastors may be the only one of the five-fold leadership (Ephesians 4:12) who *won't* be paid! A lot of today's pastors will be upgrading to apostles, prophets, and teachers.

Definitions

If you understand all my terms for the "old church" and the "new church," you don't need to read this. But if I've got you confused, I apologize—and offer the following to clarify my muddy rhetoric:

1. The **Megashift** is major transfer of responsibility and power, not a change in beliefs. The **New Christianity** has nothing to do with new doctrines.

2. **House church** refers to all the characteristics of a new church that come from the fact that it meets in a house: small size, informality, family-style relationships, etc.

3. Perhaps 95% of open churches meet in homes. **Open church** (or fellowship) refers to the dynamic of the meetings (*how* you meet), with everyone free to participate—and God allowed to break into the proceedings and redirect them. (**Closed church** denotes the opposite.) A **new church** is the same as an open church, but emphasis is on the things that mark it as fresh and distinct. Other terms are **ring, team, microchurch, simple church, organic church, body life church, participatory church, laymen's church**, and **New Testament church**.

4. In theory, a **traditional church** could meet in a house, but that wouldn't make it a "house church" as I use the term. A traditional church is one whose customs follow classical Protestantism. That includes having a building, a programmatic Sunday service with little audience participation, and a staff (paid when possible) that does much of the work. The pastor has a higher status than laymen, and his work is central to the success of the church. Though the Bible is regarded as the rule of faith and practice in the more conservative traditional churches, unwritten traditions are tacitly given more weight in a few matters.

5. **Old church** is about the same as a traditional church, but the term emphasizes the characteristics that mark it as doomed to dwindle and fade in today's world.

6. **Institutional church** connotes things like a professional pastorate office, committees with official channels of procedure, distinct departments of ministry such as Sunday school and social outreach, etc. Doctrines and practices that flow from a denominational heritage determine many institutional matters.

7. **Hierarchical churches** are also traditional, but the term emphasizes the superior/subordinate relationships among laity and clergy, including denominational superstructures.

Actually, *reverend* means "he who should be revered." But as you may have noted in browsing the Bible, God is pretty sticky about just Who gets revered.[6] In fact, Jesus specifically warned, "Don't let anyone call you 'Rabbi,' for you have only one Rabbi, and you are all brothers." (Matthew 23:8) Admit it: The titles "pastor" (shepherd) and "reverend" (revered one) are just as lofty as "Rabbi" (teacher).[7] So the next time a guy walks up to me and says, "Hi, I'm Pastor Tim," I'm going to smile and say, "Hi, I'm Layman Jim."

Dividing up the body of Christ into officers and enlisted men makes true unity impossible. It's such a beef-brained and destructive idea that it should have been deep-sixed centuries ago. The miniaturization of the layman is its most glaring effect; second-class citizenship in the kingdom of heaven is the most common curse of the traditional church. When Christ is the head, He makes sure that every part of His body, the church, functions right: no back-of-the-bus Christians. But when the *pastor* is the head, the church meeting looks like "the meat counter at Safeway, where you see chicken parts laid out in rows: a package of thighs, a package of necks, a package of legs. And none of it gives you any idea whatsoever of how a real, live chicken looks and moves."[8]

We've scrapped the titular and status-based division between clergy and laity bestowed upon us by Pope Hyginus in 140. But that

Satan's Invention?

"I don't know—but I can guess—why the devil ever invented pulpit gowns and bibs and all that sort of distinction between clergymen and laymen. I am no clergyman; there is no such distinction in the New Testament. We are all Christians if we are converted, and there is no other distinction ....

"It is sometimes asked, 'Ought laymen to preach?' Nonsense! Any man may preach if he has the ability. I do not believe, in my soul, that there is authority for saying, 'These men are to preach, and these people are to talk of Christ, and all the rest of you are to hold your tongues and listen.' No, no, no! ...

"I do believe it is the invention of Satan to lift up some few men above the rest and say, 'Only some of you are to fight the Lord's battles.'"

—Fundamentalist icon Charles H. Spurgeon in his sermon, "The Church: The World's Hope," given at Metropolitan Tabernacle, Newington, England, 1863.

does *not* mean everybody is the same. Everyone is uniquely gifted and deserves recognition and freedom to use those gifts. That's why egalitarianism is no good.

If you're in the lower tier of hierarchical Christianity, you get—sorry please—no titles. But your superiors are addressed as Reverend Smith, Apostle Johnson, Bishop Williams, Prophet Moffatt, etc. Problem: We've confused gifts and functions with titles and offices. Your service should define your position, not vice versa.

Now, Scripture describes Phillip as an evangelist, Agabus as a prophet, and Apollos as a one heck of a teacher.* And Jesus actually *named* the twelve as apostles. (Luke 6:13)** Such recognition is important. But can you imagine Jesus saying, "Good morning, Apostle James! Did you sleep well? Please wake up Apostle Peter and Apostle John, and let's go for a walk."

What started as a helpful way of describing disciples grew into a system. This system is unkind to laymen, but it grinds up pastors, too:

• 45% of pastors suffer from burnout.[9]

• 90% claim they were not properly trained to handle the octopus-like demands dumped on them. 95% struggle with discouragement.[10]

• 70% have a lower self-image after they went into the ministry than before.[11]

• 80% say their job is affecting their family negatively.[12]

• 37% say they are currently struggling with Internet porn.[13]

• And H.B. London, head of pastoral ministries for Focus on the Family, states that at least 70% of U.S. pastors say they have no friends.[14] *No friends!* Dear God, what have we done?

The modern pastor is simply not to be found anywhere in the pages of Scripture, and I've never met a pastor who would even attempt to defend the concept from the Bible. Which brings up the next issue ...

7. THE FOUNDATION: Scripture or the Traditions of Men?

Jesus marveled at the cleverness of the Pharisees: "How ingeniously you set aside the commandment of God to maintain your own traditions!" (Mark 7:9)

---

* No one is named a "pastor" in the New Testament except the Great Shepherd, Jesus Christ. Actually, the term *pastor* is more of a metaphor than a work description. The absence of even one pastor adds to the irony of our elevation of pastors to the supreme position of executive-teacher-prophet-apostle-elder-evangelist-whatever.

** Tacking on *Prophet* and *Apostle* before people's names compounds the problem we already have with *Reverend*. Worse, we demand to see an impressive track record before we use these titles. (In high contrast, Jesus in Luke 6:13 named the twelve as apostles before they accomplished *anything!*) Worst of all, we have allowed the pathway to the "office" of apostle or prophet to remain incredibly murky. The ecclesiastical fog is creeping in.

Our traditional churches still do the same—albeit less ingeniously. For example, they all set aside I Corinthians 14:30-31: "If anything be revealed to one who is sitting down, then the original speaker should stop talking. For in this way you can all speak God's Word, each in his turn, so that everyone may learn and everyone be encouraged." Try doing that in the middle of some pastor's sermon next Sunday, and the ushers will ush you out before you can say, *Nicolaitanism!* (That's the Bible name for the hated tradition behind hierarchical churches. More on this in Appendix Two.)

You'd think that by now the word "traditions" would have acquired an aroma of month-old raw oysters, but no, it still warms the hearts of millions who have spent their lives marching in little circles in the trackless wasteland of good old-fashioned churchianity. They simply have no idea of what they're missing.

The *doctrines* of most traditional churches come from the Bible, but their *practices* are of pagan origins. So when tradition outranks Scripture, what happens? Suddenly, there's no basis for unit wherever Tradition A conflicts with Tradition B. That's why we have 33,909 denominations worldwide, some of which despise each other.[15]

But team Christians who fellowship in open churches find it easy to discuss ideal church patterns—even though we are some of the most cussed-independent people on the planet. The various streams of the U.S. house church movement, for example, rarely debate "your church vs. my church." The debates are almost always about how best to understand the Bible and apply it.

Critics have sometimes stated a worry that home fellowships, lacking the sublime wisdom of a duly ordained M.Div., will surely someday fall into error and hatch heresies by the hundreds. I'm still waiting for that to happen. The boo-birds who flaunt this fear have apparently never tried to sneak a piece of theological fluff past a roomful of steely-eyed, Bible-toting, combat-ready saints. Things like the Inquisition, papal infallibility, and denying the Bible to laymen could never have been hatched out of gatherings of a dozen believers on their knees in a circle.

8. Mouse Church or House Church?

What do you want, geldings or giants?

No issue could be clearer: It's emasculation vs. empowerment.* The ordinary sit-'n-sing church brings one, a team church brings the other.

For many of us, the most exhilarating part of the new Christianity is our rapid growth in power, versatility, and knowledge. We've put in

---

* I'm not being fancy. Emasculation is the polite word for castration.

How to Twist the Bible ...
Just a Little

For centuries, Bible translators have muddied the semantics of church structure.

The King James Version, for instance, tells us, "If a man desire the office of a bishop, he desireth a good work." (I Timothy 3:1) Two problems here:

1. There is no word for a church *office* in the original Greek New Testament. The translators made it up.

2. *Bishop* should be *elder* or *overseer*. But in the time of King James, a bishopric was a cushy, tenured job that the Church of England wanted to enhance.

A better translation would be, "If anyone desires to be an overseer ..." But by some slimy political appointments, Richard Bancroft, the Archbishop of Canterbury, scattered the Puritans (the "good guys" who would have voted for better wording) among the six translation committees so they could never form a majority.

Thanks to Bancroft, who hated and persecuted Puritans and even had one of them killed, the beautiful King James Version is marred by a number of such outbreaks of editorializing. After the committees had finished their work, he even tacked on 14 revisions of his own, mainly boosting his hierarchical views.

We are told that "it is a shame for women to speak in the church." (I Corinthians 14:35) Paul was not expounding on the topic of qualifications to be a pulpiteer; he was discussing orderliness vs. confusion in meetings. He was referring to the annoying, idle *chatter* (λαλεῖν, lalein) that occurred when illiterate first-century women were clumped together and left to figure out what on earth was going on by themselves. This word for "speak" can also mean "an extended or random harangue," and who needs that!

We are also told to *"obey* them that have *the rule* over you and *submit* to their *authority* ..."* (Hebrews 13:17) Forget "the rule" and "authority." They're not in the original. And the Greek words for "obey" and "submit" are not the usual stern ones. They're a lot softer. Much better would be, "**Listen to** (go along with, let yourselves be persuaded by) **those who stand before you** (guide you, lead you by their example), **and be deferential to them.**"

By ratcheting up such phrases half a notch, making them consistently harsher, translators warped the original Christianity.

too many years in the closed-church system, which locked us into piddly roles, put a cork in our bottle, and gave us burgers and beans instead of a banquet for the soul. Now we've got a life without limits.

The house church meeting *pattern* is great, but the real goal is the house church *dynamic*, the wide-open tornado that sweeps us into action, propelling us into countless situations where we must use our gifts, take exciting steps of faith, and grow like a radish. Perhaps we'll even see more miracles soon. As someone has said, "If you want to see what you've never seen, then do what you've never done." In an open church, you fall *kersplat* on your face now and then, but you learn to stand up, wipe off the mud, and keep going. The *kersplats* are part of the lifestyle. The fast-track discipleship of the new churches is not for invertebrates.

The Holy Spirit has millions of growth tracks to choose from, and your own path of growth will depend to a large extent on what gifts He has given you. Team Christianity opens up avenues of ministry for you that will utilize the *full range* of your current gifts plus an *extended range* of higher gifts that you don't have yet. But take it from me, you'll love the feel of the wind under your wings.

We have few spectators in open fellowships. "Every-member ministry" sucks in everybody sooner than later. Call it your pilgrimage, quest, journey of faith, or adventure of adrenaline; the core reality is that you'll spend the rest of your life in uncharted waters!

The emasculation problem springs from the Christian caste system, which feeds on itself: The greater the pastor, the more that people sit back and say, *Wow! I could never preach like that.*[16] As lazy laymen dump more responsibility on the pastor, he accumulates a larger share of the church's spiritual experience, and before long, he is indeed far above his flock.*

Tragically, he may even begin to think this is God's ideal, that he is *supposed* to hover in the heavenlies and bring down to his benighted followers a weekly blessing of wisdom and inspiration. *Christianity Today*, which does run a lot of helpful articles, is a leader in this sorry trend. In 1997 they featured a cover article in which the pastor-author tried to woo readers back into pre-Reformation darkness. Excerpts:

> ... in worship, the pastor must become priest.... The pastor assumes the role of mediator, incarnating God to the people....
>
> Through our craft, we will facilitate worship.... As pastor-priest, we bring to the congregation the glory of our encounter with God. Having spent long, enduring time in

---

* For the record, the reason I don't spend "equal time" bewailing the plight of women in the traditional church is that the gap between clergy and laity is so big that it dwarfs the gap between the sexes.

the Lord's presence, we speak to our congregations out of those encounters.... And as we worship, liturgists and leaders become a priesthood, mediating God, showing the depth of their own experiences, radiating God's glory, pointing weary souls heavenward....

I remember when one of our daughters was baptized. She stood near the baptismal font as our pastor bent over, asking her questions of faith.... Later she said, "I remember Pastor coming near, and I was covered and lost in his long, black robes, and he baptized me."[17]

Mediator? Incarnating God? Lost in his robes? In such veneration, *Christianity Today* has spun out and left the track. As Paul wrote in I Timothy 2:5, "There is but one God, and one mediator between God and men, the man Christ Jesus." And Peter added that *all* of us are "a royal priesthood." (I Peter 2:9)

Am I quibbling here? Perhaps a bit. But why don't more American men attend traditional services along with their wives? Is it maybe because they've figured out that the pastor has taken on the role of surrogate husband of every woman in the congregation? Is it because they instinctively recoil from a game where they're shut out and have to play a passive part? You betcha. When there's no room left for strong men, they opt out.

Open churches offer a reason to opt back in: unlimited empowerment, which produces men of iron and women of fire.

> The mindset of the underling is hard to shake. Pope John XXIII once commented:
>
> "It often happens that I wake at night and begin to think about a serious problem and decide I must tell the Pope about it. Then I wake up completely and remember that I am the Pope."
>
> – Pope John XXIII in *In My Own Words*

9. In open fellowships, men are a slight majority.

Men go to open meetings:

• to get their marching orders from the Commander of the Hosts of Heaven.

• to model true discipleship by telling how the Lord strengthened them that week.

• to stand up and proclaim the awesome wisdom and love of the Creator who has spoken to them in Scripture.

• to take their rightful place as men learning to be leaders in the household of God.

In open churches around the world, men have a role to play, a man's role.*

Men feed on challenges. Can't live without them. We grew up and thrived in a boy culture where *I double-dare ya'!* was only slightly less impelling than cries of *Chicken!*

Someone recently wrote an update on Karl Barth's aphorism that "The Word became flesh—and then, through theologians, became words again." The new, improved version reads: "Jesus Christ turns wimps into men. And then the church turns them back into wimps again."

You don't grow strong men by making them sit in rows. You grow strong men by whacking them on the shoulder and saying, "On your feet, Pete! What has God been showing you this week?"

Strong males who are forced to be pew warmers are like the bench warmers in football: They're aching to grab the coach by the lapels, get in his face and yell, "Just put me in the game! Just gimme the ball!"

In team Christianity, as in war, everybody is in the game, and everybody gets his hands on the ball. Typically, men will do roughly 60% of the talking and women 40%. That's not something we aim for, it's just what happens—and everyone seems to like it that way.**

SIDE NOTE ON BOYS: Step one in God's plan for re-establishing fathers and fatherhood is to have a boy sitting in church next to his parents when his dad stands up, and every eye in the place is on Dad as he opens his Bible and says, "The Lord showed me something in Galatians yesterday, and I think we need to hear it ..."

As I said before, lions don't grow in small cages. And after a lifetime in a cage, it does no good to set them free, either. Zoo-born animals fed by keepers never learn to survive in the wild.

Rousseau observed that men are born free, yet are everywhere in chains. I would add that men are born wild at heart, yet our churches are filled with captured lions, tamed pew-sitters who no longer know—if they ever knew—how to feed themselves spiritually, how to defend their families from evil, and how to attack their true prey, the devil.

---

* In the West, there is about a 90% overlap between open churches and house churches. But just to show that they're not the same thing, let me mention China. Its wildly successful house churches are far from textbook examples of openness. As a result, two-thirds to nine-tenths of the Christians are women. Even among believers, religion is still seen as the sphere of women.

Yet the Chinese church, simply by meeting in homes, does offer more participation than our steeple-and-brick masterpieces. That's why it's growing so rapidly, about 9% a year. And as soon as it succeeds in opening up to full participation, I suspect it could begin to double every year.

** Well, I do have some dear friends who insist on men doing all the talking. But I've seen some small home gatherings where most of the men were gone for various reasons, leaving perhaps me and some other guy as the only pants-wearing types. I'm still waiting for them to explain to me (with a straight face) how that kind of church meeting is supposed to work. I've also seen excellent churches inside women's prisons or other odd populations that had only women. What would they recommend for these? Two hours of mime?

125

10. Passive or Proactive?

The #1 gripe of most pastors I know is, "What on earth do I have to do to get these people off their fannies?" It seldom dawns on them that they might be their own worst enemies, giving their flock an hour or two of practice every week in *sitting and doing nothing*. The Sunday morning drill in suspended animation is perfect for zombies-in-training.

Open churches offer the opposite: a 24/7 exercise in initiative. PLEASE ALLOW ME TO SPEAK IN AN IDEALIZED TONE HERE IN ORDER TO DRAMATIZE THE DISTINCTIVENESS OF THE NEW SAINTS' LIFESTYLE:

A. *We're responsible.* The Earth is the LORD'S, and if things are not right, we go to work on *making* them right. We accept stewardship for just about everything in sight, from trash in the street to trash on movie screens.*

B. *We're proactive.* The new saints take the fight to the enemy and nip problems in the bud. We don't sit around waiting for somebody to come along and tell us what to do. The world will not be won by passive peons sitting in rows and accumulating oak leaf clusters for Sunday school attendance. When Jesus said that the gates of hell would not prevail against His church, He was talking about us being proactive. I've yet to see anyone attacked by a gate.

C. *We're apperceptive.* That means we're constantly trying to act, not react. As we go through each day, we bring to each situation all that we have ever learned. Our spirits are constantly moving, reaching out to people and situations around us. We're not dinghies bobbing on the seas of life, we're speedboats cutting through the chop and making our own waves.

Consider how Jesus answered questions. In John 3, Nicodemus started off with a compliment, saying he believed Jesus was from God. The Lord replied on a different level, saying that a person must be born again. His answer reveals a vastly larger frame of reference—which includes a deep understanding of Nicodemus's needs.

So it is with us. Our conversations and actions spring from a wide frame of reference that includes all we know about God's purposes for the people and events we are touching. We don't easily get irked or sucked into the tiring minutiae of life. Much of the time, stimulus-response psychology simply doesn't apply to us. Our responses are actually "sponses" because they are a continuous part of the endless river of thoughts and deeds that flows through us from the heart of God, where every action in the universe originates.

---

* For instance, I'm on the board of reference of the Christian Film & Television Commission, a ministry that in 20 years has increased family movies from 6 to 101, increased "Christian content" movies from 1 to 116, and reduced R-rated movies from 81% to 40% of the total. New saints don't just whine anymore. We act.

The new church will keep you in sync with this majestic, mysterious flow of life. As a new saint, you won't just "face reality." You'll create *new* realities out of your matrix of mustard seed faith.

11. DECISIONS: **No voting, no decrees.**

To tradition-bound minds, an "open church" sounds like a recipe for chaos. They envision shouting matches, Old West fistfights, hellish heresies, and drooling incompetence.

Actually, we get along quite well, considering the potential for mischief in a wide-open group. And we do so without voting or resorting to parliamentary procedure. (Ever notice that the book of Acts doesn't mention *Roberts' Rules of Order*?)

It's a complex topic, but basically we try to decide things by consensus.* We learn and grow a lot that way.

Some projects and events are just too messy for consensus, so we go for sheer efficiency. For instance, when the Salem Community Church, a house church in Massachusetts, wants to hold a conference, the first thing they do is appoint a "Conference Czar" who calls all the shots.

Elders provide guidance and leadership mainly as father figures,** mother figures, or examples, not ruling executives, so they don't usually express themselves *as a group* unless something is wrong. (Then think "referee.") As long as things are humming, they function pretty much like anyone else.

In an open church, when a tricky issue is being discussed in depth, it sometimes seems like a chore. But I treasure many of those past times because they dispersed our darkness and brought us a unity that never could have come from a vote. The most glory-filled decisions are those where a single person holds out for what is right until at last the entire team opens their eyes to reality. Ballots short-circuit that process.

But whatever method we use, our strong unity springs out from our blended diversity of vision ... while out in the loveless, demanding, secular world, diversity sabotages unity at every turn.

12. Who's in charge here?

In traditional churches, the pastor is in control to a great degree. But team Christianity has a bit of disturbing news for clergy:

---

* The early church often made decisions by united prayer and discussion, as in Acts 1:23-25, 4:24-31, and 6:5-6.
** One-to-one spiritual fathering is one of the greatest needs in this forlorn and torn-up age. The new church provides a warm matrix for that. See Larry Kreider, *House Church Networks* (Ephrata, PA: House to House Publications), 2001, chapter 7, "The Role of Spiritual Fathers and Mothers."

Frankly, pastor, we already have many people in the body of Christ who have some sort of pastoral gifting. It's not that we don't need you anymore, it's just that in the New Testament, being a pastor is a gift, not a position. And, well, the new church doesn't really have <u>traditional</u> pastors.

But there's also good news:

We greatly need a whole armada of apostles, prophets, and up-to-date teachers. We're way short on these church-planting, disciple-building specialists. So here is your chance to shift into the church of the future just by changing hats.

You probably have some gifting in one of these fields of work already. Thus, you can upgrade yourself rapidly to an industrial strength apostle or prophet, or you may expand your range of teaching and make a great leap sideways as a mobile teacher who rotates through a cycle of open congregations or speaks at conferences or networking meetings of new churches.

The new churches are proliferating. Within a very few years, your pond will be large. And I think you'll be a bigger frog.

The issue, as usual in this world, is control. And pastors are hired because laymen have relinquished control, cut back on commitment, abandoned responsibility, and turned into spectators.

Traditional churches are here to stay, but to the extent they're built around a professional clergyman with a special title, special authority, special status, and special duties and privileges, they're not Biblical. And I feel they may have reached their apex. In just 12 months (1999 to 2000) the number of donors to U.S. churches fell 14%, and the average donation fell by 19%.[18] A lot of believers are hitting the silk. Meanwhile, interest in home churches is spiking upward.

Jesus wants His church back, and He's going to get it. The revival that is sweeping the world and heading toward the U.S. and Europe will be led by a million nobodies under the clear headship of Jesus Christ.

13. Free the people! Free the Lord!

Alexander Solzhenitsyn, in *The Gulag Archipelago*, gives us a memorable picture of freedom. He has been released from a prison camp in Siberia and is walking down the road alone:

And off I *walk*! I wonder whether everybody knows the meaning of this great free word. I am walking along *by myself*! With no automatic rifles threatening me, from either flank or from the rear. I look behind me: no one there! If I like, I can take the right-hand side, past the school fence, where a big pig is rooting in a puddle. And if I like, I can walk on the left, where hens are strutting and scratching ...

... my spine, which seemed bent for eternity, is already just a little straighter, my manner already a little more relaxed. In the course of those two hundred meters I have graduated to the next higher civil estate.[19]

Such is freedom for the newly free.

It is no less precious for those who have discovered freedom in Christ. Countless Christians have shed tears of joy and release when they join open fellowships and suddenly find that they are an integral and honored part of something far bigger than they are.

Such liberation now extends to all the ministry you do in an open church. Freed from the fetters of committee approval or pastoral permission, your labors for the LORD can now diversify and flow in almost any direction. Forget limits. "Nothing will be impossible for you." (Matthew 17:21)

EVEN BETTER: God is also free to do as He wants in open meetings. He has, at least in theory, total control of the agenda and choice of participants. As an American, I'm proud of my heritage of freedom. We have pioneered in freedom for two centuries, and the world looks to us for inspiration in that. But the U.S. and West European church has lagged far behind the rest of the world in miracles and church growth. Perhaps now we can close that gap as we learn to trust God for miracles and, at the same time, give the world a shining example of how a truly free church can grow.

NOTE ON FREEDOM VS. IRRESPONSIBILITY: Know the difference between a terrorist and a two-year-old? Answer: You can reason with a terrorist. Few things are more debilitating than having to deal with a one-man anarchy with the attitude of a two-year-old. *You must choose to be accountable*, either to your team or to an individual you respect, to help each other reach your goals. So accountability should be eagerly given, not demanded.

Your freedom is rooted in your accountability; bear in mind the words of singer Julie Andrews: "Some people regard discipline as a chore. For me, it is a kind of order that sets me free to fly." A Christian who is answerable to nobody is a danger to himself and a liability to the kingdom.

14. MINISTRY: Magnetic or Mobile?

Long ago someone said, "A man must keep his mouth open a very long while before a roast pigeon flies into it."

This is the trouble with a facility-based church. You spend a king's ransom on the building, then you sit and wait for the paint to peel or a visitor to show up, whichever comes first. Even if you go out and invite lots of people to come, you still have a *come-to church*, not a *go-to church*.

The new churches do the opposite: mobile ministry. We go to where the people are—in their homes, offices, cafes, and other watering holes. For instance, all 135 of the bars in my own city have been touched by believers who care. And we've gone into places that are a lot tougher than bars.

Worldwide, the old church does not have an image of being outgoing. In a 1991 survey of young people (roughly ages 15 to 25) in Amsterdam, Holland, 100% said they were interested in God ... yet only 1% said they were interested in the church.[20] Pastors who heard of this commented that something must be seriously wrong with the youth of Amsterdam. *(OK to laugh here)*

15. Expensive or Explosive?

In its schools and social outreach programs, the traditional church is way more cost-efficient than the government. Beyond that, it doesn't have much efficiency to brag about. Top U.S. statistician George Barna recited for us a sad number in a recent seminar: "In the last decade, the churches in the U.S. spent $500 billion on domestic expenses—with no growth to show for it."[21]

He paused, then added, "Now, how long would a board of directors take to fire a corporate president who went through that much money with no growth to show for it? The word *nanosecond* comes to mind."

Institutional churches can't give much of their income to missions or charity work because it gets eaten up first by salaries and expenses for the building and programs. Offerings don't vanish down a rathole, they just get siphoned off into things that merely *maintain* the church instead of multiplying it.

The new churches, meeting mostly in homes, have overhead expenses somewhere between a kazoo jam session and a dog fight. Freed from the ball and chain of institutional expenses, they can be ridiculously easy to start.

Typically, expenses are light enough that members are left with more money to give to various other Christian causes of their choice, which is liberating. Tithing, being entirely an Old Testament concept, is usually displaced by the more generous and happy guideline of

II Corinthians 9:7, "Let everyone give as his heart tells him. There should be no pain or sense of compulsion."*

Many of your offerings will go to some member with a special need (unless you're all well off). Some fellowships cache a few hundred dollars to help members through rough spots, but most prefer face-to-face giving because it really brings hearts together.

The next frontier for open churches: learning to fund those in mobile ministry. The biggest thing holding back the expansion of the kingdom (other than sin) is that we have not learned to support traveling apostles, prophets, and teachers. We are still too inward-looking. This is a major kink.**

16. THE HEART OF YOUR CHURCH: Large Meetings or Small?

The center of gravity of the world's churches is shifting. It used to be the large Sunday morning "worship service," but today there is a rapidly spreading awareness that the real matrix of growth and change is the small group, whether it's an independent house church, a cell (subdivision of a traditional church), or some other goal-oriented task team.

Even Fidel Castro—who falls a bit short of a prophet—endorsed the burgeoning house church movement last year: "We don't need more church buildings in Cuba. But Christian meetings in private households are fine as long as no more than 15 people attend."[22] That's about in the middle of 12 to 20, the range of limits advised by various house church experts.

Until the mid-1980s, the "debate" between the house church and traditional church featured a wide chasm. On the traditional side, the big meeting was the heart and soul of church life. On the house side, big meetings were shunned as the shadow of Babylon.

Now both sides are coming closer together:

• Several hundred thousand traditional churches in the U.S. have adopted the cell church model because cell life brings sorely needed spiritual and numerical growth. This is a giant step, two-thirds of the way toward the house church network model. (That's why I always applaud cell churches.) Even the world's largest church, in Seoul, Korea, has given up on constructing any more branch churches and has moved to a pure house-cell network hubbed around the Internet.

---

* The New Testament view of giving is further clarified by Luke 12:33, Galatians 6:10, I Corinthians 16:2, Acts 11:29, etc.
** "One of the weaknesses that we see as so prevalent [in house churches] is that they do not want, nor do they accept, the moderating influence of apostolic or prophetic ministries that come from outside their own fellowship." (*Simply Church*, p. 76)

Cell Church, House Church: What's the Difference?

Both kinds of churches have small groups meeting in homes, doing many of the same activities. So aren't they about the same thing?

No. A cell is a subdivision of a central traditional church (which usually receives and retains all offerings). A house church is independent, though it probably networks with other home churches and meets with them from time to time.

Both kinds can and do multiply nicely, but no matter how much you expand a cell church, you only have one church (with all the limitations and conformities of a single church). And in the central Sunday service, the wonderful, life-building dynamic of the weekday cells collapses right back into the impotence and anonymity we're trying to get away from.

A house church is a complete church, not part of a church. It's not locked into someone else's vision. Free Christianity forces you to learn to feed one another spiritually with the Word of God and seek direction from Him—rather than expecting to receive most of your nourishment and guidance from the pulpit (or the cell leader) for the rest of your life.

Your house church has the freedom to take new directions under God. It's free to:

- express the unique gifting of each member
- fulfill the dreams of all its members
- meet the special needs of its own neighborhood
- do their own weddings, baptisms, and funerals
- multiply infinitely.

• House churches have begun to network, holding occasional or monthly joint meetings. However, they're careful to avoid *big* meetings on a weekly or biweekly basis; it's too easy to get swept away by the music and excitement of a large celebration or lured into terminal laziness by the sit-'n-soak mentality of spectator gatherings.

There is a growing agreement across the spectrum that:

1. Small, participatory groups are the main source of intimacy, growth, accountability, responsibility, repentance, and new steps of faith. Also, they are the only venue where you can practice the 54 "one anothers" of the New Testament, which are the core of the Christian community.

2. But extensive networking among *all* Bible-based churches is necessary to win our cities and nations for Christ. When the churches of a city get their act together and pray and reach out in unity, God is much more motivated to move on a wide scale.

17. Who needs apostles, anyway?

A class-A, five-star apostle is a powerful pioneer—and multi-gifted.* He travels from place to place starting churches, but never settles down to supervise them long term.

His secret of success is knowing when to leave and allow the fledgling cluster of converts to start functioning and growing on their own. When left to sink or swim, most folks much prefer to swim.

If at all possible, the apostle comes back from time to time, as Paul did, taking a few days or weeks to check up on the new plant and straighten out any problems. This allows for adequate oversight without dominating or smothering.

In contrast, many traditional churches have been started by a man who settles in for the long haul as the founder-pastor. Such a double distinction wins him the esteem of an apostle, shepherd, CEO, and chief elder—a personage with whom few would dare disagree! Though the New Testament doesn't even hint at placing one elder over all the rest,** the founder-pastor is a common figure, and his successors inherit most of his formidable mantle.

Until recent decades, most traditional churches were local franchises of a denomination (hence the title, "*First* Luthobapterian Church of Podunk"). While this did reinforce brand name identity nicely, it marginalized the Biblical practice of oversight by apostles. To this day, a man who strolls into a traditional church and says, "Hi, I'm an apostle," is *persona non grata*. There is <u>no</u> place for him, and he is a threat to the tranquillity of the flock.

The problem is not with denominations, many of which have recently begun to do a fine job, given their hierarchical structures. The problem is with denominational*ism* and its mindset of control. When a traditional pastor asks, "Who is your covering?" he isn't concerned about your church's prayer support. He wants to be assured that you're under a chain of command like *his* church is. If you smile and give him the proper answer (*Jesus!*), he may henceforth view your church as a loose cannon.

We have the same problem individually. From time to time, you'll meet people driven by a spirit of control; they will not rest until you assure them that you are personally under the firm authority of some

---

* See II Corinthians 12:12 for the long-term picture. But as I noted before, Jesus also applied the term "apostle" to raw recruits who had never done anything! (Luke 6:13) So you don't have to wait until you have performed "signs, wonders, and miracles" before you can start doing the main work of apostles: calling people to Christ and planting churches.

** SMALL PERSONAL OPINION: The ancient Latin phrase *primus inter pares* (first among equals) was the longest-running insider joke in Western history until George Orwell exposed it—and topped it—in *Animal Farm* with his cute observation that, "All animals are equal, but some are more equal than others."

strong mentor or pastor. Well, the worth of a wise mentor-discipler is beyond rubies, and if you're lucky enough to have one, listen, weigh his words and act upon them. But God holds *you* responsible for what you do.

In all cases, I highly recommend you read Frank Viola's foundational book, *Who Is Your Covering?*[23] Very solid and heartening.

18. Empire vs. Kingdom

In times past, many churches were private clubs, and denominations were mega-cliques maintained for the sole benefit of their members. I could tell you sad stories of people in desperate need who were turned away to scrounge for food or seek shelter under a bridge simply because they were not members of the church they sought help from.

The past half century brought much enlightenment, and such cases have dwindled. Yes, in some areas of the U.S. and Europe, pastors still regard their churches as their own private empire, not as *one* local expression of the kingdom of God with any duties to other churches or people. And yes, a pastor or leader who is eager to build support for a citywide project may still receive from other pastors just a polite pat on the head and a promise to pray for the project. But happily, a new awareness has flooded most regions, and pastors are rapidly learning to pray for one another and work together on citywide efforts. Relationships and attitudes have been transformed.[24]

19. Better Doctrine, Fewer Fights

In a stated act of "self-cleansing" on January 22, 1998, Joseph Cardinal Ratzinger, Grand Inquisitor for the Roman Catholic Church and head of its Congregation for the Doctrine of the Faith, speaking for the church, said that their archives (4,500 big volumes) indicate a death toll of 25 million over the centuries. That's just those killed by the Catholic Church for being heretics. (And likely two-thirds of the original volumes are lost.)[25]

How could the followers of the gentle Savior cause such a death toll? It all started with doctrine. Following the early church's struggles with heresies, finely tuned systems of doctrine were hammered out. Eye-crossing, i-dotting precision was achieved, even in issues like the nature of the Trinity, the incarnation of Christ, and predestination vs. free will, all of which are beyond the abilities of men's minds to explain fully.

This battle-hardened theology was bequeathed to succeeding generations of Christians, right down to our parents. Doctrine was a war banner, a flag we waved to flaunt our differences from other denominations. Thus, our most cherished truths became our prime source of distrust and division instead of unity and love.

Today, however, doctrine is more like a foundation under our feet or an anchor to keep us from drifting away from the truth. We've learned to unite around the core doctrines we have in common.

Unfortunately, many of the large U.S. and European denominations are dying out because they abandoned any pretense of conservative doctrine and dove into the sinkhole of liberalism, whose tenets are 180 degrees off from the truth.[26] Led astray by their leaders, they have lost touch with the bedrock verities of the Bible. They have followed the perennial pattern of error crashing into the church from the theologians and power players.

The debacle led by liberal clergy is an interesting comment on the fear that lay-led congregations may become hotbeds of heresies. Fat chance! Any review of church history will reveal that the customers in the pews are virtually always more conservative than the ecclesiastical potentates promoting their personal brand of holy baloney. As Wayne Jacobsen puts it bluntly, "I'm sorry to burst your bubble here, but every major heresy that has [afflicted] God's people in the last 2,000 years has come from organized groups with 'leaders' who thought they knew God's mind better than anyone around them."[27]

Even the most doctrinally solid pastors are now falling victim to the inherent flaws in the traditional church *pattern*. In the U.S., "94% of all senior pastors claim they consistently provide their congregations with teaching that 'intentionally and systematically leads them to a biblical worldview.'"[28] *Oh, please.* A George Barna survey shows the facts:

• Only 10% of all U.S. Christians have such a worldview.
• Nearly two-thirds of them think all truth is "situational"—that there is no such thing as "absolute moral truth."[29]

The system isn't working. In fact, "a majority of people who attend a church service can't recall the topic of the sermon—much less the key points" after two hours.[30]

20. The End of Loneliness

Big traditional church meetings can be lonely crowds, whole roomfuls of isolated souls. I've sat through many a worship service not knowing the names of those on either side of me. Being a bit of a politenik, I often didn't even know what they looked like apart from a quick glance while seating, when it's proper to look directly at your neighbor.

When a pastor stands in a pulpit with every eye focused on him, the crowd appears to be one big, happy family. That is an optical delusion of the highest magnitude.

By contrast, ring churches are true teams, often with a high degree of 24/7 commitment, rich fellowship, and profuse opportunities for what we call "every-member ministry." These are the cry of the human heart, especially in the Western world and especially among Generation X.

21. Is Jesus your host or your guest of honor?

In traditional worship services, we say to Christ (in effect), *Welcome, Lord Jesus! Please take the seat of honor here while we worship You and sing your praises! Only please don't interrupt our service.* Like the queen of England, He is enthroned and admired, but not allowed to make any decisions.

A program is a program, and cannot be substantially changed— even by God—without causing embarrassment or serious consternation. Yes, order is important, as it says in I Corinthians 14:26, but when *programmed* order becomes more important than the presence and power of the Lord, then in the phrase of the British, we have "lost the plot."

Jesus actually wants to be the host of our meetings, the master of ceremonies. As the emcee, He touches one heart, then another through His Holy Spirit, producing a series of contributions that usually flows in a loosely thematic progression ... along any of a million avenues.

The flow may change direction and transpose into a new theme or mode every 20 or 30 minutes—sometimes more often—but it is still His Spirit that weaves it all together into a discernible whole. Until you have seen the Lord do this a half dozen times, you won't really believe it—not deep in your heart. But afterward, you'll come to expect this mini-miracle as the norm.

Critics who have never actually been in a truly open meeting often object, with exasperation, "Look, *somebody* has to be in charge." Well, the Holy Spirit definitely qualifies as somebody. Moreover, any church filled with liberated disciples of the One who holds the seven stars in His right hand will be jampacked with strong leadership. Count on it. Our "leaderless" meetings are far from leader*ship*less.

22. Constipation in the Church

A congregation without a working excretory system will have a lot of pain.

Sin is indigenous to the human heart, and it perpetually bubbles up from covert to overt, from latent to patent. When it comes to the surface in a church, it may produce a crisis. But even if it remains hidden, it can hinder the whole congregation and limit or block God's blessings.

Snapshots
of a few miracles...

Page 3: **Dead at five, alive at seven:** *Arjun Dass of Delhi, India, was electrocuted in April, 2001. A team of five led by Savitri prayed for him, and God resurrected him ten hours after his death.*

Arjun with his mother, Mina, in 2003

Left to right: *Jim, Arjun, Savitri, and Arjun's mother, Mina, in 2003*

Page 9:
Happily ever after: *Daniel with his wife, Nneka, who would not accept his death even though his body had been injected with preservatives.*

Page 9: **Dead for two days:** *Daniel Ekechukwu looks at his own death certificate.*

Page 22:

A demoniac in Firozpur: *In the morning, this man was so deranged that he had been kept chained to a tree for eight years. But that evening (inset) he appeared at a Christian rally to say, "Hallelujah!"*

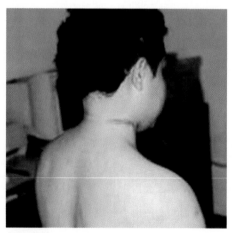

Page 32:

A slit throat, total loss of blood, and quick death: *Then God sent him back. The only part of Domingos's neck uncut was the spinal cord and the skin in back, seen here.*

Page 151:

Another veil torn: *In a move with a striking parallel to the tearing of the veil in the temple at Jerusalem, the sturdy pulpit at Christian Tabernacle in Houston was broken and tossed toward the pews while the pastor was hurled backward. (For the photo below, the pieces were put back where they fell on that morning.)*

Page 151:

Tenney and the split pulpit: *In retrospect, the torn pulpit stands out as the main object lesson. But at the time, no one paid much attention to it. As Tommy Tenney notes in his book* The God Chasers, *"We were too occupied with the torn heavenlies." God had ripped a hole in the space-time continuum to signal a basic change in how His kingdom must work in the years ahead.*

Page 151:
The pieces of the pulpit where they rest now, almost out of sight at the end of the platform.

The moral of the story: *God wants a deeper relationship with His people, but this must involve upgraded meetings in which He rules more directly, with less human interference in His agenda.*

Page 108:

From two heads to one: *Esther at one year and 19 days, with her parents Dashru and Sukhwari at home in Sukropath, Madhya Pradesh, India. She's quite normal now. But as astonishing as the miracle is, its meaning is much greater.*

FREEDOM   GOD'S PRESENCE

EMPOWERMENT   ADVENTURE

SOLUTIONS   PARTICIPATION

SUPPORT

MEGA*SHIFT*

Plainly, it's vital to have a way to continually get rid of sin lodged in the hearts of God's people. But in a traditionally structured church, the only mechanism of cleansing is for the pastor to sermonize regularly on sin and hope that the Spirit convicts people enough that they'll go home and repent in private.

Open churches have a powerful way of getting rid of sin: turning loose the Holy Spirit, allowing Him to touch individual hearts and giving floor time to those convicted by Him.

During the normal course of teaching and sharing, the Spirit will occasionally speak to one of the saints about his or her sin. The resulting confession often triggers another—and another. If you've been beating your wife for two years, and a brother sitting next to you confesses that he slapped his wife yesterday, the Spirit of God will put *tremendous* pressure on you. You'll find it almost impossible to just sit there and nod your head, pretending to be Mr. Innocence. You will feel as though you had HYPOCRITE tattooed in scarlet letters on your forehead. Thus does the LORD of the burning bush purify His people and restore them to a place of blessing.

23. Are we sinners or saints?

John was one highly sophisticated apostle.

Though he was able to fearlessly recast the good news in abstract Greek literary terms ("God is love" and "In the beginning was the Word"), he also shrugged off the Greek mania for logical consistency and presented deep, Hebraic-style paradoxes without a blink: In I John 1:8 he states, "If we claim to have no sin, we are only fooling ourselves and refusing to accept the truth." Yet two chapters later he gives us the flip side: "Whoever is born of God does not commit sin, because the very nature of God dwells within him, and he cannot sin, because he is born of God." (I John 3:9)

So which is it? Are we saintly sinners? Sinful saints? The question is a paradox, not a contradiction, and I'll bet John never lost a moment's sleep over it. Along with the rest of the church, he knew that we are the true saints of God. The biggest clue he gives us is in the original Greek of 3:9. "Cannot sin" is "cannot go on sinning" or "practice sinning" in various modern translations, which reflect John's meaning. Though we do stumble, our basic identity is Spirit-inhabited *saints*. For us, sinning is "out of character," as they say in Hollywood.

Am I splitting a hair? I think not. This is a major issue. The whole Nicolaitan system of oppression was built upon the creation of a permanent underclass of "sinners" who could be managed by an elite clergy, holy men wearing holy robes and giving holy sermons in a holy sanctuary on the holy day. Once you let the unholy herd realize they are saints, the spell is broken, freedom breaks out all over, and the whole man-eating superstructure of unbiblical traditions begins to crumble. Soon you could see a stampede toward something better.

24. Perseverance or Victory?

I love the old hymns; I sing them all the time. From memory. Sometimes all the verses!

But the hymns had their flaws. Leaf through a century-old hymnal, and you'll find a lot of the lyrics are on just being faithful, persevering in this troubled world, seeing our friends in heaven someday, and hanging on until Jesus comes back to rescue us.

Such was the unique culture of the old U.S. church from, roughly, the Civil War to the 1960s: insular yet warm, defensive yet triumphalistic, static yet always singing about heaven.

It sent out circuit-riding preachers, but offered few meaningful roles to its laymen. It vastly expanded the modern missionary movement, but ran its own churches as a holding operation. It lifted millions of black Africans out of primitive darkness, but practiced de facto segregation at home.

In short, the old church was mainly focused on stability and perseverance, while the new church focuses on overcoming and growth. The new church is changing the world, not by timidly adding a few carbon-copy outpost congregations, but by setting up independent, self-multiplying church *networks* everywhere. This "saturation church planting" is both fast and systematic. Each new network is meant to multiply from day one, not just sit and subsist as an appendage of the mother church.

Reading this one-sided summary, you may wonder why everyone hasn't jumped ship by now and joined the new networks. Well, one big reason is that fast-growing things are messy. (Look at your kids, for instance.) If you start a network of networks and plant 200 house churches next year, it won't be tidy.

Unfortunately, members of the old church are taught that orderly decorum is the root value of meetings. So if even one of your 200 churches has a few goofballs swinging from the chandeliers, your entire movement will be tainted in the eyes of traditionalists.

In the new churches we prize the Presence above everything else. If God is there in His power, love, and majesty, we can tolerate a lot of slop: inappropriate contributions, flawed thoughts from entry-level prophets, teary tales of woe, songs no one knows, etc. *Perhaps the biggest sin of the old church today is valuing order above life.* God values life above order.

25. Spiritual Growth or Stagnation

Open churches produce people who are far more mature than those in closed churches. Sitting in a pew cannot compare to the accelerated, 24/7 challenges of life in a community of believers dedicated to helping one another grow. (This can now actually be shown via testing.[31])

Typically, the high you get from 60 to 80 minutes in a traditional service is just enough to last you for the next seven days, at which time you will need another fix. An open church meeting is more like a banquet where you learn to feast continuously on the Bread of Life.

26. Hitting the Wall—or Not

Traditional churches often stop growing at a certain number of members: 100, 200, 400, etc. That's because a lone pastor can only service the needs of about 200, but with one added staffer can service 400, and so on. The principle extends to the hundreds of thousands; as long as cash flow keeps up, they can keep hiring—and growing.

Open churches fall under a broad category, *metachurches* (not megachurches), a term coined by top church consultant Carl George in his classic *Prepare Your Church for the Future.*[32] A metachurch is any church (even traditional) structured so as to constantly generate its own new leaders. They tend to keep growing because they endlessly hatch new leaders out of the incubator of small affinity groups based on relationships that (unlike cells) are fairly natural.

Aspiring leaders in open fellowships don't have to go to seminary, get voted onto a board, or be appointed to a key committee post. We have *servant* leadership that percolates up from the grass roots and flows through the entire regional network.

True Biblical authority doesn't just sit like a golden crown upon the brows of the ecclesiastical elite. It flows and grows as elders and equippers help others develop their gifts. (See Ephesians 4:11-12 for God's answer to a leadership shortage.) Here is a tough question for traditional pastors: While you are occupying the pulpit, preaching a sermon, are you *enabling* your people to do what you're doing? Or are you *preventing* them from doing what you're doing?

THE RULE OF THUMB: As you become *able* to strongly serve a wider range of people, you should be allowed to *do* your ministry work for wider and wider circles throughout the kingdom. With no stained-glass ceiling to hit their heads on, the new saints are upwardly mobile.

27. The Devil's Worst Nightmare

The revival that I expect to unfold soon across the U.S. will eventually produce a lot of things we've never seen before:

• Stadiums across the land will be filled nightly with capacity crowds singing, praying, and sharing testimonies—mostly from ordinary, unknown people. These rallies may even displace many sports events.[33]

• Such gatherings and other broad efforts will involve a wide mix of churches: traditional and new, open and closed, Evangelical, Charismatic, Pentecostal, plus some elements of the more liberal denominations.

• A new harmony will bring together house church networks, megachurches, and family/community churches, all working in synergy. See Larry Kreider's *House Church Networks* for an optimistic yet plausible vision of cross-church teamwork.[34]

In addition, two new categories of leaders will flourish:

• A host of merit-based point men and point women, the *five-fold leaders* of the church. (Ephesians 4:11) Four of these types are mobile and thus will circulate locally, regionally, or nationally: apostles (pioneers), prophets (pathfinders), evangelists (spearheads of progress), and teachers (fountainheads of wisdom). In short, they are the glue that holds together the new move of God. (The fifth type is pastors, whose ministry is mainly in local assemblies. In the new churches, they are mostly non-professional.)

• "Elders of the city," a category so new and widely misunderstood as to require quotation marks. These leaders are not elected, they are simply recognized. They command such respect from a wide range of believers that most everyone looks to them as spokesmen and reliable helmsmen for the church of the city.* They rise above their denomination or congregation. They seldom meet as a discrete group or issue joint statements, partly because their status is fuzzy and always evolving. But in times of trouble or opportunity, all eyes shift toward them for direction or encouragement.

Now please pardon the bold face type here, but this next point is the least understood principle in the book:

Most house church leaders recognize the importance of having large, <u>multi-church</u> gatherings from time to time, but few have perceived the importance of broad-based participation in them.

In planning stages of a big meeting, the word "celebration" usually pops up, paralyzing the thought processes of all involved. The final result is often a ho-hum experience, a series of well-known leaders mouthing expectable verities—all punctuated by an abundance of trendy Christian music played loudly enough to drown out any

---

* The hazy phrase *church of the city* is best clarified by a trick question: "How many churches are there in this city?" The correct answer is, "One! It just meets in 350 places."

A Prophecy on the Megashift

I realize that I am a mere teacher/writer, so it's nice when I find my words echoing those of a true prophet. At the risk of spraining my arm by patting myself on the back, here are some lines from Rick Joyner, one of the most well-known prophetic voices of our time:

"A revolution is coming to Christianity that will eclipse the Reformation in the sweeping changes that it brings to the church. When it comes ... the way that the world defines Christianity will be radically changed.

"What is coming will not be a change of doctrine, but a change in basic church life.... When this new church emerges, she will be so different from what is now perceived to be the church, that the whole world will not even recognize that there was ever a connection between the two.

"Ultimately home-groups will become the foundation upon which the entire church will be built. Home group ministry teams will actually provide the bulk of the work in equipping the saints, including teaching and pastoring.

"The church has been bound by forces that have greatly inhibited her from becoming all that she was created to be. Control spirits have dominated and crushed creativity. However, even under this extreme pressure, a transformation is taking place ... There is about to be a jailbreak! ... [A] great people are about to emerge from the present forms of church that have been built upon the ways of men, and they will risk everything to seek that which God is building....

"[A] true union of the church is not possible until the forces of spiritual slavery are defeated and all people are set free to follow the Lord in their own quest.... This is not the license to depart from sound doctrine, or to rebel against God's established authorities. However, there is about to be a clear distinction between those who have received their authority from above, and those who have promoted themselves, or been promoted by institutions.

"The future leaders of the church are now being given a vision of radical New Testament Christianity being restored ... It is time to heed the call and allow the Lord to lead His people to the new wineskins that will be able to hold what is about to break out upon the earth.... The new dynamic of church life will overshadow the Great Awakenings in their social impact, transforming cities and even whole nations."[35]

sense of group singing. It is non-relational. The life-transforming magic of small groups is totally absent, having been sacrificed to the phantom concept of "celebration," and the net impact is anything but ground-breaking.

It is imperative that leaders creatively bring in powerful contributions from the rank and file and give them center court, not cameo spots. Only in this way can the fire of God be spread to the whole community. Only in this way can those in the trenches rise to spheres of wider and wider ministry.

28. The Old Church Gets Older, the New Church Gets Newer

Old-line denominational churches tend to fossilize. Why? Because they *cannot* reform. They can't make fundamental changes, they can only tinker.

For seven years I beat my head against a lot of lovely, ivy-covered church walls, trying to pour new wine into their old wineskins. Open Church Ministries, which I founded in 1990, tried until 1997 to get traditional churches to open up to full participation. But the Lord Jesus was right about putting new wine in old wineskins (Mark 2:22). It doesn't work. The pastor won't sit down, and nobody else will stand up!

So today, Open Church Ministries is almost wholly devoted to helping people plant networks of new churches composed—preferably—of new Christians or church dropouts. It's far more fruitful.

However, it's also a slippery process. Gerald Coates, the most recognized leader of what are called the "new churches" in Britain, said it well: "Jim, if you don't keep listening to Jesus, pretty soon you're not part of the new church anymore. You're part of the old church."

Why should we keep changing? Because the world is changing daily, and God is rapidly opening up:

- new ways of doing church
- new methods of dismantling the kingdom of darkness
- and a wide new range of miracles.

Old wineskins simply will not hold new wine. And in places where people are already stampeding into house churches, like India and China, growth would slow to a tenth of today's rate if they had to stop and put up buildings and hire staff for all the new churches.

Semper reformanda, the reformers said, *always reforming*. And they were right.*

29. So what do you want, bosses or brothers?

Enough of linear argumentation. In these last two sections, let's talk *relationships*.

---

* It is not claimed that an open format will solve all problems. But it does open the door to the Holy Spirit and give *Him* the freedom to solve them.

"Help, I'm Trapped in a Traditional Church!"

Maybe you're so firmly planted in an institutional church that you're part of the woodwork. Maybe you fear that your mom would put out a contract on you if you left. Maybe you're married to the pastor— or you *are* the pastor. What can you do?

The standard option in recent decades has been to go to the cell church model, a hybrid form that brings many of the advantages of a house church. That's a big step forward.

But now a whole new strategy has popped up out of nowhere (probably meaning that the Lord is behind it). It's a very logical strategy, and it's being pioneered by some of even the largest megachurches and denominations. In a nutshell, it's *using your traditional, facility-based church to plant open fellowships, networks of pure, independent house churches!*

This new move has come as a total shock and astonishment to house church veterans, some of whom still bear scars from being booted out of Old First Church for roiling the waters.

But it's a really logical step because it fits in so beautifully with a tradition that all Christians understand perfectly: *sending out missionaries*. Missionaries aren't expected to fill the pews or coffers of the mother church, they're just expected to do their job of winning souls and building the kingdom. So sponsoring a network of house churches will not be viewed as *competing* with your church, but as part of its missions program.

Moreover, this strategy enables the mother church to flex its considerable muscle by mobilizing, motivating, and utilizing its "early adopters," those few restless souls who are always eager for something new and challenging ... while allowing its majority of contented traditionalists to stay in their accustomed roles without being bothered by the new "outreach program."

It's a win-win outcome ... unless you include the Lord, which would make it a win-win-win.

Honestly now, do you really feel a need for a hierarchy of church authorities telling you what to think and how to behave? Or would you rather have a warm circle of devoted friends who are tenaciously committed to standing by your side no matter what kind of doo-doo life throws at you?

Take comfort: Nowhere in the New Testament will you find a verse that says one believer should be another believer's *boss*. Neither Peter nor Paul taught a brand of Christianity that puts one person over others. Yes, we do need powerful leaders, submissive disciples, towering authority, church order, and an unbending proclamation of absolute truth. But we need these things as an integral part of an organic reality, not as a hokey remedial superstructure jerry-built onto a rusted-out bureaucracy.

My friend Frank Viola points out some numbers that help you imagine what it *felt* like to be part of the early church:[36]

- The noun *pastor* shows up just once in the New Testament.
- *Overseer* appears four times.
- *Elder* is used five times.
- *Brothers* (which of course includes sisters) comes up 346 times.

Got the picture? Gene Edwards summarized it thus:

> Counting all types of written documents and correspondence, archeologists have about 500,000 specimens from this [early Christian] era, with about 25,000 of them categorized as "Christian" or "probably Christian." ... *Not one of these pieces of papyrus, etc., makes any reference to a clergyman. There is absolutely no mention of a "minister" or "priest" or "pastor" or any other term for any office or any kind of leadership.*[37]

You don't have to be Columbo to get a feel for the relationships in early house churches. We had great leaders then, but we were *family*. It was years before we started appointing bishops over bishops over bishops, displacing Christ and setting up a hierarchy of titled dignitaries claiming to be the bouncers at the gate of Heaven.

30. The Church Where You Matter

I did my time in the pews, fifty years plus—and most of that in pretty darned good churches. But somewhere along the line, I began to ask myself, "What if I didn't show up next Sunday? Would anyone besides my personal friends miss me? And would the service be any different? Even one syllable different?"

I had to conclude that my absence would be like a missing spoonful of snow in Siberia. There was little sense of belonging and less sense of ownership, as in, *This is my family.*

But in a typical open fellowship, you are important. You are needed. You are loved. And when someone isn't there, you have a *definite* sense of loss. You find yourself saying, *I sure wish Jody were here. She would have had something great to say about this topic. She would have made a difference.*

The open church is a connected church, a family. And it's full of Jodies. And they all matter *a lot.*

Sitting in my hotel room in New Delhi a month ago, I listened spellbound as my host, Joshua Pillai, reeled off story after story of Jodies in that part of the world. There was Mannu Lal, 55, who started a thousand house churches in India in four years. There was Tawpaun, 33, a wife and mother in China, who planted 233 churches in one year—and baptized 12,000. There was even a 90-year-old Chinese lady who led 5,000 people to Christ simply by putting up a little sign at a notorious "Lovers' Leap" saying, "Before you commit suicide, come see me at _____ (her address)."

Who are these heroic figures? Superman? Wonder Woman? No, they're just serious Christians who see with the eyes of Christ and understand with their hearts how extremely important people are.

Take a quick look in your own heart. See any unmet needs there? OK, now, see any compassion there for the thousands of folks in your town who are living stunted lives and struggling with problems they just can't handle? Well then, if you have a Bible, you're probably qualified to go out and draw together a brand new branch of the family of God. May God bless you as you go.

The need is there on every corner.

I used to attend a good traditional church in Newport Beach, California, home of the world's largest small-craft marina. The pastor was Joe Aldrich, a young man wise beyond his years and a veteran of thousands of counseling sessions with the sophisticates of that wealthy city. One morning he was speaking about the desperate needs in the hearts of people everywhere. With a vague wave of his hand toward the million-dollar homes on the nearby hills, he stated quietly, "Knock on any door. It'll bleed."

A good open fellowship can stop the bleeding. If it doesn't, you're in trouble. As a poet said:[38]

> So if this is not a place where my questions can be asked,
>   then where shall I go to seek?
> And if this is not a place where my heart cry can be heard,
>   then where shall I go to speak?...
> And if this is not a place where tears are understood,
>   then where shall I go to cry?
> And if this is not a place where my spirit can take wing,
>   tell me, where shall I go to fly?

---

1. David Barrett and Todd Johnson, *World Christian Trends* (Pasadena: Wm. Carey Library) 2001, pp. 303-306.

2. Cf. Eph. 2:2-3

3 George Barna, *Barna Update*, April 13, 2004: The average giving from born-again adult Christians in 2003 was $1,411.

4. Barrett, *op. cit.*, vol. I, page 841. It's

worth footnoting that Mozambique is in the midst of the (relatively) biggest revival on earth, with 3,000 new churches springing up in the last 18 months. That's equivalent to having 44,000 new churches in the U.S.A. The Barrett/Johnson figure for the worldwide average cost of one baptism is $359,000 (www.gem-werc.org/gd/findings.htm). And it takes 85 U.S. church members a year to reach one person for Christ. (Thom Rainer, interviewed in "Understanding the Unchurched," *The Lookout*, 1/11/2004, vol. 66, no. 2, pp. 7-9.)

5. Jamie Buckingham, "Please Don't Call Me Reverend," *Charisma*, June, 1981.

6. Graham Cooke, founder of United Christian Ministries in Southhampton, England, has wisely observed: "The difficulty right now I think is that a lot of leaders cling to their titles like apostle, prophet, bishop, reverend, minister, pastor; and those are not *titles*, they're *functions*. There's no hierarchy in the body of Christ of *status*—not when Jesus could say He came down and laid down His sonship and took upon Himself the form of a servant. In Scripture there are only three titles that God gives us: the first one is servant, the second is steward, and the third one is bondslave. So you get promoted to different levels. You start off as a general servant. Then you get promoted down to being a steward.... After stewardship there is a promotion ... another series of death into slavery." (*Second Wind*, Box 7, Gresham, Oregon), Spring, 1998, page 10.

7. We always need good pastor-shepherds in the church—that is, people who *function* as pastors. What Jesus says we *don't* need is the title.

8. A recycled quote from my book, *The Open Church* (Portal, Georgia: Open Church Ministries), 1992, page 173f.

9. Charles Crismier, "The Significance of Serving," *Ministries Today*, Jan./Feb. 2001, p. 68.

10. Shirley Dobson, "Ministering to the Minister," *Christian American*, Sep./Oct. 1997, p. 12.

11. From a survey by the Fuller Institute of Church Growth.

12. *Ibid.*

13. *Leadership Journal*, Winter, 2001.

14. Crismier, *loc. cit.* You can, in fact, still find seminaries teaching that a pastor should never have any close personal friends in his own church.

15. Barrett, *op. cit.*, Vol. I, p. 18.

16. Paul Tournier, the great Swiss psychiatrist, said it best: "Even the most saintly and humble person—the revered and much loved leader of a devoted congregation—inevitably makes his followers dependent upon him, like little children. It is not his faults, but his virtues, his fame and his richness of spirit, which hold them back and prevent them from growing up themselves. They will do so only when he is gone." (Quoted by Stan Jones, *Faith at Work* magazine, Feb., 1979, p. 37)

17. Gary M. Burge, "Are Evangelicals Missing God at Church?" *Christianity Today*, October 6, 1997, p. 20ff.

18. Barna Research Group, quoted in *Ministries Today*, Sept/Oct., 2001, p. 10.

19. *The Gulag Archipelago* volume 3, page 417.

20. Wolfgang Simson, *Houses That Change the World* (Waynesboro, GA: OM Publishing), 2001, page 2.

21. Cf. his press release June 4, 2002, at www.barna.org.

22. Baptist Press, cited in *Friday Fax* #32, 2000.

23. Frank A. Viola, *Who Is Your Covering?* (1405 Valley Place, Brandon, Florida 33510: Present Testimony Ministry), 1998. Also available at www.ptmin.org, or

write ptmin@aol.com. This establishes, in scholarly fashion, the Biblical legitimacy of the house church. He also has written *Rethinking the Wineskin*, which likewise establishes the illegitimacy of the institutional church.

24. See Otis, *op. cit.*, page 72f.

25. *Women's Summit 2000*, unpublished 2000 manuscript by Bindu Choudhrie, page 18.

26. The best book comparing the two views is the classic by J. Gresham Machen, *Christianity and Liberalism*, now available for free downloading at http://homepage. mac.com/shanerosenthal/reformation ink/jgmchrandlib.htm. Also published by Rosetree Press.

27. Wayne Jacobsen, *Why I Don't Go to Church Anymore*. Contact Wayne through www.koinonianet.net or e-mail him at waynej@lifestream.org. He is echoing a thought from Roland Allen a century ago.

28. George Barna, president of Barna Research Group, in "The Great Disconnect," *Rev. magazine*, Nov./Dec. 1999, page 75.

29. Barna, *loc. cit.* Also, *Ministries Today*, May/June, 2002, page 11.

30. *Ibid.*

31. I helped develop a paper-and-pencil test to measure spiritual maturity. The test has been analyzed and proven to be scientifically valid. However, it must be graded by a professional, so it is not sold directly to the public. If you wish to use it to discover the maturity level of an adult individual or group, please contact the developer, Dr. Nancy Rivas at the Erickson Institute in Chicago, nancyemr@sbc global.net. Your cost for the grading of each test will be $10.

32. Carl F. George, *Prepare Your Church for the Future* (Grand Rapids: Revell), 1991.

33. This is the essence of a vision seen by a number of today's prophets.

34. Larry Kreider, *House Church Networks* (Ephrata, PA: House to House Publications), 2001. Larry is a highly experienced churchman whose words command respect in both house church and institutional church circles. He is the international director of Dove Christian Fellowship International, an apostolic (not denominational) movement.

35 This is a blending of three quotes by Rick Joyner. One is from "Revolution" in *The Morning Star Prophetic Bulletin*, May, 2000, as cited in *Kreider, op. cit.*, page 88. The second is from *Joel News International*; you may access it by sending this exact message (including hyphens) to lyris@xc.org: get joel-news-international joyner-megatrends-1. Leave the subject line blank. The third is from http://his-people.soc.ru.ac.za/messages/sermons/gar eth/old/nt_wineskin.htm.

36. Frank A. Viola, *Who Is Your Covering?* (Brandon, Florida: Present Testimony Ministry), 1998, p. 28.

37. Gene Edwards in James H. Rutz, *The Open Church* (Portal, Georgia: Open Church Ministries), 1992, p. 51. Emphasis in original.

38. Adapted with permission from Gary Smalley and John Trent, *The Blessing* (Pocket Books), 1990.

5

The New Meetings

Nineteen Things We Do
in Open, Body Life Gatherings

Then what is the right course, brothers?
Whenever you [the whole church] meet,
every one of you has something to contribute:
a song, a piece of teaching, some special information
God has given him, a message in an unknown language,
or an explanation of what it means.
I Corinthians 14:26, with a phrase from 14:23 in brackets

The "veil" in the temple at Jerusalem was perhaps six inches (15 cm) thick, a bit like a meeting room divider in a modern hotel. When the Lord Jesus died, God tore it from top to bottom to signal the end of the separation of the common people from His presence in the Holy of Holies, where only the high priest could go. (Matthew 27:51)

*I could be quite wrong, but to my knowledge
there were no further supernatural signs to signal
any basic change in the status of believers after
that—until October 20, 1996. On that day, God
—or some angel with a deadly karate chop—split
an equally hefty "veil" in two, signaling the end
of the separation of common Christians from the
power center of traditional ministry, where only
a pastor normally could stand: the church pulpit.*

In any decent church service, you can count on the Lord Jesus
Christ being there—at least as a quiet observer. Wherever the Bible
and worship are part of the program, God is pleased, and His Spirit
may do great things.

But on occasion, when He is allowed to completely take over the
running of a meeting, His presence can be so heavy and wonderful that
you feel like you're swimming under a hundred feet of living water.

The folks at Christian Tabernacle, a 3,000-member charismatic
church on the east side of Houston, found out what that's like on
October 20, 1996.

Even before the start of the 8:30 a.m. early service, the presence of
God was overwhelming. The air was so thick they could hardly
breathe. Some of the people didn't even make it to the sanctuary; they
collapsed to the floor just inside the doors. The ushers were hard
pressed to keep the doorways clear by dragging away bodies and prop-
ping them up against hallway walls.

Yet this was no "mass hysteria" phenomenon. Without knowing
why, some began weeping uncontrollably the moment they drove onto
the church property, and they barely managed to walk across the
parking lot.

On the platform, the music team got so choked up they couldn't
keep playing their warm-up music. The worship leader was slumped
over the keyboard, crying.

Throughout the tastefully done auditorium, the silence was broken
only by quiet sobs and prayers. Even the children weren't making noise.

No one had to announce what was happening. Every soul in the
place was face to face with the Eternal Presence met by Moses in the
burning bush.

Time for Humans to Take Over?

Clearly, God was in full charge of the meeting—and liking it.
But frail humanity is often boggled and befuddled by a sudden

encounter with Ultimate Reality. Sitting impatiently in the front row was the church's pastor, Richard Heard, a very godly and modest man, and next to him was my friend Tommy Tenney, the soft-spoken evangelist who had been his guest speaker for the previous two Sundays.[1]

After about fifteen minutes of this massive but nondirectional encounter with God, the host (being a pastor, trained to take charge) leaned over and whispered to Tenney, "Come on, Tommy, isn't it time for you to step up and take the meeting?"

With tears streaming down his face, Tenney replied, "I'm about half afraid to go up there because I think something big is about to happen." And he didn't budge. (Not the sort of cooperation you expect from your visiting speaker!)

So after a moment, Heard stood, walked shakily across the soft-padded red carpet, mounted the 28-inch platform, grasped the pulpit with trembling hands, and read from II Chronicles 7:14:

> ". . . if My people who are called by My name will humble themselves, pray, seek my face, and turn from their wicked ways, then I will hear from heaven, and will forgive their sin and heal their land."

Heard commented, "What the Holy Spirit is saying to us is that we should seek God's face, not His hand. We should not be seeking just His benefits, but seeking to know *Him*."

At that instant, a loud thunderclap of noise hit the sanctuary. Heard was picked up and thrown backwards. The heavy cast acrylic pulpit was split into two pieces, then flung toward the congregation in two directions, landing about six or seven feet apart, as you see in the photo.

See photos in photo section.

When God Moves, He Moves Quickly

The action was explosive in its suddenness. Most of the 14 witnesses I interviewed at some length afterward exclaimed, in virtually identical words: *It all happened so fast!*

Heard was unhurt, but flat on his back eight or nine feet away and thoroughly "slain in the Spirit," as the Pentecostals say. Only a twitching of the little finger on his right hand for the next 2½ hours showed he was still alive. (It took four men to carry off his limp form, and, reaching his office, they too collapsed under the weight of God's glory.)

The half-inch-thick, cast acrylic pulpit fared not so well. It lay in two pieces, with a jagged, lightning-bolt edge running down at about a

60° angle from top to bottom (see photo in photo section). The base and top were unscathed, but the stem middle was severed.[2]

The congregation was instantly hit by the tangible terror of God, as if a bomb had exploded. For a moment, they were awestruck, with jaws dropped and eyes popping. Then they began weeping and wailing. Many went to the front and fell on their faces. Some avoided the aisle traffic by climbing over the pews.

Many people approached Tenney and insisted they be baptized on the spot. So he and the church staff baptized people for hours, and the meeting continued in fits and starts till one A.M.

Over the following weeks, there were a number of healings, deliverances, and an array of other charismatic-type occurrences. For example, seven cases of cancer were cured. And on one Sunday morning, three people were healed of profound deafness while being prayed for by a 7-year-old boy who had just been healed of deafness himself the week before!

Seven nights a week, for the next four weeks, hundreds of people stood in line to repent and receive Christ. Tenney freely admits that, professionally speaking, his preaching was kind of pathetic. Yet after he would stumble awkwardly with a message for 15 to 20 minutes, the Presence would come, and people would stream forward, fall on their faces, and cry out to God.

In the end there was, of course, great celebration. Even on the morning of the split pulpit, repentance was followed by sights like businessmen pulling off their ties and dancing like ballerinas! Godly sorrow always leads to joy.[3]

Why Tenney Didn't Budge

"I wasn't afraid that God was going to strike me down, or that something bad was going to happen. I just didn't want to interfere and grieve the precious presence that was filling up that room!

For too long we humans have only allowed the Holy Spirit to take control *up to a certain point*. Basically, whenever it gets outside of our comfort zone or just a little beyond our control, we pull in the reins (the Bible calls it 'quenching the Spirit' in First Thessalonians 5:19). We stop at the tabernacle veil too many times."

—Tommy Tenney in *The God Chasers*, page 6

Christian Apartheid
and a God-Like Bear

The modern pulpit is the most obvious visible symbol of the separation of the "laity" from the place of ministry. If you're a "layman"[4] in a typical church, you may never be allowed to stand behind it and give your friends a message from your heart—or the Lord's heart—not even ten words. Not once in your lifetime, no matter how urgent.

Stay with me because here's where it gets tricky: *By striking and destroying this symbol of spiritual apartheid, God gave us a peek inside His heart.* Tommy tells me it was "a slap in the face for overly tight human control of the church."

Yes. But at the same time, God didn't intend a blanket condemnation of Christian Tabernacle. If so, He would have struck the pulpit and pastor without moving them. Instead, He *separated* the two, flinging them in opposite directions. He also rendered the pastor temporarily silent and the pulpit forever unusable.

Nor was this event a mere display of general anger. If God were to single out a church that makes Him angry, there are millions of churches that deserve His displeasure more. Indeed, He chose Christian Tabernacle because they are *unusually receptive* to His voice. Ever since this sign was given, their staff has spent far more time waiting on God and almost totally abandoned rigid plans for services. (I was dismayed, however, to learn that they quickly brought in a replacement pulpit.)

So then, what motivated God to make this unique sign? Simply this: *The meeting was 100% in His hands, the people were deeply in touch with His heart, and suddenly it was all taken away from Him.*

A few quiet evenings ago, I was writing at my desk in my home at the edge of a forest when I heard a *thump* outside. Walking out onto the balcony, I discovered that I had left the trash can outside, and a bear had helped himself to the contents. Clenching a plastic bagful of garbage in his teeth, Mr. Bear was happily ambling off into the bushes.

I yelled, "Enjoy, you big, hairy pig!" But I didn't run down to retrieve my trash. I would not have gotten my trash back. I might not even have gotten my *hand* back. He was a nice bear and didn't crawl in my window to loot and pillage, but at that point he viewed the trash as *de facto* 100% his.

God is a bit like Mr. Bear. He's willing to respect our turf, to let us have our pre-programmed, human-led, pulpit-centered meetings. He even graciously adds great blessings to them if our hearts are in the right place. But when a meeting is totally under His control and wonderful things are happening, He gets royally riled if someone takes charge and jerks people's attention away from Him.

That doesn't mean He wants silence. As you'll see in this chapter, He wants us to learn dozens of ways of speaking in meetings. But <u>He</u> wants to be the Master of Ceremonies.

Same Lesson, Different Country

The aforementioned David Hogan once had an experience similar to Richard Heard's.

At 8:15 A.M. on October 27, 1995, Hogan arrived at a 450-person conference in progress near his mission area 75 miles southwest of Tampico, Mexico. The scene was like the split pulpit aftermath, with many people crying and apologizing to each other for past offenses, while others were being healed of blindness, cancer, lupus, epilepsy, demonic possession, etc.—without anyone even touching them.[5]

It was a bit much, even for Hogan. Walking in and stopping ten or twelve feet from a table up front, he looked around and said, "God, what are you—"

That was all. He woke up hours later *under* the table, and his legs wouldn't work for a while. God wasn't entertaining questions.

Same Lesson, 90 Years Earlier

The modern Pentecostal movement dates from the explosive Azusa Street Revival in Los Angeles, starting in 1905. Frank Bartleman chronicled their heavy struggle to keep the meetings open in the early days:

> Those were Holy Spirit meetings, led of the Lord ... . When we first reached the meeting, we avoided human contact and greeting as much as possible. We wanted to meet God first ... .
>
> No subjects or sermons were announced ahead of time, and no special speakers ... No one knew what might be coming, what God would do ... . We all wanted to hear from God, through whomever He might speak ... .
>
> The meetings started themselves, spontaneously, in testimony, praise, and worship ... . We did not have to get our cue from some leader; yet we were free from lawlessness ... . Someone would finally get up, anointed for the message. All seemed to recognize this and gave way. It might be a child, a woman, or a man ... . No one wished to show himself. We thought only of obeying God. In fact,

there was an atmosphere of God there that forbade anyone but a fool from attempting to put himself forward without the real anointing—and such did not last long ... . The Spirit ran the meeting from start to finish. There was no program, and hardly a chance for even necessary announcements ... . [There was] neither pulpit, nor organ, nor choir ... .

God came so wonderfully near us that the very atmosphere of heaven seemed to surround us. Such a divine "weight of glory" was upon us that we could only fall on our faces ... .

We had the greatest trouble with strange preachers who wanted to preach. Of all people, they seemed to have the least sense and did not know enough to keep still before Him. They liked to hear themselves ... . But many a preacher died to self in these meetings ... . The breath would be taken from them. Their minds would wander, their brains would reel. Things would turn black before their eyes. They could not go on. I never saw one get by with it in those days. They were up against God ... He wound them up in short order. They were carried out dead, spiritually speaking. They generally bit the dust in humility ...[6]

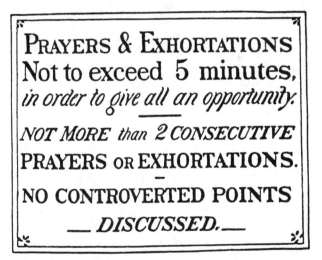

PRAYERS & EXHORTATIONS
Not to exceed 5 minutes,
in order to give all an opportunity.

NOT MORE than 2 CONSECUTIVE
PRAYERS OR EXHORTATIONS.

NO CONTROVERTED POINTS
DISCUSSED.

One Way of Maintaining Order: *In 1857 a great, laity-driven revival broke out in New York City. Spontaneous participation in the large meetings fueled the fires, but apparently the people didn't quite have the hang of it. So this sign was posted in the Fulton Street Church.[7]*

Bartleman then explains the decline and fall of the revival:

But at this time old Azusa Mission became more and more in bondage. The meetings had to run in appointed order. The Spirit tried to work through some poor, illiterate Mexicans, who had been saved and baptized in the Spirit, but the leader deliberately refused to let them testify, crushing them ruthlessly. It was like murdering the Spirit of God. Only God knows what this meant to those poor Mexicans. Personally, I would rather die than to have assumed such a spirit of dictatorship. Every meeting was now programmed from start to finish. Disaster was bound to follow, and it did so.[8]

What Difference Will the Split Pulpit Make in Your Future?

1. *Freedom*. Jesus wants His church back. He is pleased to be our guest of honor, but really wants to be our emcee. And when He is free to do His thing, He will set you free to do *your* thing. In fact, He will push you into doing stuff you never thought possible.

Across the U.S., programmed, non-interruptible meetings will begin to wane in popularity. Participation will everywhere be at the heart of the new Christian lifestyle of responsible freedom. You will learn to step into His unveiled presence, spread your wings, and fly.[9]

2. *Growth*. God has signaled the end of the lazy game in which laymen treat pastors as the entertainers and "pack mules" of the church, dumping on them heavy burdens that no person should have to bear alone.

From now on, we're *all* ministers, and we *all* must take orders from the Lord who lives in our hearts. That means learning to use our gifts, learning to work together in love, and taking steps of faith as a daily habit. You'll soon take on roles that were impossible till now. In five years, you may barely recognize who you are today!

3. *Versatility*. Under the traditional, two-tiered system of Christianity, the pastor was a jack-of-all-trades, which left the layman as a one-trick pony with a job description of *Pray, Pay, and Obey*. If you could hold down a pew cushion for 90 minutes and move your mouth a little during songtime, you were a passable, commercial-grade Christian. If you were deeply enmeshed in the system, it often hurt your life more than it helped. Many of those dropping out today state that they are leaving to *preserve* their faith, not because they've lost their faith.

The old Christianity will not die out. Most humans are not fond of change, and so the system will limp along, with scattered improvements, till Christ returns. Those of us in open fellowships wish them well, and in fact will eagerly continue to work and pray with them at every chance. But make no mistake. When God split that pulpit, He intended it to mark the blooming of an era that finally establishes the "kingdom of priests" He has longed for since the Exodus. (Ex. 19:6)

You're looking at a serious shift in paradigms here. If you opt to shrug off the split pulpit as some kind of oddity, remember whose sign you're shrugging at. And if you have any lingering doubts about how real all this is, you can do as I did: Catch a plane to Houston, take I-10 east to Normandy, go north to Wallisville Road, then left ¼ mile to Christian Tabernacle. Walk in and run your hand along the torn razor-edge of that pulpit.

Bring along a Band-Aid.

What Does the Bible Say About This?

As a Christian, you're free to hold any kind of special meeting you see fit. It's wide open. Wherever two or three are gathered, Jesus is there.

But the Bible nowhere authorizes you to systematically freeze every future gathering of your church into a programmed agenda dominated by privileged individuals speaking non-stop to a passive audience of disenfranchised listeners.

The same conclusion has been reached by a 2002 study at Fuller Seminary on the topic of open, interactive meetings: "There simply is no other model for Christian church meetings found in the Bible. Strictly speaking, there is no Biblical justification, not even one passage, for conducting typical closed, non-interactive church meetings."[10]

Just the opposite: As you saw in the verse at the start of this chapter, empowered saints are expected to participate *whenever* the body of Christ comes together, be it a small group or large. I've seen participation work beautifully in groups as big as 20,000.[11]

Moreover, God himself is expected to barge in and interrupt the meeting by giving messages for people to relay to the group, as Paul mandates in I Corinthians 14:30-31:

> If someone sitting in the meeting receives a message or idea from the Lord, the one who is speaking should stop. For in this way, you can *all* have an opportunity to give a message, one after the other, so that *everyone* will

learn something and *everyone* will be stimulated and encouraged.

Stained-glass Christianity rests on a wobbly foundation that consigns these verses to the historical dustbin or the "millennial bucket" (a handy repository for verses that could only work in a future Millennium paradise). Not so. Open meetings are quite practical. Done well, in fact, they're lots more exciting, educational, life-changing, and just plain fun than old-fashioned services. Most important, the open pattern sets both you and Christ's Spirit free to act in great power.

If your gatherings are truly open, only one problem can hold you back from experiencing a stunning variety of "God things." That problem is ...

People Stick to What They Know —And They Don't Know Much

The typical Christian in the U.S. today hugs his comfort zone like a war orphan clutching her doll—and that zone is about the size of a hamster cage. Why? Because the Christian has almost no experience in taking action in a meeting.

That's where you come in. As a true scholar who has read this book, you are my choice to lead him out of the wilderness and into the promised land.

Seriously, your biggest challenge is simply to broaden his horizons. The most common mistake of someone in your position is *failing to help people experience the full range of constructive activities*. The 19 most important ones are listed for you in this chapter, but there are *thousands* of things you can do that will:

1. Invite a strong presence of God
2. Lift everyone's spirits
3. Enable them to overcome sin in their lives
4. Help them to face and solve their problems
5. Teach them the whole counsel of God
6. Empower them to do things they've never done
7. Build them into a true team.

Meetings will be the focal point of your team life, but it's rare to find a list of what you should do in them ... and rarer still to find help on *how* to do each mode of activity. That's why I think the following tips—which took me 40 years to collect—comprise the most important chapter in this book.

You must have a *feel* for each mode, so read with your heart, not just your eyes. Let this advice sink deep into your soul, and you'll be able to launch not just one ring (or team or "church" or fellowship), but a whole network of ever-growing teams.

What Does an Open Meeting Look Like?

Shakespeare has a scene where a mob of ignorant revolutionaries is plotting a comically naive utopia. One of them, Dick the Butcher, suggests as a start, "The first thing we do, let's kill all the lawyers."[12]

In that same spirit, I would suggest: *The first thing we do, let's kill all the sermons.* Right off the bat we save the better part of an hour, thus allowing everybody to sleep in and arrive at church in a nicer mood.

That sure beats having people sleeping in mid-service.[13] Moreover, it frees up time to do the exciting, Biblically legitimate things that honor God and produce changed lives. The remainder of the chapter reveals 19 of these activity modes, along with their pluses and pitfalls.

1: Encourage! Challenge! Admonish! Uplift!

The Roman believers who received Paul's letter didn't have Bibles, and they were mostly illiterates anyway. (The population of Rome was two-thirds slaves.)[14] Yet he strongly states to them in 15:14, "I am quite certain, my brothers, that you are full of goodness, complete in knowledge, and *competent to instruct one another.*"

Wow. This radically fresh idea is a foundation of the new Christianity. It means that ordinary, run-of-the-church Christians are now qualified to instruct (admonish, teach, counsel) *each other* rather than relying on a more gifted person to do it for them.

In medieval times, the church said that only priests could instruct.[15] Then in 1517 the Protestant Reformation brought back the doctrine of "the priesthood of the believer," which gave permission for ordinary believers to do anything a priest could. In theory.

However, Martin Luther soon became disillusioned and gave up trying to implement this doctrine, simply because he could not find the capable, responsible believers to flesh it out. He reverted to a more traditional model, where clergy are laden with most of the burden of ministry, while laymen sit and watch as an audience.

But now, thanks to the rise of small groups, cell churches, house churches, underground churches, and other open fellowships, we have a whole new type of disciple: millions of men and women reared in responsible freedom and empowered to teach their neighbors and friends.

This means you can expect each player on your team to exercise his or her right and privilege to exhort, stimulate, needle, and encourage all the others. *The Holy Spirit will use this mode of action as a prime power channel to prod your team forward.*

A LITTLE SECRET: The number one cause of collapse of participatory groups is the members' failure to bring something to contribute and lift up the saints.

If you're a long-term survivor of the traditional, pastorized church, you've heard Hebrews 10:25 quoted perpetually to promote attendance:

> Let us not forsake the assembling of ourselves together, as
> the manner of some is, but let us encourage one another ...

Notice that the opposite of *forsake* is not *attend*, but *encourage one another*. That's a megashift! To the writer of Hebrews, it was the essence of what happened in church.

And where do you get the raw materials for an encouragement, challenge, or admonition? Just keep your eyes open, and you'll find them in your own life—also in news magazines, the Christian media, and most often, the pages of Scripture. Train yourself and your teammates to ask yourselves *daily*, "What can I bring to the family this week?" Ultra important.[16]

Exhorting and challenging will be the bread and butter of your meetings. "When it comes to revival, we are often waiting for God to show up and do the miraculous; however, God is waiting for us to show up and do the obvious."[17]

2: Testify

In most religions, a priest is someone who has special access to his god and represents that god to other people. But in Christianity, if you became a true, born-again Christian yesterday, then you are a priest or priestess today:

> But you are a chosen people, a royal priesthood, a holy
> nation, a people belonging to God, that you may declare
> the praises of Him who called you out of darkness into His
> wonderful light.[18]

Note God's main purpose for making you a priest: to represent Him to others by talking about how great He is and what He's done. (Keep in mind that when a *human* demands lavish praise, he has a sick mind, but when God does the same, it's 100% appropriate—and a blessing. In fact, He is opening the door of heaven for you; when you praise Him, you join the angels.)

Now, testifying to the work of God in our lives isn't hard. Most of us like to talk about ourselves, and the warm, friendly atmosphere of an open fellowship meeting is the ideal place to learn this easy avenue of ministry.

But there is a problem: Gratitude is the thinnest of all human emotions. We quickly forget or discount what Yahweh-Jireh ("the Lord our provider") has done for us. SOLUTION: *Get your team to count their blessings daily,* and they'll soon have a new mindset—and a growing pile of praise reports. Such reports can turn your meetings into all-night parties!

3: Confess

> Confess your sins to one another and pray for one another so that you may be healed. (James 5:16)

> Bear with each other and forgive whatever grievances you may have against one another. Forgive as the Lord forgave you. (Colossians 3:13)

Now I come to the least appealing part of your meeting: fessing up to all those dirty deeds you've done.

In the early days of John Wesley's "class meetings" in England, the first item on the agenda (after an opening song or prayer) was for each of the 12 or more people to confess his previous week's sins. Not exactly an upbeat way to start! But at least they got the hard part out of the way first and enjoyed the benefits of COMMUNAL RIGHTEOUSNESS for the rest of the meeting.

Large, anonymous meetings have no mechanism for producing communal righteousness. You can't sanctify an audience. You can't even know the spiritual condition of the person who comes in and sits next to you. But in both the Old and New Testaments, there were times when 100% communal righteousness was an absolute must. See the stories of the sin of Achan in Joshua 7 and Ananias and Sapphira in Acts 5 for a couple of horrifying lessons in the importance of group purity to Yahweh Sabaoth, the LORD of Hosts.

Among Protestants, it's common to feel sympathy or disdain toward Catholics attending the confessional. It seems so artificial and so at odds with the verse from Colossians quoted above. Frankly, however, I must point out that when we dumped the confessional booth, we dumped *all* public confession along with it. And unconfessed sin can fester.

Private confession between you and God is basic and good. But it brings no immediately visible *assurance* of forgiveness, and it sometimes leads to a false public image of personal holiness. If people don't know where you've failed, they can't help you in that area. Moreover,

What's Your Job as a Leader in Team Christianity?

Job One is to know the purpose of a church.

Now, I hope people will turn to Christ and be saved in your meetings. Lots of them! But that's not their overall purpose.

I hope your people learn the Bible in depth. But that's not your main goal, either.

I hope you'll have great times of worship. But even that is not the primary objective.

You'll find the number one aim of your meetings stated most succinctly in I Corinthians 14:26. After Paul lists a few of the activities that happen when you have total participation, he summarizes: "Let all things be done for edification."

So what's that? The King James Version (1611) said, "Let all things be done unto *edifying*," and by "clang" association over the years, the word blended into *satisfying*. But they aren't the same. To *edify* means to *build up*, as in constructing an edifice.

Keeping edification as your purpose is a great safeguard. It will keep your team from being warped into:

- A committee to get a Christian elected mayor
- A working platform to promote home schooling, prolife causes, teen virginity, frontier missions, etc.
- A spearhead effort to get the U.S. church up to speed on prophecy, the Hebraic movement, spiritual warfare, etc.
- A hand-holding club to endlessly psychoanalyze childhood traumas, marriage messes, multiple layers of unhealed memories, etc.
- An enlightened forum to iron out the ragged edges of classical theology, such as predestination, the timing of Christ's return, or modes of baptism.

I'm not trying to make fun of these important causes and issues. I'm simply pointing out that you need to stay alert to the very real danger of drifting away from Christ-centered meetings.

a strictly private confession has no price tag and thus feels insignificant. *Hey, God, I'm sorry!* bounces off the walls of an empty room and costs you nothing in tears or repentance. The guilt is gone, yet the guilt *feelings* may remain. But telling a roomful of friends that you just gambled away Junior's college fund—now, that's painful! The good part is, it allows a public confirmation of God's forgiveness and starts the healing process. That's why James 5:16 says that healing waits upon confession.

ONE QUALIFIER: A major confession will often trigger a chain of confessions from others. And that's good. The motivation is usually pure.

The revivals at Christian college campuses in the mid-'90s sprang from chapel confessions that in some places went on for 48 hours.[19] Students with spotless reputations would even dart out to their rooms, gather up their drug and porn stuff, bring it back, and drop it at the altar or burn it. Obviously, you don't want to interfere with such a genuine move of God—even if it does last for days.

But be aware: Copycatting often starts within an hour or so. Just to get on the bandwagon, someone with no biggies to confess (or nothing he *wants* to confess) will admit, with sad demeanor, that six months ago he failed to cover his mouth when he yawned—in the bathtub. That's the time to call it a day.

4: Be Reconciled

The church must show the world the true path to peace. The planet's power elite will never find it on their own.

How do open church people find peace? Through reconciliation to the triune God of peace and to each other.

Here's how it works: When you have team members on the outs with each other, the Holy Spirit usually handles it himself. You seldom need to play referee. Chances are that the next time the subject of forgiveness and reconciliation comes up, the Spirit will speak to one or both of the parties without anyone's prompting. (Actually, any subject will do if it touches even remotely on the trouble issue.)

Typically, what happens is that the one who feels most convicted about the rift will apologize before the group. Often, this takes the form of kneeling before the other—on one knee or two—and asking for forgiveness. As you can imagine, this is an encouraging and emotional event for the whole fellowship.

In fact, reconciliation is now happening on a large scale between historic factions in the church. At reconciliation gatherings across the U.S., repentance and confession of past wrongs has occurred between whites and blacks, anglos and native Americans, men and women, etc. These events are major building blocks in the coming U.S. revival.

5: Teach

> Let the word of Christ dwell in you richly, in all wisdom, as you teach and train one another. (Colossians 3:16)

> ... put that teaching into the charge of men you can trust, such as shall be competent to teach others. (II Timothy 2:2)

Your open meetings are an exciting opportunity to create something that has rarely been seen in the history of traditional churches:

a full-participation team where every member is capable of giving a clear, impassioned presentation of important truths.

Interactive teaching is needed, sermons aren't. Sermons are a difficult art form that demand long preparation. In a traditional church, who would want to see an untrained beginner try to preach the sermon? The pastor is probably the only one they'd want to listen to for long—if at all.

Traditional meetings produce listeners, not speakers. An open fellowship has one tremendous advantage in developing strong leaders and speakers: You can offer floor time. You don't produce spiritual giants by having them sit in silence. You produce giants (or at least good speakers) by saying something like, "Speak up, dude! How can we solve this problem? What does the Bible say we should do?"

TRUE STORY

How the Holy Spirit Brings Instant Reconciliation in Open Meetings

Lightning bolts flashed from Ramona Bevel's eyes as she sat down in the back row and folded her arms that Friday night in North Carolina.

Seething with defiant anger, she could hardly wait till the seminar on open-style church participation was over. Across the room, her husband Charles imagined he saw little wisps of smoke coming out of her ears. He had dragged her to the weekend-long seminar, and she wasn't having any of it. Ten years of marriage had bred a deep-seated resentment toward Charles, and the stresses of having three children only made it worse.

As she sat with pursed lips, she plotted the dramatic *coup de grâce* to their marriage: At the end of the weekend, she would announce to him the fact that she had filed for divorce yesterday.

Meanwhile, the other couples in the room were happily answering the theme question: "What did you bring to share with us tonight?" They enjoyed a wide array of songs, prayers, blessings, and new truths learned.

On Saturday morning, the theme question was, "How is your walk with God?" Several eagerly shared both struggles and exciting breakthroughs. Phil led a familiar song that described his walk with the Lord, and others joined in. Jed reported that his walk was such a blessing that he wanted to speak a blessing over his wife, Julie.

Jed turned to her, took her hands in his, and looked her in the eye. "Julie," he began, "I am so proud you are my wife. You were fashioned for me long before we met 25 years ago. You bring me joy in every way. And what a good mother you are! Even our granddaughter lights up when she sees you. I want to recommit myself to you as your

164

This kind of challenge has an especially strong impact on men. (And the creation of a new breed of powerful, secure, competent men is also bringing sighs of relief from the women.)

In many open meetings, teaching (or counseling, warning, advising) will be the main activity. Over time, the variety and depth of that teaching will rise dramatically.

Of course, you won't get instant expertise. In team Christianity, *small is beautiful*. Don't ask members to give full-length talks. Encourage, coax, and prod them to start with five- to ten-minute bits. Or even one to three minutes. We all have to start somewhere!

How can a member know if a topic is good to go? Basically, if it gets him or her excited, it will get everyone else excited.

husband and say that I will always be there for you. I love you so much!"

As they embraced each other, tears could be seen in some eyes—but not Ramona's. In fact, she looked as though her inner turmoil would explode at any moment.

At that point there was movement from the opposite side of the room. It was Charles, slowly making his way across to his wife. He pulled up a chair in front of her, sat down, put both of his hands on Ramona's shoulders, and said, "Darling, what a fool I've been. Instead of blessing and affirming you, I've cursed you with my silence and ingratitude. I was wrong to take you for granted and to demand things of you that I withheld. I've sinned against you by openly withholding my love and affection. I *do* love you and the kids, although I haven't been there for you much of the time. My commitment to you today, Ramona, is to change all that and put you first in my life—for the rest of my life. I love you very much!"

A stunned Ramona responded, "Charles, why didn't you *tell* me that you loved and appreciated me? All these years, I thought you didn't care and didn't need me. All these years, I've been longing to be the kind of wife you need." She searched his eyes and added, "Maybe ... maybe we *can* start over this morning."

Start over they did! Charles's confession and commitment opened up their communication again and brought restoration with healing.

On Sunday afternoon, the others in the seminar threw Ramona and Charles a surprise reunion party, complete with a wedding cake and a bouquet of flowers for Ramona.

One weekend, two transformed lives. God works fast when you let Him.

An unusual incident? No, things like this happen daily when you open your meetings and allow the Holy Spirit to take charge of the order of events. The God of Surprises does things that simply can't happen in planned or program-driven meetings. In team Christianity, life-changing meetings are the rule, not the exception.

What kind of formats can they use? The variety is endless. For example, they can:

• Teach a skill, such as how to have a quiet time or how to lead someone to Christ

• Tell a story—from life, from history, from the Bible, a fictional/allegorical tale from their own imagination, etc.

• Drill the team in the memorization of a few verses of Scripture

• Give a dialogue sermonette, a ten-minute, interactive talk built on a deductive (topical) Bible study

• Discuss and denounce a trend or event in society that Christians should be confronting or praying against

• Read a Bible passage and comment on it

• Read a key passage from a book—or give a full-on book report

• Bring a news report with an explanation of its meaning to the kingdom

• Announce important news from a mission work

• And the never-failing favorite: Tell something they've learned about God or His dealings with us.

Teaching sparks teaching. As Sam Silent and Barb Bashful watch ordinary believers come alive and teach with enthusiasm week after week, the Spirit of God will ignite their souls to begin sharing little bits here and there. Be sure to give them a verbal pat on the back.

HERESY WATCH: What if someone drifts into a topic that is controversial or even borderline erroneous? It depends. Some subjects are so controversial, they're like lighting a fuse to dynamite; schism could follow quickly. And in rare instances, some errors are so far off from truth or so destructive that you have to stop them in progress. Your call.[20] There's a fine line between a brave discourse on a tough topic and a fatal foray into a theological swamp. The general principle here is that you don't alienate them or boot them out, you simply tell them not to teach what they're teaching.[21] Happily, heresies have been a rare problem among the new saints.

6: Pray

By and large, traditional prayer meetings used to be pretty awful. Today, many are still awful, but many are much improved. Even old-line prayer meetings now tend to have better balance:

• More praise and thanksgiving instead of nonstop petitions
• More sincerity and fewer clichés (or at least newer clichés)
• Above all, more focused, effectual prayers.

The new outpouring of group prayer since the '80s has been honored by God with vast advances of the kingdom around the globe.

166

How long should your meetings run?

Across America and around the world, interactive gatherings of Christians typically average 2½ hours—plus time for optional food, breaks, and socializing.

Don't people get bored or tired? Not often. But if the meeting does drag for some reason, there's a quick solution: Fix it or end it!

As a rule, open meetings centered around Jesus Christ are so exciting and fast-moving that nobody wants to go home. Veteran church-goers who would normally start to look at their watches at the 60-minute point get so turned on they just won't quit—and some meetings *do* go on all day or all night. (We joke a lot about needing tire irons to pry people's fingers off the furniture and cattle prods to get them out the door.)

Often, time disappears as people get caught up in the drama of lives being transformed before their eyes. If there is a persistent problem, it is not boredom, but the challenge of getting a word in edgewise.

But we have miles to go before we reach a semblance of ideal praying. So here are five steps you can take to make your meeting's prayer time more realistic, lively, and powerful:

A. Dump the orations. Do conversation.

Old-style prayer is starting to fade because so few really *like* it. It's unnatural and foreign to the way humans converse. It's Greek oratory, not Christian conversation. It's a series of mini-speeches, not a woven dialogue. It's based on stand-alone individual efforts, each of them impervious to the contributions of others. It's performance-oriented, giving you a warm feeling of success if you get louder *Amens* than anyone else. Plus, it's terminally boring. (Just ask your teenager.)

Worst of all, it's highly intimidating to those who've never prayed in public before. That's the killer. When you have unsaved seekers in your midst, oratorical prayer is a tall cactus fence around heaven.

In contrast, conversational prayer is so natural that everyone tends to get swept in without a struggle. Probably hundreds of thousands of Americans have been saved this easy, painless way. There's nothing to learn, no holy lingo to master, and no need to think up an impressive, two-minute speechette before you open your mouth.

SPIRIT-LED PRAYER IS TOPICAL. Anyone who so desires can lob in a few words on a subject, then the conversation moves on. Just like home, where conversation ricochets around the dinner table like a billiard ball. (But try to imagine a family with one person talking on six topics, followed by the next person covering the same six topics, and so on. That's traditional prayer.)

167

In conversation, we all can build on the prayer of the previous person. Mary's hesitant request draws out Harry's solid request, which encourages Scotty's bold request. That's faith building—in seconds, not years.

Team prayer builds up the team and centers attention on the Lord. Performance prayer builds up the individual and centers attention on him or her.

LAST RESORT: If your team has too many hidebound traditionalists and not enough new saints, it may keep sliding back into oratorical prayer. If so, try this: a ten-minute experiment in *one-sentence prayers*. If someone objects that he or she can't even cover one subject in a single sentence, smile and reply, "Bingo! For these ten minutes, you're going to depend on the others to finish your thoughts *for* you!" Backup support becomes mandatory. It's a radical cure for that oratorical Greek hangover, but it's great fun, and I guarantee it works. They'll go a lot longer than ten minutes!

For deeper study, I recommend you get a few copies of the little million-seller classic, *Prayer: Conversing with God* by the late Rosalind Rinker. They will change your ring forever.

B. Bring the Holy Spirit into the action.

Jesus said, "My sheep hear my voice." (John 10:27) Base your prayers on this fact.

Learn to wait on the Spirit and listen to what He wants. Sometimes that requires a time of silence *before* you pray, but usually He steers *while* you pray. You start out praying for one thing and quickly find yourselves shifting to a different strategy or even a whole different request. It may feel natural, but it's totally supernatural.

Once you let God direct your hearts to the right prayer request, the actual asking may be a stroll in the park. Yes, really *big* requests may sometimes take hours of persistent, fervent prayer, but it's a lot worse if you're asking for the wrong thing.

A rhetorically challenged family friend once dismissed a certain effort as "barking up a dead horse." In that same vein, I implore you: Don't waste your prayer time flogging the wrong tree. Listen to the Spirit!

C. Remember the big picture.

Most of your group's prayers will be about themselves, plus friends and family.

That's good. In fact, you should limit the quantity of daisy-chain, third-hand prayers. It's enervating to have a lot of prayer requests for total strangers, like Sally's neighbor's friend's uncle's boss's wife's cat.

Never forget that your circle is part of a larger task, the transformation of your neighborhood, your city, your nation, and the world. We're all connected in this. Devote some time to changing the high-level spiritual control of the people and institutions around you.

D. Be ye thankful.

Yes, the squeaky wheel gets the grease, as Jesus said in Luke 18:7. Yes, there is a time to be whiny as a four-year-old in a toy store. And yes, you have to ask, seek, and sometimes knock till your knuckles bleed.

But prayer is *not* an adversary proceeding! Your team needs to be persistent, but this is not a you-vs.-God war that you win by sheer volume and group gripe. Your heavenly Father is an *actual person*, and as such appreciates a little gratitude and warm love now and then. So when you talk to Him, try at least to remember to kick things off with some thanks and praise. If you don't, there's a danger of focusing 100% on what you *don't* have, and that can create an atmosphere of negativity and doubt.

E. Do follow-ons.

"Again, I tell you that if two of you on earth agree about anything you ask, it will be done for you by my heavenly Father." (Matthew 18:19)

One of the bummers of oratorical praying is that it hardly allows for agreement; each prayer is a steel-plated masterpiece unto itself, impervious to attempts to nail it together with other prayers.

Instead, teach your people to use the conversational interplay to reinforce, validate, support, and intensify one another. You know how it hurts when you pour your heart out with an anguished request, yet nobody cares enough to back you up, and they casually go on to the next request, leaving your soul twisting slowly in the wind. Don't *ever* let that happen in your circle.

7: Bless

Now I come to the most ignored mode of all: the spoken blessing. If you're looking for a life-changer with raw power, this is it!

Giving a blessing is *not* a clever, new innovation. Look at Genesis 1:27-28, and you'll see that the very first thing God did after He made Adam and Eve was to give them a blessing. Why? Was the creation flawed? No. It was because He wanted to add DIRECTION and STRENGTH to it.

Likewise, today *you can massively redirect and revitalize what exists!* You can enable people to:

- restore forgotten dreams
- revive love for a spouse
- bring conviction of sin and repentance (indirectly)
- unlock silent, long-dormant feelings

- set people free from demonic strongholds
- encourage and release people to launch a new ministry.[22]

Look at your hands. As shocking as it may sound, you can use those hands to alter people's IDENTITY (who they are) and change their DESTINY (what they will make of their lives).

In contrast, an absence of blessings can cause a person to become:

- performance-driven (workaholic)
- shallow in relationships
- sexually addicted or frigid
- chronically depressed or feeling empty
- morally adrift and ethically myopic
- confused about life and purpose.

Suppose you have a truly outstanding young man in your ring, but you see him waffling, wobbling, and floundering a lot. At your next meeting, you can stand him up, take his hands, look him in the eye, and say something like this:

> Tyler, you are one of God's favorite men. He loves to watch you in action when you minister to people, and He has marked you for a high mission in life. Nobody in this city has a greater heart for suffering people than you do. When you reach out to someone at the mission downtown, that person *knows* he has been touched by the Savior's love. Before most folks even wake up, you are out driving around to pick up donations from bakeries and stores for the soup kitchen.
>
> Because you seek the welfare of others more than yourself, God is able to entrust you with more responsibility than He can give to most of us. In the months ahead, Tyler, you are going to see your ministry to people jell and take on a clear direction and purpose that will inspire others and even draw them to your side as you minister together. You will know instinctively where to put your time and effort.
>
> You are already full of compassion, Tyler; **I now bless you with the perseverance, confidence, and wisdom to make your compassion produce the fruit of more and more changed lives.** May God add His blessing to this breakthrough in your life and make you into a giant cottonwood tree that men will run to for shade and rest and renewal of life.

Notice three things: First, you didn't echo his problems back at him or speak one word of negativity into his life. (E.g., *May the Lord help you with your stupidity problem.*) Although a blessing is not an exercise in positive thinking, you must avoid poisoning your own words.

Second, this had a tinge of prophetic authority to it. We're assuming you gave this blessing because you knew the truth of these things in your spirit. You can only give blessings like this* if you truly know someone or have a special spiritual gift for it. You can't base your blessings on your personal wish list!

Third, this was not a prayer. You invoked God's blessing at the end (which you should always do), but this was mainly *your* blessing from *your* hand. That's a long-lost but legitimate power and a prerogative of the saints. Compare Luke 10:5: "Whenever you enter a home, give it *your* blessing." Jesus didn't say to stand in the doorway and pray, "O LORD, please bless this house." Christ commands us to bless even those who curse us. All power flows from God alone, but He does entrust a portion of it to us.

(And if you think giving a powerful blessing is scary, look at verses 10-12, where Jesus delegates the power to give a devastating curse! Also see Genesis 49, Deuteronomy 33, and section 14 of this chapter.)

Look at the patriarchs, and you'll see how their blessings changed history. Look at the entire history of the Jews, and you'll see how their Friday evening family blessing ceremony (called the *benshen* service) has kept them together, made them strong leaders, and enabled fathers to pass on to their sons and daughters a strong identity and sense of purpose even in the face of deadly persecution.

We desperately *need* a blessing at crucial points in our lives: birth, weaning, starting school, conversion/baptism, puberty, graduation, leaving home, starting a career, getting married, making a big decision, facing trouble, taking a step of faith, illness, widening our ministry, etc. But anytime will do!

How to bless someone. Your blessings will have most or all of these seven parts:

A. Meaningful touch. Where culturally appropriate, you'll want to hold your friend's hands or—less often—rest your hands on his head or shoulders.[23]

B. Eye contact. Look your friend straight in the eye. Peter told the lame man, "Look at us!" as he prepared to bless him with healing. (Acts 3:4) Paul gazed "intently" at a lame man before healing him. (Acts 14:9)

---

* There are more general sorts of blessings, such as when Jesus blessed all the children. Even the shortest blessings are always welcome. But we need to learn how to give a *full* blessing as I outline here.

C. <u>Positive description</u>. This concerns IDENTITY. Always attach a *high value* to the one you're blessing. You may want to tell how he or she looks to you, to God, and to others. It's OK to be lavish in your praise, but avoid flattery and exaggeration.

D. <u>Symbolic picture</u>. Whenever you can, give a metaphor or visual illustration of your friend. A vivid image sticks in the mind long after the words have faded. See how Jacob used pictures in Genesis 49.

E. <u>Future sketch</u>. This concerns DESTINY. Unless you have a prophetic gift that enables you to see distinct events in the future, stick to the *basics* of how this person's life and ministry will unfold, given his character, motivation, opportunity, etc. *Avoid fortune-telling*; just listen to your *own* spirit. (I'm assuming that your spirit is in close touch with the Holy Spirit.)

F. <u>Invoking God</u>. Except for very brief blessings, it's always wise to call on the Lord to give your friend some specific blessing related to your blessing. This usually involves a sentence starting, "May God ..."

G. <u>Your commitment</u>. If you're blessing someone you'll have an ongoing relationship with in the future, you may want to state your active commitment to helping him, praying for him, or making your blessing bear fruit. If you're not sure about the future relationship, skip this part.

WARNING: Don't rush to give an ornate blessing if you lack anything clear to say—even if it's a big occasion for your friend. Speak what you know, or you may be guilty of misleading.

8: Sing

The devil hates good music. It brings believers in tune with God and one another.

The Presence of the Living God

Always try to make sure the LORD shows up for your meetings! If He doesn't, something is amiss.

Yes, the idea of having a church gathering without God sounds kind of absurd, but trust me—people do it all the time! It's amazing how we get caught up in talking *about* God or doing things *for* God ... without having the actual *presence* of God.

A group of Chinese pastors visited some noted U.S. churches a while back. At the end of their tour, they were asked about their biggest impression. "What really amazes us," they said soberly, "is how much you Americans can accomplish without God."

Ouch.

That's why we're told to "... speak to *one another* in psalms and hymns and sacred songs ..."[24] Unfortunately, we're doing a dismal job of that today, even in most of our sharpest meetings. Christian singing needs a major overhaul—except for the few remaining tunes in a minor key, which of course need a minor overhaul.

I can hear you saying, "Surely, Jim, you're not going to harangue me for three pages about music." Ah, but I am. The need is too painful and the potential payoff is too grand. So at no extra charge, I humbly and tactfully offer these suggestions to you and your local horde of tone-deaf barbarians:

A. *You do need some kind of music.* Team meetings without singing soon acquire the stale air of a college lecture hall. Even if half your members are earless wonders, you need *some* occasional singing. A musically challenged team can get along nicely on just one or two songs or hymns per meeting, but they should be chosen with sensitivity and a bit of old-fashioned democracy.

B. *Scatter your music.* Singing eight or ten songs or hymns in a row can be edifying as long as it doesn't cause a charley horse in people's brains. But a long string of music has one weakness: The selections are usually arbitrary, so the words have no relevance to any current topic or action of the fellowship.

It's more helpful to sing *ad hoc* selections. For instance:

• A word of strong testimony can ignite a song of praise.
• A confession of sin can spark a hymn of appreciation for God's mercy and pardon.
• A plea for help can trigger a musical appeal to heaven.
• A slow or droopy meeting can be perked up by a good song or hymn—as long as it's not *too* jarring or out of place.

This connects singing with real life. As much as possible, keep your music spontaneous, not programmed, and related to the action. Spontaneity, for most groups, means *a cappella*. The average Joe or Jane musician can't pick up a tune wherever the group happens to start it. And it kills the momentum when Joe has to pick up his guitar and pluck around searching for the right key. Instant-response singing doubles the impact. Don't even preface a song with, "Why don't we sing, 'And Can It Be?'" Just lead off! The rest will chime in. (By the way, picking just the right song is a gift, and you'll find that many of your songs may spring from one or two gifted women. And yes, it most often is a woman.)

C. *You can't please everyone, but you can avoid making them miserable.* In your fellowship, you can't resolve the debate between hymn lovers and contemporary chorus lovers.

Some hymn fans react to contemporary praise songs and choruses as they might to "Jesus Loves Me" in Swahili. To them, they sound shallow, prosaic, and often tuneless. Rex Humbard calls chorus singing "7-11 worship" (7 words sung 11 times).[25]

To fans of Hosanna/Integrity music, most hymns are an embarrassment. They may be bored or turned off by the hopelessly unrealistic lyrics and the incredibly outdated tunes, which they categorize with funeral dirges.

Now, some folks are broad enough to enjoy everything from Gregorian chants to doo-wop. But most have preferences. Those at either extreme should, in love, make an effort to appreciate what's going on in the hearts of their brothers and sisters who enjoy other music. And it will help greatly if the selections are among the *best* of each genre. Draggy hymns and hokey choruses will only make things worse. Music must unite, not divide.

Let's sing wisely, as Paul said: "I will sing with my spirit, but I will sing with my mind also." (I Corinthians 14:15) Don't be like the birds in the limerick:

> There were three little birds in the wood
> Who always sang hymns when they could;
> What the words were about
> They could never make out,
> But they felt it was doing them good.

D. *Avoid musical sorcery.* Both hymns and modern songs can be used in an attempt to conjure up the presence of God. But He cannot be conjured, only invoked (called upon). I have seen some music leaders, in a desperate effort to maintain a certain aura, make a congregation repeat the same thing for 15 to 20 minutes. That's hypnosis or conjuring. Your ring doesn't need that. God doesn't need that.

E. *Never stop learning!* When it comes to music, <u>lots</u> of people are cross-grained diehards. They don't want to learn any songs they don't already know. And this goes double for learning any *types* of singing they don't know, such as *a cappella*. But trust me, they'll come around. When they begin to discover the joy and beauty of pure vocal harmony, they'll repent. The sound may be a bit ragged for a while, but *a cappella* singing <u>can</u> be learned. It often takes some months, but it's worth the wait. And meanwhile, work on learning a new song or hymn every week or two. Life is growth.

F. *Don't suppress people's spirits with loud instruments.* Whether it's a 300-pipe organ, a 1,000-amp keyboard, or a window-shattering electric guitar, instruments can be your enemy. The same goes for quad stereos with speakers bigger than your SUV. When cranked up beyond the 100-decibel level, they may excite your soul, but they *will* suppress your spirit. Stick to acoustic strings, soft electric piano accompaniment, or just voices. A meeting of hearts is different from a performance; whether you have 2 or 20,000, the instruments are there to *support* the singing, not *lead* it.

> During the Welsh Revival of 1904, Evan Roberts observed that "When there comes a pause in the services, then is there a danger of someone swinging the pendulum instead of raising the weights" (for those readers who are strictly digital, it is the weights which drive a grandfather clock, not the pendulum). To express this danger in contemporary terms, when there is a lull in the revival, there is always someone who thinks that turning up the volume on the PA system is an adequate substitute for the anointing.
> —Maurice Smith,
> The Parousia Network

NOTE ON HAVING A SINGLE "WORSHIP LEADER": Bad idea. The same goes for a married one. Even the nicest inevitably replace Jesus as the meeting leader. And the worst remind me of the hairy dude with the whip on a Roman slave galley.

HEADS-UP: In the larger meetings (which you won't want to have more than about once a month), your leaders need to be prepared to step in after a certain amount of singing and cut it off if the Spirit so leads. Otherwise, people may sing themselves into the middle of next week. (See the article on "God Is in the Transitions" on www.megashift.com.) Singing can quickly turn into a juggernaut and become an hour-long institution—even if only 10% of the people really want to sing that long.

9: Wait on God

We talk about it, but we don't do it.

"Waiting upon God" sounds like an inspiring and exalted activity, but not very American. Sitting in silence is not what we do best (unless a TV is on).

I promise you, however, that waiting on God has a better chance of suddenly transforming your group than anything else you could do. Just two or three minutes of total silence and submission before Him will bring more of His splendor, power, and love into your meeting than you could imagine.

You can enter into a period of silence in two ways. First, someone may call for a time of silence/contemplation/worship/listening or whatever you want to emphasize. That's the norm. But even better is to train your team to look for such moments. An especially moving contribution may flow naturally into silence and focusing on God, and in those times, His presence can be overwhelming.

10: Worship

Wouldn't it be great if there were a string attached to God so we could pull Him down and put Him in the center of our ring?

Well, we can. The string is called *worship*.

We're talking *pure* worship here, not the generic eleven o'clock "worship service," where participation means following the emcee's instructions to bow your head, pay your dues, and sing the predetermined songs.

Perhaps the highest privilege of being in a ring with teammates who are eager for the presence of God is that you get to participate in *real* worship, where the Lord speaks to every heart—which He likes just as much as you do!

Studies of church dropouts show that their main problem was not shallowness, backsliding, heresy, or rebellion. More than anything, they just missed God and the glory of His presence in the Sunday service. (Yes, wherever two or three are gathered in His name, He is there; but being omnipresent, He is in Antarctica, too. I'm talking about His strongly felt presence, where time stops, tears flow, people are reluctant to speak or even move, and He gives deep words of life and encouragement to each person. People will drive 300 miles for that kind of worship.) In the famous words of A.W. Tozer, "Worship is the missing jewel in the Evangelical church."

Any kind of worship is good, but the purest worship is not just a by-product of praise or singing, it's deliberate. Look in the Old Testament, and you'll find that often the word "worshiped" follows "fell down and" or "bowed down and." It's difficult to touch the hem of Jesus' garment when you're standing up and jumping around (though that's good, too).

If only a few of your meetings have a time of pure worship, something is haywire. Yet if 100% of your meetings have such a time, something else is haywire; legalism and tradition have taken over, displacing the rule of the Holy Spirit, who makes every meeting different. The solution? Learn to *enjoy* worship! When every soul in your circle is eager to walk through that golden curtain and kneel around the Father's throne, your ring has become a doorway to Heaven.

11: Share Communion and Other Symbolic Acts

In your fellowship you can celebrate the Lord's supper in a hundred fascinating ways, most of which would be impractical in a large meeting. For one example, instead of merely passing the elements, you can have each member answer some set question *as he or she partakes:*

- What are you thankful for right now?
- What does the death of Christ mean to you today?
- What is the greatest thing about being part of the body of Christ?
- Now that your sins have been paid for, what part of life is different for you?
- What does it mean to you that you will live forever?
- Lead us all in a short prayer for an unsaved friend of yours, asking that the blood of Christ will soon cover his or her sins.

PRACTICAL NOTE: If sharing a common cup brings a health concern, you can just dip the bread in the wine (or grape juice).

Foot-Washing: This has made a comeback in recent years as a deeply moving ceremony that creates humility and instant closeness. I'd say that on average, someone will find a reason to wash someone else's feet about every year or two.

Recently in China a young woman was kicked out by those of her own religion (YiGuanDao) because she has a harelip. She felt crushed. Two months later, she visited a house church, and they immediately washed her feet, treating her as the guest of honor. Overcome with emotion, she burst into tears as she told of her previous rejection. Afterward, she was overjoyed and became a Christian. No argument needed, no objections offered.[26]

Candles: There are scores of reasons to light a candle!

- To symbolize a prayer as it is being spoken
- To bring an event or person to memory
- To dedicate an offering or sacrifice
- To show unity or reconciliation
- To pledge a change in behavior or a new direction in life
- To symbolize the presence of the Holy Spirit
- Or simply to provide light! For many people, evening candlelight meetings fulfill a great need for ceremonial majesty, depth of meaning, or visualizing the mystery of Christ among us.[27]

Anointing with oil: As a Biblical symbol of the Holy Spirit, olive oil can be used in many ways: to dedicate someone for a task, to mark someone (or something, like a home or business) for protection, to claim physical healing in someone, or even to bring down something like a pornography shop or X-rated theater.

Boundary markers: If God leads you to claim His special lordship over a certain property or area, you may want to reify this claim by piling up a few rocks or driving stakes at the boundary corners.

Combined with prayers, communion, and other special ceremonies, this has been a powerful means of starting and solidifying a dramatic change in the spiritual environment of a region.

Benshen service: This traditional family ceremony has been a mainstay of Jewish life for centuries. At the start of the Friday evening Shabbat meal, the mother of the family lights two candles, and the father conducts the service, which is centered around the spoken blessing and uses four elements: bread, wine, salt, and oil. The father blesses the mother, the mother blesses the father, and the father blesses each child. (Kids love it!) Easily adapted to Christian usage, it can be an oft-repeated part of your meetings. It's so rich in symbolism on several levels that I couldn't do it justice here, so I'll have to refer you to a standard work on the subject, *Benching and the Early Christian Meal*, by Douglas A. Wheeler.[28]

Other symbolic acts: You have seen in the Bible that the Hebrew people had a fondness for symbolic actions, especially in naming things and dramatizing prophecies. Your open format gives you a similar opportunity to improvise with symbols. Your fellowship can invent new symbols that no one ever heard of. Use your imagination: Bring special symbolic tokens to give to each person ... join hands in prayer, not with a circle, but with a many-handed high five ... hand out yellow ribbons (or whatever) to pin on to signify a unity of purpose about something ... give a gift of appreciation to someone who has done something outstanding for the team or for others ... make a cake or other national dish from a country the group is involved with, and give out pieces halfway through the meeting, and so on *ad infinitum*.

THE BOTTOM LINE ON SYMBOLIC DEEDS: If your leadership tires, meetings can degenerate into one long answer to the opening question, *So how'd your week go?* The resulting flatness can make your meeting drag. But inject a few symbols, and the meeting can snap back to life and re-center around the Lord.

12: Eat!

Food is one of those universal languages. A good meal or refreshments can cover a multitude of procedural sins in your meeting!

It's asking a lot of one hostess to prepare a meal for your whole team every week. But if you rotate hosts or share the work, a full meal is possible, at least now and then. Many teams have a meal at every gathering. Potlucks are good; they avoid harmful "competition" for Hostess-of-the-Decade status.

Snacks are *always* possible, though you should respect the feelings of the growing numbers of people who are trying to eat healthy. If the family of God is always fed junk, things are not right. Don't try to be a culinary highbrow, but respect others' bodies as temples.

Train your people to favor spiritual topics during food time. Talking about sports, work, or trivial matters is good … in moderation. That's how we touch antennae and relax. But endless small talk is a trap. As Paul warns, "Avoid empty and worldly chatter, because those who indulge in it will become more and more ungodly."[29]

With the aid of a full meal (or just a few drinks and munchies), your post-meeting times can be better than the meeting itself. People will clump into little groups, and you may see world-changing prayer—or resolutions of problems that wouldn't even be brought up in a meeting.

A beautiful example happened in Jakarta, Indonesia, recently. A new Christian started visiting a house church, and during their meal-time afterward, Jesus appeared to her in a vision.

Now, this lady had lost her son eight years before. Literally. At age four, the boy had simply walked out of the house, wandered away, and hadn't been found since. You can imagine her anguish.

In the lunchtime vision, Jesus told her, "Go to the Jakarta National Monument now. You will find your son there. Today I have answered your prayer."

She immediately left for the monument, which is actually a big park about two square miles (5 square kilometers) in area. So she prayed, "Lord, this is so large! Where will I find him?" Looking around, she saw a big tree in the distance, and she sensed Jesus telling her, "Under that tree."

She walked to the tree and found a boy who looked about 12. "Daniel, is that you?" she asked. Daniel immediately recognized his mother. They hugged and were reunited.[30]

Jesus' first miracle was at a wedding feast. He loves meal-times!

13: Care and Share

A single mother of three was lamenting the hardships of getting around town without a car, so a woman with an extra car handed her the keys and gave it to her. In

Eat Your Way to Success

"We have been involved with church in homes for over 30 years, and we have come to the conclusion that there is one factor more important than any other in determining whether a group will be successful: Those that eat together invariably do much better than those that do not."

—Felicity Dale, M.D.
Editorial Board,
House2House

the new churches, that's a common type of event. Interactive body life in open meetings can be dynamite. Things can happen that would be procedurally impossible in a large traditional assembly.

Of course, larger assemblies can do some amazing things too. Two years ago, I was at a semi-open meeting of 200 in Colorado Springs. The leader was led to ask, "Does anyone have a special need today?" After a longish silence, a single mom stood up and admitted that she was broke and couldn't pay her bills.

He had her walk to the front of the group. As she stood there sniffling into a handkerchief, people walked up, put money at her feet, and gave her big hugs. This is Biblical: "Bear ye one another's burdens, and so fulfill the law of Christ."[31]

One of the core values of America is privacy, which is enshrined in our maxim, *Mind your own business*. But in team Christianity, privacy is limited to personal matters, family secrets, business issues, and small details unrelated to the team. When a teammate asks you, "So how's your walk with God these days?" he is not out of bounds. (Yes, there are nosy people, but you can restrain them.) If Bob is led by compassion with discernment, Bill's business is Bob's business. We're all in this together. We're family now. We've got to learn sensitive ways to help one another.

Simple as it sounds, one of the most helpful things you can do is just to keep your eyes open during the meetings. (Men especially need to hone their awareness.) When someone shows subtle signs of distress, pray or take action. At the next juncture, say, "Mickey, what did you think of that?" Asking for an opinion may open a hurting heart.

14: Spiritual Warfare

There are so many sources of evil in society—ideologies, governments, institutions, movements, personages—that we must learn to come against them in prayer, asking God to restrain them, knock them down, or destroy them. Scripture is replete with such actions.[32] (If you're put off by "warfare," think of it as resisting, fighting, blocking, or bringing down something destructive.)

Your team can be a battering ram to break down any fortress of evil in your city. Premier researcher George Otis has discovered that the most universal factor in the worldwide revivals that are transforming their communities today is *Christians uniting in persistent prayer against the main source of evil*, whether that is a spirit, a false god, a power establishment, or even, occasionally, a person.* His videos,

---

* Note again that spiritual warfare is not against individuals, except in cases of people consciously dedicated to evil goals—and even then, the prayer is not that God would destroy them, but redeem them.

Transformations and Transformations II, give very powerful examples of this. They are changing lives, cities, and nations.[33]

I recognize that prayers against evil may not set well with quiet souls who prefer warm fuzzies, but as long as we live in an evil age, we must be part of what God is doing to defeat that evil. We are not to become judgmental or "play God," but as a team founder, you must model leadership in calling upon the Supreme Commander to block or pulverize any forces that raise themselves up to destroy His kingdom, damage His world, or cause suffering.

15: Advance

Avoid stagnation: Take steps of faith. Don't shut your eyes to reality, but trusting in God, walk into the unknown and ask Him to guide and provide. Choose a course of action bold enough so that if God isn't in it, it will fail!

When you're getting ready to take a step, announce it to your fellowship. Use them as a launching pad, as a support base, as an anchor to be accountable to.

The new churches function as a support team. If you're isolated and struggling on your own, there's no one to pick you up when you fall. If you're part of a team, you're unstoppable!

Out of the 23 million born-again Christians in the U.S. who don't go to church anymore, how many of them do you suppose had a strong support group to help them onward and stand by them at the tough turning points of life? My guess: practically none.

If you want to do something fascinating, take a survey of folks you meet at the mall, supermarket, airport, or wherever. Ask them this:

> How would you like to have a team of fifteen sharp people who are committed to helping you in every way possible, a team that would stand by you, no matter what, in any kind of trouble? They would all pledge to be there for you at the big turning points of life and help you to reach your highest possible levels of success, solve your toughest personal problems, and become the kind of person everyone admires. If you were in trouble, you could call on them day or night, and they wouldn't rest until you were OK. In return, all they would expect is the same sort of loyalty from you. Would you like to have that kind of group around you?

That should be an interesting poll.

Let me know when you find someone who says no.

Charismatic Activities

*(If the gifts below are not a significant part of
your meetings, you may wish to skip this section.)*

16: Team Prophecy

When Christ leads by moving individual hearts in concert, His
presence becomes palpable, and the effect can be beyond earthquakes
or tornadoes. An open, Spirit-driven meeting fulfills the Scripture:

> If all prophesy ... the secrets of [an unbeliever's] heart are
> disclosed; and so falling on his face, he will worship God
> and declare, "Truly, God is among you."[34]

Notice that the unbeliever is not impressed at the presence of God
on any particular person, but he's *floored* by the fact that God can be
seen *among* us; that is, in the electric *relationships* of an interactive
team.

Key Insight: Paul isn't talking about a salad of unconnected
prophecies, which could be shrugged off as babble, but a Spirit-orches-
trated, harmonic message aimed straight at the unbeliever's heart.
When three or four strangers proclaim to you closely related
messages—and all of them are humanly unknowable—falling on your
face is a pretty rational thing to do!

Your team's prophecies need not foresee the future. A prophet is
simply someone who speaks for another, as in Exodus 7:1, where God
says to Moses, "Aaron thy brother shall be thy prophet." So prophecies
need only reflect the mind of the LORD.

Three earmarks of a true prophecy:

A. *It's fitting and becoming to the mood and content of the meeting.* If you've ever heard a long, loud, off-the-wall prophecy that makes
everybody wrinkle their brows and cock their heads like the RCA
Victor dog, you know what I mean.

B. *It passes the Bible test.* If it somehow seems out of sync with
Scripture, it probably is.

C. *It passes the sniff test.* First Corinthians 14:29: "Let two or three
prophets speak, and let the others weigh what is said." Weighing
means taking time out to react and discuss. If the group doesn't have
an "inner witness" from the Holy Spirit that it's true and relevant here
and now, table it and go on. (In practice, however, the majority of
prophecies are so innocuous and generic that they don't need any more
evaluation than a nod of the head.)

WARNING ON WARNINGS: I'm happy to report that the great
majority of prophecies today are positive, supportive, and confirming
of what the recipient may have already known or felt (such as a change

of job, a move out of state, or a wider ministry). This matches I Corinthians 14:3, which says prophecies should be constructive, stimulating, and encouraging. But there are always a small number of wannabe prophets who keep coming up with warnings of dire events that will ensue unless the recipient takes serious remedial action. These sad, troubled souls feel shut out and insignificant, and this is a simple way for them to gain some sort of power. Almost always, they are so deluded that they truly *believe* their own gloom and doom. My advice: Don't listen to them. You'll only invite a repeat performance. Prophetic warnings *can be* real, of course, but they must pass the above A-B-C test.

17: Healing

Over the years, you will do a lot of praying for people's healing, and you should expect lots of great results from the merciful hand of God.

I have four suggestions that will help.

First, always ask the ill if they would like to be healed (assuming they're conscious!) Asking *May we pray for you?* is a bit like asking *Would you like to receive Christ?* Divine healing is not something that you shove at people. Fortunately, you rarely will hear anyone say no.

Second, read them some Bible verses about healing.

Third, unless your group is solidly in favor of it, do not *command* a person to be healed or command a spirit of sickness to leave their bodies. Instead, tell them that in obedience to Scripture, you're simply going to ask God to heal them. (It's Biblical to use oil if you wish.) Then trust Him with the results.

Fourth, intensity is not a magic trick, but it does count. "The <u>fervent</u> prayer of a righteous man has a powerful effect." (James 5:16)

He will heal—again and again. Remember, however, and be encouraged: You may have to pray at length, or more than once. Even the Lord Jesus Christ himself had to pray twice for a blind man. (Mark 8:25) Healing through prayer is not rocket science.

18: Deliverance

> And though this world, with devils filled,
> Doth threaten to undo us,
> We will not fear, for God hath willed
> His truth to triumph through us.

Ever since Martin Luther wrote these words, the awareness of demons has been a basic part of the Protestant tradition. Today, however, there is a wide divergence in views of just how numerous and problematic those demons are. Some feel that true demonic manifestations in the U.S. are a rarity; others see demonic activity almost constantly.

Your ring will not resolve this great debate. But you *can* adopt a stance that will allow you to help deliver people from demonic oppression or outright possession regardless of a divergence of views among your team members. My general advice is not to go looking for demons. However, if you encounter aberrant behavior in someone—behavior that is not explainable by what is commonly known about abnormal psychology—you can assume that you likely have a case of a demonic presence of some sort.

This is such a complex subject I can hardly even open it here. But I can pass on to you five tips from Open Church Ministries president Lynn Reddick that can save you years of frustration and failures:

A. If you can at all avoid it, never do a deliverance by yourself. And if the victim has a background of involvement with the occult, use more than two people.

B. Ask the victim if he or she *desires* deliverance: "Do you want to be free?"

C. Demonic influence is usually a far more serious problem if the victim is unsaved.* If you've assumed that the victim is a born-again Christian, but the deliverance process is dragging out without result, you may need to go back and recheck that. Ask about the details of the conversion, the change in his/her life, etc.

D. Unless you're facing an emergency situation, such as one in which demons have taken total control of the victim's body movements, don't be rushed. Both you and the victim may need as much as two or three weeks of preparation for the deliverance. Much can be done during that time in terms of prayer, instruction, fasting, etc.

E. Check up on him after the deliverance. The former victim must become a part of your ring or some other accountability group. Never send a newly delivered person out into this evil world to face the future alone. Demons love to come back in force, so fill that vacuum in his heart with the presence of Christ and the loving warmth of new teammates.

TOTALLY DIFFERENT ALTERNATIVE: Many times, demons will flee on their own when their victim enters into deep worship with a group of Christians. Over time, in fact, you may see more results through worship than through deliverance sessions!

19: Tongues

When the Azusa Street revival began the Pentecostal movement in 1906, a common feeling among participants was, *Finally! Something that's going to unite the church!*

---

* Please notice the subject is *influence* here. It is rare (many would say nonexistent) to find cases of outright demonic possession of Christians—by which I mean a takeover of a believer's central nervous system.

Alas, it hasn't exactly panned out that way. Today, no issue has caused more ground-level dissension than speaking in tongues.

Thankfully, with the rise of team Christianity, this division is beginning to fade. Chances are fairly high that you will have a few of both charismataic and non-charismatic players in your open fellowship. You *can* function as a mixed but united team. Uniformity, no; unity, yes!

So what to do? With fear and trepidation, I offer you five guidelines:

A. *Don't become anti-glossolalia.* You should lobby against the *misuse* of the gift of tongues, but I Corinthians 14:39 is quite clear: "... Do not forbid speaking in tongues."

Moreover, there does not seem to be an expiration date attached to this command. Many well-meaning brothers and sisters have suggested A.D. 95 as an expiration date because it was about then that John completed the New Testament by writing down his Revelation. (Their idea is that the Bible replaced all the gifts.) And I Corinthians 13:8 does say that tongues (and knowledge) will pass away; so, although knowledge is still alive and well, they insist that the gift of tongues has been withdrawn, and current examples are all bogus.[35]

Theirs is an awkward position to defend (except for the idea that *some* messages in tongues are less than genuine!) It claims that in the midst of the eternal Word of God we have a totally defunct section in I Corinthians 14:39 that was, in fact, only "funct" for about 40 years— from around A.D. 55, when the letter was written, to A.D. 95 ... thus leaving the entire church to scratch her head for 1900 years over a dead passage. That's a stretch.

B. *Discourage loud displays of uninterpreted messages in your meetings.* First Corinthians 14 is equally clear that without an interpreter, speaking in tongues is a gift for private use, not public. Not many Christians today will be grievously offended by a few quiet glossa words during a time of simultaneous (concert) prayer, but beyond that level, tell your tongues-speakers to be sensitive. Many fine charismatics and Pentecostals feel that speaking in tongues is so wonderful in private, why withhold it in public? In other words, they just kind of ignore I Corinthians. As a responsible leader, you can't afford to do that.

C. *Interpreters are key people.* A well-interpreted message in tongues is akin to a prophecy. Because fully gifted prophets are scarce, it behooves us to cultivate our interpreters.

D. *Emphasize the fruit of the Spirit.* The internal, eternal evidence of the Holy Spirit's working is love, joy, peace, patience, kindness, goodness, faithfulness, gentleness, and self-control. Taken all together, these are far more valuable than any gift of tongues I've ever seen. Keep your team's attention on the most important things.

E. *Let love run the meeting.* If all the above seems too confusing, just re-center the group's attention on the Lord Jesus and let His love draw them together. Love never faileth.

I Have Called You Friends

I've always been overwhelmed by Jesus' announcement, "No longer do I call you servants, for the servant does not share his master's confidence. But I have called you friends ..." (John 15:15)

Friend is an exalted position in life, sometimes closer than *brother* or *sister*, and a ring church is, at the human level, a warm circle of committed friends. I hope this chapter has helped you understand how your Christian family can blend together in true friendship.

I used to have a golden-hearted doctor named Terry Lilly, who was a true friend to many. On his office wall he had these words in a carved antique frame:

It is my joy in life to find
In every turning of the road
The strong arms of a comrade kind
To help me onward with my load.

And since I have no gold to give
And love alone can make amends,
My only prayer is, "While I live,
God, make me worthy of my friends."[36]

---

1. Tommy Tenney, *The God Chasers* (Shippensburg, Pennsylvania: Destiny Image) 1998, page 8.

2. Bill Silva, a Christian Tabernacle member who is a materials specialist familiar with Dupont cast acrylic specifications, told me that such a pulpit would easily withstand 57,000 pounds per square inch (4000 kg per square centimeter) of pressure—and even then would only shatter into tiny splinters like glass. But he insisted there is absolutely no way it would *ever* split along a diagonal, lightning-like line, regardless of the pressure exerted.

3. For a representative example of how repentance turns to joy in the context of an open meeting, see www.ptmin.org/chile2.htm.

4. Please pardon the quotation marks, but this is an illegitimate term that evolved to make a false distinction between the priestly class of Christians and all the rest of us. In the Bible there is no such dichotomy. "Laity" (Greek: λαος) simply means the people of God, including ministers and pastors.

5. See a fuller version of this event at www.pastornet.net.au/renewal/journal9/9g-hogan.html.

6. Frank Bartleman, *Azusa Street* (New Kensington, PA: Whitaker House), 1982, pages 58-61, 75f, 99.

7. The sign is courtesy of the Billy Graham Center in Wheaton, Illinois. Ominously, the Fulton Street Church was on the site of the World Trade Center.

8. *Op. cit.*, page 120f.

9. The split pulpit was a lesson in what *not* to do. It didn't even begin to show what we *should* do in meetings. The remainder of this chapter will open up that subject.

10. From a doctoral dissertation by Jeffrey Edward Short, *A Strategy for Planting an Interactive Church in Las Vegas, Nevada,* chapter four: "The Theological Case for the Interactive Church."

11. For example, I once visited Jack Hayford's "Church on the Way" in Van Nuys, California. They had four microphones in the audience, where any of the four or five thousand attendees could walk up and speak. To filter the contributions, they stationed an elder by each microphone. If you wanted to say anything, you first had to whisper the gist of your message in the elder's ear; he would then decide if you should give your message now, later, or not at all.

An interesting side benefit: When the church started this, they were afraid it would inhibit people. What they actually found was that members would hesitantly summarize their contribution, and the elder would often say, "That's *exactly* what this congregation needs to hear! Go for it!" The member would then step up to the mike with great confidence and boom it out.

12. *Henry the Sixth*, Part II, III, II, 86.

13. Trick question: What's the Greek word for *sermon*? Answer: There isn't any, at least in the New Testament. Classical sermons didn't appear until after about three centuries of church institutionalization.

14. Graydon Snyder in *Opening Day in the House of God*, p. 186. Available only through Open Church Ministries as part of *The Future Church*. See bibliography.

15. Even today, some Catholic Bibles state up front: "Not to be read without the presence of a priest."

16. SIDELIGHT: Many Americans, even believers, are infected with a cynical spirit of scoffing. Their conversation is one long running gag, with the standard punch line being some variant of "Life is crummy." It is a sophomoric sickness that never seems to fade. But if you will train such people to start bringing positive, helpful, uplifting bits of encouragement (not scolding tirades), you'll see the beginnings of a miraculous transformation in their lives.

17. Dean Comerford of Future Church Ministries, Invercargill, New Zealand. Quoted in Joel News International. Send an e-mail to lyris@xc.org with the command in the message box: get joel-news-international comerford-massive-blessings.

18. I Peter 2:9

19. Various sources. See *Friday Fax* #32, 1995.

20. In a team with a few mature, well-informed members, you don't have to be the doctrine czar. Just make sure they know they're supposed to share in the responsibility of keeping the less mature from wandering into hidden quicksand.

21. I Timothy 1:3; Titus 1:11.

22. These thoughts and experiences are from Dr. Lynn Reddick, president of Open Church Ministries, in his new book, *The 2 Minute Miracle: Releasing God's Power, Protection and Prosperity with Spoken Blessings* (Portal, GA: Portal Publishing Co.), 2003.

23. See Genesis 27:26, for example.

24. Ephesians 5:19

25. Quoted by George Otis in *God's Trademarks* (Grand Rapids: Chosen Books) 2000, page 86.

26. Source: an unnamed Chinese Christian, via Open Doors (Germany office). Fax: 49 (5384) 90978. Cited in *Friday Fax* #44, 1999.

27. For the most part, dead ceremony and meaningless ritual are exactly what we're trying to get away from. The new church is replacing these with the living presence of God and strong relationships with other believers. However, we are also seeing a widespread, persistent yearning for the majesty and mystery of symbolic ceremonies—which can be powerful *if* they are rooted in here-and-now events: a song, a commitment, a repentance, a major event like a birth or wedding, etc.

28. Download at www.restorationfoundation.org/volume%2010/43_28.htm.

29. II Timothy 2:16

30. Source: Samiton Pangellah, Abbalove. Fax: (62) 21-6018408. E-mail: contact@abbalove.or.id. Cited in *Friday Fax* #10, 2001.

31. Galatians 6:2

32. In the Bible, outright cursing starts in Genesis 3:14 and runs through Revelation 22:19.

Now, we are specifically commanded to bless others instead of cursing them. (Luke 6:28, Romans 12:14) We should be known as people of blessings. Yet curses are enshrined in poetry in Psalms 35, 55, 58, 59, 69, 83, 94, 109, 137 (esp. vs. 8f), and 140—some of the "imprecatory" psalms.

If these seem out of step with the mood of the New Testament, you might recall Jesus' eight "Woe unto you" curses in Matthew 23. Or His zapping of the figless tree. And the curses on two sorcerers, Simon and Elymas. Or the words of Peter that struck down Ananias and Sapphira.

Even as we establish righteousness and justice throughout the world, we are also destroying evil. So a balanced view of curses is important. One decent example is at http://www.theocentric.com/originalarticles/imprecatory.html.

33. Available from The Sentinel Group, P.O. Box 6334, Lynnwood, Washington 98036. Phone: (800) 668-5657 with credit card. E-mail: info@sentinelgroup.org. Web: www.sentinelgroup.org.

34. I Corinthians 14:25

35. Genuine examples abound. For instance, in a prayer meeting in Latvia in 1989, a Latvian girl suddenly spoke loudly in Estonian, "Lift your eyes because your hope and Savior is coming soon!!" Visiting evangelist Kertu Gasman from Estonia later went to the girl and told her how surprised she was that she could speak Estonian (a very different language). The girl replied, "Estonian? I can't speak a single word!" *Source*: Liv Kuldvere, YWAM Norway. Fax: 47 (526) 72972. Cited in Friday Fax #15, 1996. Also, read the stirring account of an historic turn in African mission work when many natives suddenly spoke out in flawless French, German, English, and other languages. (Pete Greig, *Awakening Cry*, [London: Silver Fish Publishing], 1998, page 58)

36. Frank Dempster Sherman, 1860-1916.

EPILOGUE:
Mad Max, Zorah, and the Lady in Pink

Saturday Evening, June 6, 2012

As you fold your umbrella and jostle your way into the crowded high school gym, you suddenly realize that none of these hundreds of happy, noisy people would have been here except for you.

With your first step onto the floor, you look around, and your heart leaps into your throat as it hits you: Your problem-stained life has turned out to be a bases-loaded home run.

You push toward the middle of the floor, where a round, low platform sits among chairs and bleachers on all sides. A familiar face pops out of the milling crowd: a wiry, gray-haired doctor who helped you get all this started when it was just eight people in your living room.

"Mad Max!" you shout over the din, "where did you find all these warm bodies? In your waiting room?"

"Nope, they found us," he answers with a hug. "About half are new Christians, and half came looking for a church where they could be part of the action instead of just spectators. We've got an extremely active kind of believer here. I'd bet a third of them will be itching to say something tonight."

"No way! You must have close to a thousand people here."

Max glances around. "Actually, looks like a little more than that tonight. We told them *you* were coming."

"You what?"

"I announced that the founder of our original church planting team in 2005 was finally coming back for a visit, so of course they all want to hear—"

"You *what?*" You feel blood draining from your face.

"Hey, you're an apostle figure to them—even though you were only here for the first two years before you had to move out of state. They want to hear how you started all this." Max grins. "Tell them how easy it was."

"Oh yeah, right. How easy it was. I'll tell them about the time Old Man Hanski next door called the cops because you were yelling at me."

"Well, you could skip that part."

"Look, I'm not the star here anymore. In fact, to be honest, Max, sometimes I was sure that our little home church would fizzle."

"Or explode. But God sure knitted us together, huh? And look at it now. There's 93 home fellowships represented here tonight."

"All growing out of our little circle?"

"Yup. And it looks like they're getting ready to start. See these kids here by the platform?"

You turn and see a clump of about 15 teens. In the middle, a petite black girl in a red skirt starts squealing and jumping up and down.

"Well!" he says, "it looks like they've picked the kickoff person for tonight. Every week, we let the kids choose one of their own to start the meeting."

"Doesn't that kind of set the tone for the early part of the meeting?"

"For the *whole* meeting, sometimes. Last fall a boy started us off by confessing he'd stolen a car. The Holy Spirit used that to launch a whole string of confessions. Except for some quiet crying now and then, you could almost hear a pin drop for the next five hours."

"Five hours! That must have changed a bunch of lives."

Max nods. "Sure did. But usually, a kid will just begin with a song or prayer or Scripture or testimony. Each kid who wants to kick it off tells what he wants to do, then all the others listen to their hearts and decide who should lead off. But hey now, we saved you a seat up in front."

Vincent and the Traffic Jam

As you start to move, the girl hops onto the platform, picks up the mike, and yells, *"LET THE PARTY BEGIN!!"* A boom of cheers and applause laced with laughter fills the gym.

And a party it is. Immediately, some people at the top of the bleachers start a fast-paced song, and it spreads in seconds to everyone. You holler in Max's ear, "Nobody *ever* lets kids do that!"

He yells back, "It's our own thing. These new churches are all different. God's getting very creative."

When the song ends, another begins, from who knows where. Then another and another, each one fitting beautifully, like a medley.

After ten minutes, the mood softens as a slow, haunting tune sweeps the crowd:

On a plain without water or pathway to guide us
We were wandering with death in our eyes, through the sands
When a Stranger came by and stretched out His arms, saying,
"All the roadmarks you need are engraved in these hands ... ."

By the time the last verse fades away, four men and a woman have come forward to say something. They speak in the ear of a silver-haired man in the front row. As he listens to each one in turn, he gestures toward some reserved chairs beside him.

"When the traffic gets heavy, we use Vincent to sequence people," Max whispers. "We've all learned to stand up and speak, flowing with the mood and the topic, but with five at once ..."

Vincent waves the last man to the platform. But as he picks up the mike, he sees something at the back. Without a word, he puts it back down and returns to a seat by Vincent.

A torrent of murmurs and quiet gasps floods across the gym as all heads turn to gaze at a small figure near the back door, inching her way to the front.

You and Max crane your necks to see.

"Who—?" you ask.

"Oh, dear Jesus. It's Mary Alice! They've let her out of the hospital, probably for the last time."

"Who *is* she?" you ask.

The murmurs quickly die away to an electric silence, an awed hush that fills the room with the presence of God and a glory that everyone feels like a weight of gold.

Leaning over to your ear, Max says in a barely audible whisper, *Mary Alice Parker, age 97. Missionary who planted house churches in China from 1930 until World War II. She and her husband were put in a Japanese prison compound, where he died. After the war, she kept* planting churches until Mao took over in '49. Left Shanghai on the last boat and went to India, where she planted more till she was 85. When she came here, she taught a lot till the cancer got her. But she still counsels eight or ten people a day from her bed.

Wearing a pink sweater, the tiny, withered woman slides her walker forward six or eight inches at a time. The loudest sound in the building is the slow *click, click* of the walker.

"It's time for your next step."

Seeing that Mary Alice has refused her wheelchair and will need a few minutes to reach the platform, a tall, graceful lady in a long blue dress steps forward and onto the platform. She picks up the mike and walks to the edge, looking down the aisle at Mary Alice.

In a rich contralto voice, she sings *a cappella* a song she has written to the tune from the classic movie *The High and the Mighty*:

> *You were sent from Heaven,*
> *Sent from God above to reveal His love.*
> *Now you've come that we may become*
> *The priests we were meant to be.*
>
> *Teach us words from Glory,*
> *Carry burning coals to our weary souls.*
> *Don't hold back, that we may not lack*
> *In hope that can set us free ...*

A few verses later, a couple of young men are helping Mary Alice get up the two steps and to the center of the platform.

Pausing to catch her breath, she looks around and says, "Jesus is here." Hundreds of soft amens echo back.

She briefly strokes her silver hair, then leans on her walker. "I'm kind of wet. Monte let me ride over here with the window down. I'm afraid his car's pretty soggy now, but ... I just wanted to feel the wind and rain on my face one more time.

"In a hospital bed, you hear the Lord more clearly. And He's been telling me to come back and say something."

As she continues very slowly, her listeners sit like frozen statues.

"You probably know ... this gathering was started as a mission church ... by a very fine traditional church across town, where services were always planned in advance." She gestures toward you. "I see your founder is here tonight." You feel a thousand eyes turn toward you.

"Well, right from the start, they bravely gave you all permission to meet with just the Lord Jesus in charge of things. And you've done

192

well. You've grown. You've learned how to be the body of Christ here—with Him as your head. You've brought many newcomers to the kingdom. And your lives have been changed. But—it's all been so wonderful that you've settled in and gotten comfortable!

"Well, I think it's time for your next step now. I suppose about half of you have visited me and shared your hearts, so I know many of you are ready. Right now I'm looking into the eyes of several dozen dear friends who need to step out in faith and turn your home or office into an open church. You need to start inviting in neighbors and office friends for a meal or a visit ... and show them how to wrap their lives around Jesus. It's time.

"Since I never had children, I've kind of adopted you as my own. So may I give you a word of motherly advice? *Life isn't about comfort; it's about making a difference in spite of pain.* Don't wait for your life to be calm and pain-free. Begin your greatest work now.

"For just a few minutes, I want to meet with you out in the hall. I want to hold your hands and look into your eyes and give you a mother's blessing. You know who you are because God has spoken to your heart." She looks toward the back door. "I ... I guess I'll have to have my wheelchair now."

About a hundred people stand and start moving toward the hall.

"And all of you," she adds, "allow the Lord of the wind and the rain to bring storms and discomfort into your life ... in the form of some needy friends ... for the sake of the kingdom. As a symbolic prayer of dedication, you may even want to take a drive sometime with *your* windows down. You and your car will get wet, but you'll dry out. And you'll always remember that you gave permission for the King of Heaven to bring His whole stormy world into your life."

As the two young men spring up to help her, an old man's thin voice floats through the air, starting the congregation on a hymn popular in Mary Alice's youth:

> *God be with you till we meet again,*
> *By His counsels guide, uphold you,*
> *With His sheep securely fold you,*
> *God be with you till we meet again.*
>
> *Till we meet, till we meet,*
> *Till we meet at Jesus' feet;*
> *Till we meet, till we meet,*
> *God be with you till we meet again.*

Trying to swallow the lump in your throat, you realize that it's the end of an era ... but you ponder how much better it is to mark it publicly—in triumph—rather than letting it sputter out silently in an empty, sterile hospital room.

Billy Joe's Impossible Announcement

By this point, another two dozen people are making their way to the platform. You lean over to Max. "How do you *do* that kind of singing? New Christians today *never* learn those old songs!"

"Yes, well, nobody wants a steady diet of oldies anymore, but we decided that lots of them were too good to forget. So we often call in a worship team just to teach some new and old songs—and get the tunes into our heads."

"Then how do you get the *words* into your heads?—"

"Oh, we just print 'em up and hand 'em out. We take the sheets home and use them in our quiet times. Works for us."

The platform is now ringed with people, mostly in their twenties or thirties, sitting restlessly on its perimeter. They all start turning their heads toward Vincent. He extends his hands palm upward, shrugs his shoulders, and laughs.

Everyone glances around the circle as suppressed giggles run through the building. After a moment, two men and a woman stand up hesitantly. They look at the circle, then at each other. As if on cue, they stride to the center. They talk for a few moments and nod their heads vigorously. Then two sit back down, leaving a slightly built young man in a pale blue sweater.

"I'm going out to the lobby and get one of Mary Alice's blessings before she runs out of them," he says as the sound man bumps up the volume to catch his soft voice. "But first, I just have to say something about this 'making a difference in spite of pain.' My name is Billy Joe Waldencroft.* Many of you know me by now.

"Until I was 20, I was homosexual. But by that point, the lifestyle got to be pretty sad for me. And lonely. The only person in the world I felt I could talk to was my uncle Rod, who was a Christian. Unfortunately, he'd been paralyzed by a stroke and was slowly and painfully dying. But for two years, every time I went to see him, he just radiated the presence of God. And he'd always tell me about Christ and the great plans God had for me.

"Well, about 18 months ago, he convinced me to start meeting with your downtown group on Sunday mornings. Of course, they all accepted me with open arms. And yet there was such an atmosphere of purity and strength that I felt really weak and corrupt. So inside of a month, I confessed my sins and turned to Christ ... and He totally turned my head around—my emotions, my thinking, my desires, everything.

---

* Based on the true story of a New York couple I met, but with names changed.

194

"Just after that, I started coming here to your joint meetings every third Saturday. And so did Diane.

"Now, if I was a mess, she was a triple mess—a lesbian prostitute with alcohol and drug problems. A hard, tough woman. But God totally cleaned her out and softened her up. By the time I met her here, what a changed lady she was! I'd never felt drawn to a woman before, but Diane was special. When we got married a year ago, I knew I was the luckiest guy in the world. We had to be the match of the century, right? What a pair!

"Now, I come from a big family, and I've always liked kids. But Diane made it clear that she'd never used any precautions on the street, and she was sterile as a rock. Still, I loved her, so we just planned to adopt.

"But I'm standing here tonight to"—his voice begins to choke up—"to show you the power of God. Brothers and sisters, tonight is ... the proudest moment of my life. I want to present to you my beautiful, loving, saintly wife Diane ... and our new baby girl, Sarah Marie Waldencroft!"

The gym explodes with a roof-rattling roar as the crowd bolts to its feet, screaming with joy. A thousand pair of eyes turn to a woman in a bright yellow dress holding a little bundle of pink as she strides toward the platform, head held high and streams of tears coursing down her face.

The clapping and cheers last for over a minute until they are drowned out by a lilting chorus set to the tune of "Mockingbird Hill."

> *O God of Surprises! Miraculous King!*
> *For this gift we praise you, we gratefully sing!*
> *We bless you, we thank you for presents that last,*
> *O God of the future! O God of the past!*

Miguel: A Fighter for God

During the noise and singing, the platform sitters are moving around and huddling, kneeling in chattering clumps, comparing notes. After a few final gestures and stage whispers across the platform, they seem to have settled their sequence, more or less. The next speaker is a freckle-faced girl.

"I'm Katie Carmichael, and I'm seven, and my mommy and daddy didn't think I was ever possible either. And when I was born, they had to pray for me a long time so I'd be able to walk. And I want to thank Jesus for making me able to walk and run."

As she walk-skips back to her seat, the mike is picked up by a beefy Hispanic man in his mid-twenties. He appears to be about six foot four, and his black T-shirt and jeans lend an imposing air. "Well, I never had no trouble being born, but I sure gave my folks plenty reasons to wish I hadn't of been. I'm Miguel Mireles, and I been a gang leader for a long time now. I've done a lot of pretty bad stuff. The gang was my life, you know? But last fall my little brother Javier, he got killed in a knife fight. And that got me thinking a lot. I was really down about it.

"Then Rita, one of the girls in *El Faro al Mundo*, the Lighthouse in the barrio, she ask me to come to a meeting at Benito's house. I wasn't too wild about that, you know, but she was pretty excited, so I went.

"Well, this could be a real long story, but what I want to say is, I met Jesus Christ there two weeks ago. And my life don't look nothing like before. It feels all different too. Jesus is my Lord now, and I follow Him.

"I told my whole story in El Faro already, all the bad stuff. But I felt like I ought to come here and tell the whole world, 'cause what I done, the robberies and all that, it kind of hurt the whole world, you know? Anyway, I'm really sorry. But you guys are great. I feel like God forgives me cause I feel that from you. Nobody ever accepted me like this before. So I praise God. Hallelujah!"

Before he can leave the platform, a voice calls out from ten or twelve rows back, "Hold it a minute!"

It is another Hispanic, a dark-complexioned gentleman old enough to be Miguel's father. He trots forward and onto the stage, right past all the waiting speakers, and puts an arm around the shocked young man.

"Miguel, you remember me, don't you?"

"Yeah, I guess I do."

"I was the main witness in the trial that sent you to prison for two years. When you were 21, you put a gun in my face one night and took my wallet. I recognized you and turned you in.

"Well, tonight I want to say that you're my younger brother in the Lord now, and I forgive you. I accept you as a full partner in the gospel. In addition, I want to give you my blessing."

He stuffs the microphone in his coat's breast pocket, takes hold of Miguel's hands, and looks the astonished youth in the eye. "Miguel Mireles, you've always been a brave young man—sometimes for good, sometimes for evil. But now you've given your brave heart to God. You're a fighter. So I bless you as you begin to enter *spiritual* battles, encounters where ordinary men would run and hide. May the Commander of the armies of heaven give you a supernatural knowledge of what to do and say every time you stand up for Him, speak for Him, and pick a fight against hatred with His love."

As they embrace, Miguel begins to sob, and the people break out with:

Amazing grace, how sweet the sound
That saved a wretch like me! ...

A Human Flower with Thirty Petals

The next speaker comes up and quietly slips the mike out of the older man's pocket. When the song fades away, he booms out: **"If any man is in Christ, he is a new creature!"** Then more softly: "And I want to tell you about another man who found forgiveness and a new life: *me.*"

He tells his story—about a life gone wrong, about a corporate takeover whiz obsessed with wealth, willing to destroy anything in his path to success, running from God until He finally cornered him in a bankruptcy court.

Then a stream of people continue on, taking center stage, some for as little as ten seconds, others as much as five minutes:

—A couple who have recently launched their twelfth open church network in three years says, "Give it your best shot! If God puts certain people on your heart, invite them over for dinner and let the Lord turn them into family."

—A high school girl newly arrived from Vietnam responds, "I have many friends in my heart, but they all back home. Maybe you pray with me for them? And for Vietnam?" She prays for about a minute with some difficulty and considerable emotion, and several people around the gym chime in with their own impassioned prayers for her people.

—A single mother of three tells how God taught her a lesson: "As I said Sunday in our home church in North Park, I was having a lot of trouble keeping my kids in line, trying to be mommy and daddy at the same time, and it just caused constant rebellion and tension. But then God showed me that, for better or worse, I'm the priest in our home. So every Friday now, we have a special dinner and a special time when I put my hands on each child, tell them what I see as their potential, and bless them with that. I also give them blessings to be able to handle their problems at school and so forth. The kids love it. Now they see me as their biggest supporter, so we seldom fight."

—A portly couple speaks to this mother of three: "Amen! And the reason for the change in your family is that you're bringing the presence of God into your home in a very real way. In Moses' day, the presence of God was centered in the ark of the covenant. And over the ark were two cherubim facing each other with their wings stretched out toward each other. So their wings marked out a special space for God's presence. Right now, we want to invite anyone to come down here and re-create such a special place for God."

They turn and face each other, holding out their arms with their fingertips almost touching. "As a way of welcoming His presence, this will be a holy event where you bring to this circle an offering or a sacrifice—not money, but a *specific* offering of repentance from a sin ... or a sacrifice of a new devotion. Are you ready? Now, we've already started—by giving up to God our right to eat sugary foods and some other things. We've lost 60 pounds between us so far! Feel free to join us. But be brief because we can only hold out our arms for so long!"

A teenager scampers up and says, "Lord, I give you the many hours I waste on empty TV programs." The couple widen their "holy space" by moving one of their almost-touching sets of hands toward the youth. He raises his arms, making a trefoil, like a three-petaled flower when viewed from heaven.

He is followed immediately by others:

"Father God, I give You all my cigarettes—for the rest of my life."

"I give You my Saturdays—for *your* work, Lord."

"I'll give to You the first hour of my day, to spend with You."

"For Your kingdom, I give up all my doughnuts, cookies, and coffee."

"I give You my pride, as I go to Detroit to apologize to my family."

"I give up my three-wheeler, which I never needed in the first place."

"I offer up to You my Tuesdays, to work in the Skid Row mission."

Within three minutes, the platform is filled, a flower with over thirty petals enclosing a round, wide space for God's shekinah glory, which the whole church feels with awe.

Then the oldest person still waiting, a forty-something man in a tweed jacket, walks to the center. "I'm Hal Frank, and my wife Lisa and I teach philosophy and psychology at the college," he says in a rumbling professorial bass. "I'd like to add onto what's happening tonight by relating it to the gospel.

"You see how lives are changed when you allow a holy God to come in. That's the gospel, the good news in action.

"Here's a homework assignment: Find every statement of the gospel in the New Testament, such as John 1:12, 3:16, and Romans 10:9. Then see how many basic *elements* the gospel has. Then place those elements into two groups.

"You'll find one man, the Lord Jesus Christ, in two roles: as savior and lord. You'll find two events: the cross and the resurrection. You'll find two results: salvation *from* hell and salvation *to* an eternal, abundant, transformed life—such as you've seen here tonight. You'll find two processes: forgiveness and transformation. You'll find in John 1:12 that there is some*one* to receive and some*thing* to believe. You'll find two identities for yourself—formerly a sinner and now a saint.

"When you received Christ, you received a savior from sin *and* a lord of your abundant, holy future. This is the everlasting, two-edged gospel that the Father wants us to bring to our city."

On and on the divine drama unfolds for the next two hours, punctuated by response prayers, an occasional song, and an incredibly noisy fifteen-minute break for coffee in the hallway. During the break, you ask Max, "How do you keep such order with all these kids? And do you have any problem with long-winded people or trouble-makers?"

"Naw, the windbags and critics usually get straightened out at the house church level. Just occasionally, one of the elders will have to cut someone off or ask them to wrap it up. And the kids you're looking at are about half the total—the less fidgety ones. The others are over at the cafeteria having their own meeting and activities, usually headed up by a guy."

After the break, the waiting speakers have reprioritized themselves. They take up where they left off, with more testimonies, teaching, and prayers, but little singing.

The contributions are now less dramatic but more intense. After all this, you're wondering what you're going to say.

Zorah and the Mayor

Finally, nearing the three-hour point, the sitting ring of would-be contributors has dwindled to a handful. You've been admiring the physical stamina of one of them, an olive-skinned, athletic-looking woman who has been kneeling on the floor in prayer with her face on the platform the whole time. At this point, she stands up and steps to the center.

Now you are able to see that she is wearing an ankle-length dress rich with purple, gold, and brown. Her roman nose, long hair and large earrings, and a cascade of necklaces and bracelets give her a sharply Middle Eastern appearance.

Max grins. "Brace yourself! Something always happens when Zorah gets up there."

"As I have been praying, my friends," she says with an Arabic accent, "a picture has come to my mind over and over: a prominent official of the government coming to see us. I do not know who it might be." She slowly turns 360 degrees, smiling as she surveys the still-packed gym. "But I hope it is not the fire marshal."

The group laughs appreciatively at this small break in the intensity. "There is also a song in my heart. I know none of the words, but I think it is an old hymn of yours. Perhaps someone will come and sing it for us." She begins to sing, *la la la ...*

Before she finishes the first two bars, heads are nodding everywhere, but no one steps forward. As the tune ends, a man with a cane stands and shuffles toward the center. The only sound in the building is the muffled crying of one woman in an upper corner of the bleachers.

His head shakes slightly as he walks up to Zorah and takes the mike. "Well, I'm no government official, and I'm long past being a singer. But I sure do know the Navy hymn. I was in the navy during Pearl Harbor, Midway, Corregidor, Okinawa, Iwo Jima, you name it. And I'll be proud to try one verse as best I can . . ."

> *Eternal Father! strong to save,*
> *Whose arm hath bound the restless wave,*
> *Who bids the mighty ocean deep*
> *Its own appointed limits keep:*
> *O hear us when we cry to Thee*
> *For those in peril on the sea.*

In the ensuing silence, heads begin turning toward the top row of the bleachers, where a couple of about seventy is walking down hand in hand. The woman is crying into a handkerchief nonstop, and her husband, in a dark suit, is biting his lip very hard. Zorah and the old man walk away.

Max is awestruck. "I don't believe it. I don't believe it."

"What?"

"The mayor. The last guy in the world I'd expect to see here."

After picking up the microphone, the mayor stands with bowed head for a few moments, then clears his throat and says, "I'm Leo Lockhart, and this is Sandra. You know me as the one who led the effort to block the renewal of your lease and keep you out of the city arena. I came here tonight to satisfy myself that you were a bunch of nuts, as I'd been saying.

"Well, it looks like I'm the nut here. I'm truly sorry ... I—" He stops, then clears his throat again. Before I retired and moved here, I was a career navy officer. But I never was religious. Sandra was, but I never cared anything about church. I was more of an establishment man, a man of the world. The Navy hymn was the only Christian song I ever cared for—and that's just because it reminded me of the old days at sea.

"I've seen things tonight that I never would have believed. And now this hymn—" He shakes his head several times.

"I know I'm going to have to make changes in my life. This is going to bring our home together … and our city, if I have anything to say about it. The lady in the pink sweater talked about letting the world into your life. Well, here's a man of the world letting God's people into his life. I never knew church could be like this. For sure, God is here among you."

Your Apostolic Message

With this last phrase, something like a lightning bolt goes through your chest, and you jump to your feet. You know you must speak *now*. With your head spinning, you accept the mike from the mayor as the couple walks off.

"Yes!" you proclaim, "God is here among us! And for three hours, you've *seen* Him—reigning as the head of His church. And now Mayor Lockhart has just quoted the very verse I was reading this morning in First Corinthians:

> But if everyone is proclaiming God's message when some unbeliever or ordinary person comes in, he will be convinced of his sin by all he hears, his secret thoughts will be brought into the open, and he will bow down and worship God, confessing, *Truly, God is here among you.*

"Thank you, your honor, for being obedient to the voice of the Spirit and speaking your heart to us. In turn, you have opened up a thousand hearts here to you.

"It also sounds like you're inclined to open a wider door of opportunity for us. If you do, I think we're ready to walk through it. God can solve many of the social problems the city faces. We'd also love to quadruple the Lord's visible presence here by filling the city arena every month if you give us that chance."

You look around the room and up into the bleachers. Many are nodding their heads. Everyone is looking at you with a sense of anticipation, as if some giant step were about to be taken across an invisible chasm. You feel in your spirit that now is the time for a major group decision—but how, with 1,200 people?

The spark of an idea starts to flicker across your consciousness. You take a deep breath and begin, "You know, folks, until tonight, I never thought of myself as even faintly resembling an apostle. That always seemed to be a pretty lofty word. But one thing apostles are is a catalyst for action, and, well, here I am, standing in front of you at a critical point in your history.

"God has challenged us in a dozen ways tonight to consider doing the difficult—or the impossible. So are you ready to talk about it?" Rumbles of assent and *Amens!* fill the room.

"OK, here's the challenge I think the Lord is giving us. For the next five minutes, I want us all to talk with those around us. Ask each other two questions. First is, *Are you ready to take responsibility for the spiritual condition of this town, to roll up your sleeves and establish beachheads for the kingdom in every needy area of the city?* And second, *Assuming we can get a date for the arena in a month or two, are you ready to make good use of it—by filling it up?*

"Those are tall questions. But I think the time is past for us to be waiting for the government to solve all our problems for us. The time is here to bless and send out couples from our home groups to plant new churches by the dozen every week, calling people to turn from sin and toward the Savior. Are we ready to move together on this? Five minutes. I'll signal when you've got thirty seconds left. Ready? Do it!"

The sound level builds quickly to a solid roar—and continues for the full five minutes.

As people drift back to their chairs, you pick up the mike. "I know most of us already have full plates. I didn't come here tonight to twist your arm. This is your decision; it's not a vote, so we won't raise our hands. But if God is leading you to take these two steps of faith, would you please just stand?"

Silently, the crowd stands as one man. You can't see even one person still seated.

You turn slowly in a full circle, nodding your head. "You have spoken! You have spoken in unity, and the God of all power will bless you with His presence." You return to your seat.

For half a minute, there is complete silence and a powerful stillness as God wraps up the evening by speaking to each heart. Then, as though the Holy Spirit had spoken an *amen*, the people quietly gather their belongings to leave.

Some minutes later, as you walk slowly out the door with Max, you raise your umbrellas to ward off the warm summer rain. You stop at the curb and turn around to face him, your umbrellas almost touching as you watch the faces of people leaving the gym.

"Maxwell, old buddy, I'm very glad you didn't give up on me in those early days."

"And I'm glad you kept praying for us. None of us knew what we were doing, really. Maybe we still don't. But we can sure see what God is doing now."

"Yes. He's building a citywide church that knows how to work together and let Him be the head of His body so that ..."

You suddenly realize that Max isn't listening to you. His mouth is open, and he's looking over your shoulder at something in the parking lot. You turn around to see what it might be, but you can't spot anything other than cars and people.

In silence, Max puts his hand on your shoulder and stands beside you, watching.

You glance at him. "What is it? All I see is—"

And then it dawns on you. A long line of cars is going home, lights on, heading toward a new life in the world. And nearly every one has its windows wide open.

Appendix One

Invitation to Life

In my hand I hold a newspaper clipping, a faded photo from 1963. I look at it from time to time to remind myself of what love really is, and even after all these years it brings tears to my eyes.

The central figure in the crowded scene is a pretty blond girl, nicely dressed, clutching a shiny black handbag and wearing atop her hair a perky bow of that era, a satin ribbon I imagine as blue, perhaps a favorite little touch of her boyfriend.

But the girl seems to be sobbing in anguish. She is bent low and leaning heavily on the arm of an usher. The caption explains:

> *Paulette Lewis, 15, was near collapse at the funeral yesterday in Santa Monica of David Brimley, 17, her sweetheart, killed Sunday while saving her life. He was hit by a car as he shoved her to safety.*

When a car is bearing down on you fast enough to kill you, you don't have time to review your priorities; you can only act on what is settled firmly in your heart. And this much is sure: David loved Paulette more than he loved life itself.

Don't Let True Love Pass You By

Becoming a real Christian is not a matter of changing your theological opinions, cleaning up your act, or joining a church. It's a grateful response to Someone who loves you very, very much and died in your place.

Yes, there is a price to be paid. Getting saved does require more than a simple, *Hey, thanks, Jesus. The cross was a nice gesture on Your part. I guess we're cool now, huh?* You definitely do have to accept Christ as your Lord, based on a deep understanding that He is Lord of *all* life, that He is able to save you from death (because of His sacrifice on the cross), and that He is the eternal Son of the ever-living Father who dwells in unapproachable light.

When you switch your allegiance to the Father and His only-born Son, the Father sends His Spirit to live and reign in your heart.* Thus you "participate in the divine nature" (II Peter 1:4), and that's completely incompatible with kicking the dog, abusing your wife, or wasting your life on TV or other useless pursuits. But notice the order of events: You don't reform yourself to be worthy of heaven on your own merits; you come to God as you are and let *Him* clean you up. Major difference.

What I'm trying to say here is that correct belief and repentance from sin are essential for getting into heaven, but the central drama is your heart's response to someone who loved you so passionately that He willingly stepped down from heaven, slogged around in the mud with us earthlings, and finally let Himself get hung from a cross when He could so easily have called down a hundred thousand angels to incinerate the entire Roman Empire.

Most people have the vague idea that there's safety in numbers, that they'll glide safely into heaven someday if they're above average compared to others. Indeed, the Bible does say a lot about good people going to heaven and bad ones to hell. But don't confuse cause and effect: It's talking about good deeds that spring from a genuine, committed <u>relationship</u> to the Son of God.

Jesus himself was quite plain in Matthew 7:14: "Small is the gate and narrow is the road that leads to life, and *few* there be that find it." That's major scary. And nine verses later, He speaks the most horrifying words in the Bible, words I pray you'll never hear, words He says He will speak to most of the human race on Judgment Day: "I never knew you. Go away from me ... !"

---

* This is often a truly astonishing experience. Until you've given yourself to Christ, you can't believe what it feels like to wake up the next morning and find that your most basic attitudes and feelings have shifted. It's like you're suddenly a different person.

Open Your Hand

The last four thousand years of human history have come down to this: Countless events have been woven together into a long scarlet cord, which I now put in your hands.

All the great ones—from Sargon to Socrates, from Abraham to Alexander, from Caesar to Stalin, from Moses to Mother Teresa—have had a hand in history, weaving their little threads of bane or blessing into the greater cord of life on earth. Now it is your turn to take that cord firmly in your hands and decide what kind of color you will add to it.

Most of the threads are mere wisps of dull neutral, scarcely visible at all. But many are bright with love and hope, a delight to the eyes—and some are dark indeed. From where you stand today, you can scan the whole cord and see the rise and fall of nations from Sumer to the USSR, the flow of ideas from the crudest writing to the Genome Project, the heights and depths of man's morals from the abolition of slavery to the unspeakable evils of torture rooms. In short, you know the difference between good and bad because you've seen it work out in world history—and in your own life.

Why Scarlet?

Every thread of vivid red reminds us, *This is the color of life.*

Since the day Christ was crucified, the cord has grown brighter—because in that supreme sacrifice the Lamb of God canceled the ancient law, "The soul that sins shall surely die," and on the first Easter morning, the dominion of death was shattered at last by the power of the life of God. Death could not hold the Lord Jesus in the tomb because He didn't deserve to be there in the first place. He died not for His own sins, but for yours.

Since that day, His scarlet blood and pure white forgiveness have flowed out to the wide world—and now they have reached you. So let me ask …

What Will You Do with the Greatest Gift in History?

Membership in the kingdom of God is a gift with more facets than the Hope Diamond. At the risk of producing a mishmash, I'll try to squeeze its biggest blessings down to one page for you.

First off, *you never die!* Your response to God's offer is a matter of life or death, and a life that goes on for billions and trillions of years is something far too great to pass up.

I'm not talking about the cartoonist's picture of people sitting on a cloud and strumming a harp. That would be dull as mush. I'm talking about you sitting next to the Lord Jesus Christ and ruling along with Him (Revelation 3:21), taking a part in the adventure of developing and directing new worlds our science fiction writers never dreamed of. Life doesn't come to an end in heaven, it starts there. Jesus referred to entering heaven as *entering life.*

When you take the big step of committing yourself 100% to being under the lordship of Jesus Christ, He forgives all your sins—past, present, and future—and accepts you as part of His family. This is wonderful enough by itself, but it also gives you an "insider" status with God which, over time, enables you to get more and more of your prayers answered as you become more in tune with Him and figure out what's good to ask for and what isn't. *Hint:* Start small and work your way up.

Salvation Is Transformation

When you come to the Lord and trade in your old life, He gives you a new one—a fresh start, like a heart transplant, like being born all over again.

You'll soon find you have a new direction and new purpose for living. Fears, anger, bitterness, addictions, or other problems that perhaps may have crippled you will crumble away as the Holy Spirit renews your heart and mind day after day, year after year. He will also open up solutions to your external problems, such as those in your family, work, school, or finances. (But don't expect *instant* solutions for everything.)

Your new life will be punctuated with miracles—most small, some larger. Expect them. Ask for them. Ask God to enable you to overcome temptations, pet sins, and other problems that trip you up. Ask Him for the power to do things you never thought possible. He will give it to you.

If you have been plagued by feelings of emptiness, you will now find your heart filled with the happiness and peace of a child of the King. Of course, you'll still be subject to most of the headaches and heartaches that civilization dishes out so generously to all of us, but now life will be different: With encouragement and help from your believing brothers and sisters, you'll find yourself crossing new frontiers, being fulfilled in new ways, dreaming new dreams, and perhaps even recovering some old dreams you had given up as lost. The daily headaches will be eclipsed by the daily triumphs.

Your new adventures may be part of large and exciting moves of God. I pray they will. But at the very least, they will be your chance to grasp that scarlet cord and weave into it the brilliant, blazing colors that can only come from the hand of one who stands next to God.

It's good to start your new life with a prayer. Your own words are best, but if you are stuck for thoughts, you may speak aloud to the Father something like this:

God of mercy, Lord of life, eternal Creator of the farthest stars ...

My prayers have come to Your majestic throne before, but today I come to You with the most serious of all matters: my commitment and obedience to You and my purpose and identity in this world.

Father, I declare to You without reservation three things ...

*You are infinitely holy, and I merit none of Your mercy or grace. I deserve only death.

*At the cross, You showed your great love to me by paying the ultimate penalty for my sins, putting to death Your own Son as a sacrifice so that *I* would not face death. I love You, too, and gratefully accept Your forgiveness. I ask You to make Your home in my heart and mind as Lord, forever and ever.

*Through your great power, You raised Your Son from the grave to eternal life. I repent of my sin and eagerly and thankfully turn to You, asking You to send Your Holy Spirit to come live in me eternally and give me that same power—to do good instead of evil all my days.

May it please You, Lord, to bless me as I begin to become a true 24/7 disciple of Your Son, the Lord Jesus Christ. In Your lovingkindness and compassion, please give me wisdom and strength to solve the problems in my life and achieve the worthy dreams and goals in my heart. And if some of these things are beyond my ability, then I ask You to take care of them by Your own mighty hand. I cannot be my own savior; today I trust You instead, looking in faith toward a life filled with Your protection and power, now and always.

I pray in the name of Your Son, and for the sake of His kingdom. Amen!

Appendix Two

How did we ever get into this mess in the first place?

Trivia quiz: Which of the following are based on the New Testament?

- ☐ programmed services
- ☐ the CEO pastor
- ☐ choirs
- ☐ Welch's grape juice
- ☐ starting at 11 A.M.
- ☐ sermons
- ☐ buildings with fat mortgages
- ☐ stained-glass windows
- ☐ vaulted ceilings
- ☐ jazzy costumes
- ☐ seminaries
- ☐ denominations
- ☐ dressing up for church
- ☐ sitting silently in rows
- ☐ divisions based on pet doctrines
- ☐ Sunday school lessons
- ☐ Rudolph and the Easter Bunny

Awwww, that was too easy, wasn't it? You already knew those things all crept in *long* after the Bible was finished. Most of them came after Emperor Constantine issued his Edict of Milan in 313, making Christianity legal (and profitable).

A harder question: Now shut your eyes and try to imagine today's church *without* any of the above bric-a-brac. What would it look like?

Tough, isn't it? About all that's left is you and the Lord and some good friends having a great time together! Well, that was the early church: just Jesus and singing and swapping stories around the fireplace and sharing your lives (and of course, dinner).

In other words, **almost everything in today's church is foreign to the Bible!**

That doesn't mean it's all bad. Just distracting, perhaps. Or expensive. Or maybe a colossal, monumental, hippopotamic waste of time.

At the least, we can say this with confidence: *The traditional, Western, institutional church of today rests solidly upon a foundation of digressions from Scripture.*

Now for the handful who are still with me, let us explore the obvious next question: Where did the Gospel Train leave the tracks? Who left the back door open so the skunks could wander in? When did the first guy line up the chairs so everyone would face *him*? In leaner terms, **Who's to blame for this fiasco?**

First, let me recant my former views. In my last book, *The Open Church,* I pretty much blamed everything on Constantine, the first "Christian" emperor, the man who began pouring government money into the church, sparking a non-stop church construction program and transmuting the body of Christ into a Roman institution that could be *managed*—made to sit up, speak, roll over, and play dead. Mostly play dead.

I've come to see that Constantine was indeed the final nail in the coffin, but that gangrene (or perhaps rigor mortis) had already set in much earlier.

Perhaps the simplest approach to this puzzle is people's response to Jesus' teaching, where He was saying ...

The kingdom of God is like a mustard seed ... or a lost coin or sheep or hidden treasure or ...

The Lord was getting blank looks. A *lot* of them.

So He kept grinding away: The kingdom is like fertile soil ... like a wedding feast ... like a field of wheat and weeds ... like a lump of yeast ... like servants given talents ... like ten virgins ... like a netful of good and bad fish ... like ripe grain ... and on and on.

They obviously weren't getting it. The only kingdom they could understand was the longed-for military machine led by a Messiah who would drive out the hated Romans.

Ironically, that Messiah himself was trying <u>so</u> hard to get the point across: the fact that the real kingdom would be run by God, not by men; the battle would be in the heart, not in a field; and the weapon of conquest would be love, not a sword.

212

For perhaps three years He kept hammering the point. And finally, when His task was done, when He had died and risen and spent an additional forty days talking mostly about the kingdom, He gathered the Eleven on the Mount of Olives.

Sensing that something major was at hand, they said to Him, "OK, Lord, so *now* are you going to restore the kingdom to Israel?" (Acts 1:6)

I have this private theory—which nobody agrees with—that Jesus wasn't actually planning his ascension right at that moment, but when He heard that, he said, "Father, beam me up *before I start banging heads together!*"

The Basic Problem: WE WANT A KING!

You can see that the problem was around a long time before Christ.

God's original blueprint was that *all* His people would be responsible followers with a personal relationship to Him and direct access to His holy presence. One of the highest points for Yahweh in the Old Testament was in 1447 B.C.,[1] just two days before He gave the Ten Commandments. In a moment of joy and excitement He said to Israel, "You shall be my prized possession, dearer to me than all other peoples! For all the earth is mine, and you shall be for me a *kingdom of priests!*" (Exodus 19:6)

Did He ever get that kingdom of priests? I think not. He has always had a few outstanding giants of the faith here and there, but only in our day (see chapter three on "The New Saints") is He starting to see the emergence of a *broad spectrum* of disciples *worldwide* with the authority, power, understanding, and sense of responsibility of people with special access to the Holy of Holies. (I think especially of those with the gifts of apostle, prophet, intercession, and miracles, who are driving the new move of God.)

Whatever hope God had for a kingdom of priests got put on ice 407 years later when Israel told Samuel flat out: "No! We want a king over us, that we may be like all the other nations, with a king to lead us and march in front of us and fight our battles." (I Samuel 8:19-20)

Whenever God's people reject ...

- His offer of freedom under His direct lordship, as in I Samuel 8:7
- their birthright of priesthood
- the burden of thinking and acting for themselves
- the work of self-governance

... there will always be a few who are all too eager to jump into the vacuum and take the roles of kings, archbishops, pastors, etc. But the fault is not entirely theirs.

Sure, there are a few pastors who are control freaks. And as Bible teachers (who should know better), they come in for their share of the blame. But the great majority are simply trying to do the job they were asked to do by their flock. The fact that their gallant efforts are inherently doomed by the unbiblical job description they received is not their fault—nor does that fact even dawn on most of them.

Even the Lord Jesus Christ, the Son of God, was unable to break this king/peon mentality among his followers. So He sent His Holy Spirit to "teach us all things," including how to be a royal priesthood.

The Spirit was more successful in this, and it appears that the early church understood Him widely—yet probably not in depth. Before the ink was dry on the last book of the New Testament (in 94 or 95), spiritual problems were erupting in various congregations across what now is Turkey. See Jesus' letters to the seven churches in Revelation 2 and 3.[2]

The worst of the lot—which Jesus said He *hated*—was a movement called Nicolaitanism. The word comes from the Greek *nikos* (to conquer or control) and *laos* (people). It cannot be proven that the main flaw of this bunch was elevating one leader over everybody else; but that seems a good bet. Whatever the Nicolaitans may have written to explain their beliefs got trashed pretty early in the game, so the only clue we have (other than their name) is a few thundering denunciations by their opponents, who accused them of licentious behavior. Of course, licentious behavior is exactly what you get when you elevate one person to be *the* president or overseer or *sola pastora*, the lone "holy man," the one true priest who is close to God. That simply secularizes everyone else.

But enough of these generalities. Let's get down to specifics.

Let's Name Names

The early church fathers were great men of God. Most died as martyrs, before their time, yet they rank among the most notable saints of any age.

Their one tragic failing was that they departed from the Apostles' teaching in church matters, pared down the delicate concept of servant leadership (John 3:13-17), and brought in the old mentality of *Give us a king.*

On their behalf, though, I'll first present the main reasons for their lapse in judgment:

1. They had big trouble: Gnosticism! The most popular heresy of that day (217 forms by one count), Gnosticism threatened to take over Christianity. In some areas, there were more heretics than Christians!

2. The scattered but recurrent persecution by the Roman government created a felt need for a strong central leadership to hold the church together.

3. By about 150, the books of the New Testament had been *mostly* agreed upon at the grass roots level. All the books had been copied widely. But until 367 there was no official, *universally* accepted text to appeal to in disputes. (The greater blame for today's mess lies with theologians of the third and fourth centuries, who should have reviewed the church fathers' actions in light of the full New Testament and said, "Hey, we made some mistakes." But by that time, all initiative had passed from laymen's hands, and the clergy hierarchy juggernaut was unstoppable.)

Because of these things, the church allowed control-minded elders to elevate themselves above the others, becoming "bishops" or "presidents" of some big-city congregations.

The first major spokesman for this kind of thing was ...

Clement

Writing probably in the same year that John wrote the Revelation (A.D. 95), Clement of Rome wrote his own epistle to the Corinthians, in which he declared his opinion that:

> The high priest has been given his own special services, the priests have been assigned their own place, and the Levites [meaning *deacons*] have their special ministrations enjoined on them. The layman is bound by the ordinances of the laity.[3]

This kind of caste system did not exist in 95 in very many places outside of Clement's imagination. Clement was part of a tiny, elite segment of the Rome church, the well-to-do who were comfortable with dragging in Roman ideology and mixing it with the Jewish Levitical priesthood to create a Christian hierarchy (with himself at or near the top, as Bishop of Rome). It is fairly likely Clement even had connections to the emperor.

Though his views were way out of step with the great majority of believers at that time, they did eventually grow and prevail, producing the Roman Catholic Church. His split between clergy and laity was like fastening the wrong button at the top of your shirt; by the time you get to the bottom, everything's out of kilter. Think of the traditional church as a mile-long shirt with 10,000 mismatched buttons.

Ignatius

Roughly 20 years later, the bishop of Antioch, now known to the world as Saint Ignatius, was condemned to be fed to the lions in the amphitheater in Rome (about 117).

On the way to Rome, he composed letters to seven churches. They contained many helpful ideas but also began to fine-tune Clement's hierarchical system:

> Let the laity be subject to the deacons; the deacons to the presbyters [elders]; the presbyters to the bishop; the bishop to Christ, even as He is to the Father.[4]

> Your reverend presbytery is tuned to the Bishop as strings to the lyre... . We should regard the Bishop as the Lord himself ...[5]

> I advise you to always act in godly concord with the Bishop, presiding as the counterpart of God... . you must do nothing without the Bishop and the presbyters.[6]

> ... it is not permitted to baptize or hold a love-feast independently of the Bishop. But whatever he approves, that is also well-pleasing to God.[7]

Already you can hear a tone that is far, far removed from the New Testament epistles. Ignatius seems to have coined the term *monarchical bishop* as part of a sanctified power grab that, in Jim Petersen's phrase, "put the average believer out of business in terms of his or her ministry in the gospel. The freedom experienced in the New Testament period vanished as the authority of the bishops grew."[8]

Note Ignatius' two biggest innovations: The elders, who were supposed to oversee the *general* affairs of an open, interactive fellowship of saints, are now "bishops" in charge of every *meeting* of an institutional hierarchy. Also, baptism has been ripped from the hands of laymen and locked under the tight control of the priests, a move that has not one breath of support in the New Testament.

All this only 20 years after the New Testament was completed! It was a fast slide.

Irenaeus

As bishop of Lyon in France, Irenaeus (c. 130-212) became alarmed at distortions of the gospel. So he wrote a treatise that played a new trump card against heretics—or anyone with the nerve to dispute a matter of theology: *apostolic succession.*

His idea was to refute opponents not on the basis of Scripture or logic, but on the fact that they couldn't trace their spiritual heritage back to Christ. He stated that the Lord taught the Twelve faithfully, and they taught others likewise, and so on. Thus, if you were not ordained and approved by a pedigreed bishop, your views were "held in suspicion." Irenaeus triumphantly proclaimed, "We do put to confusion all those who ... assemble in unauthorized meetings ..."[9]

The idea had merit—and still does. Innovators with views floating in the outer ectoplasm, who had no connections with true Bible believers, deserved to be suspect. But notice how the idea collapses in two instances:

1. If your bishop drifted into theological error, you had a choice: You could become a heretic by following his mistakes, or you could become a heretic by splitting off from him and starting a new congregation without his blessing.

2. If you had to move to some town 50 or 100 miles from your home church—far enough to be out of touch—and there were no Christians, you were in a fix. Suppose you started reaching out, bringing people into the kingdom. In that situation, you could not gather them to meet as a group because your meetings would have been *unlawful*—no matter what you taught!*

Apostolic succession is itself a heresy (of ecclesiology or orthopraxis). By its light, the ministry of the apostle Paul (for one example) was illegitimate. In later centuries, the "right of succession" was sold to the highest bidder, and sometimes clergy even murdered each other for it.

Tertullian

The brilliant, fiery bishop of Carthage, Tertullian (c. 160 to c. 230) wrote a lot of great things. In some ways he was an amazingly independent thinker, but in other ways he was grease to the slide into centralized hierarchy—never more so than in this foggy line:

> It is the authority of the Church, and the honour which has acquired sanctity through the joint session of the Order, which has established the difference between the Order and the laity.[10]

---

* Let me see, now, how does that verse go? "Wherever two or three are gathered in My name, there am I—if the bishop authorizes Me to show up."

Translation: "In the matter of dividing the church into clergy and laity, we're making this up as we go along. We are now our own authority."

Also, by about 200, the clergy stranglehold on baptism reached this point of absurdity:

> The unwed should be deferred, for temptation is waiting for them... . Let them wait until they marry or until they are strong enough for sexual abstinence.[11] (my paraphrase)

So if you were single, your baptism (which also meant your *salvation*, they said) was on hold for years (or decades) until you got hitched—or somehow managed to con the bishop into thinking you were gifted with eternal immunity to hanky-panky. What bilge!

This sort of theological compost smothers the naive notion, often voiced by clergy today, that open fellowships are dangerous because they might fall into heresy without the watchful oversight of a professional pastor. MAKE A NOTE: Heresies are not born out of a tiny group of laymen earnestly studying the Bible, but by a church hotshot with a crowd of followers who will swallow anything he feeds them.*

Cyprian

Cyprian died only 12 years after his conversion in 247, but ten of those years were spent as archbishop of Carthage in North Africa. He wrote voluminously, even though for much of his reign he was forced to work underground by the fierce persecution of Decian and Valerian—who eventually caught and beheaded him.

Reared as a Roman aristocrat, he became the staunchest defender of the unity of the church in the first 300 years. Yet he insisted on "equal dignity" with the pope and addressed him as "Dearest brother ..." He felt that "No one should make himself a bishop of bishops."[12]

A local deacon wrote of Cyprian:

> Neither poverty nor pain broke him down. The dreadful suffering of his own body did not shake his firmness... .
> His house was open to every comer. No widow returned from him with an empty apron. No blind man was unguided by him ... So much sanctity and grace beamed from his face that it confounded the minds of the beholders.[13]

---

* That is why much of the power of the Reformation came through Gutenberg and Caxton putting the Bible in the hands of laymen.

I am moved with awe by the greatness and humility of this man of God. Yet I am dismayed by the fact that his response to the persecution and schism of the church was to encourage further institutionalization and fall back on apostolic succession, even pushing it one more deadly step:

> How can he be esteemed a pastor, who succeeds to no one, but begins from himself? For the true shepherd remains and presides over the church of God by successive ordination. Therefore, the other one becomes a stranger and a profane person, an enemy of the Lord's peace.[14]

In other words, he branded as a heretic anyone who could not meet the challenge of Tertullian: "Produce the original records of your churches; unfold the roll of your bishops from the beginning."[15] (my paraphrase)

Cyprian's final verdict: "He cannot have God for his father who does not have the Church for his mother."[16] In today's terms, does that mean Protestants cannot be saved? Exactly that.*

Augustine

As the greatest Christian thinker of antiquity, Augustine could perhaps be called the founder of Christian theology. He harmonized Christian theology with Greek philosophy, which was either the greatest achievement or worst disaster ever to befall Christian thought, take your pick, and you'll be right in either case.

Augustine's influence on Calvin and Luther was so heavy that he has also been called the father of Protestantism, though his conflict with the Donatist heretics positioned him forever as the greatest champion of loyalty to Roman Catholicism.** While bishop of Hippo in North Africa for the last 35 years of his life (395-430), he became the foremost apologist for the new, laity-smothering, Constantinian "establishment" church.

Again, I am not trying to blacken church history here. I'm simply focusing solely on the church's worst aberrations. With that reminder, and begging your pardon, I shall skip lightly past all Augustine's voluminous and helpful writings and take a glance at the main damage he caused.

---

* Withal, I deeply appreciate the change in stress of Vatican II and Pope John Paul II from calling us "our *separated* brethren" to "our separated *brethren*." Let's hope this shift finds its way to the grass roots in every nation.

** His argument against the Donatists was basically, *Just because we're wrong, that doesn't mean you have a right to leave Holy Mother Church.*

Augustine blended church and state, and in the process became the apostle of persecution for the next 1,400 years. Emperor Theodosius had proclaimed Rome a Christian empire in February of 380, compelling everyone to become a Christian, and the slaughter started the next year, with the first executions for heresy.[17] The empire had started that century with perhaps 5% true Christians, but the phony influx of official "Christians" by the end of the century raised that to almost 100%—the difficulty being that almost no one got saved; they just diluted the church to the watery condition you see today.

Under Augustine, the church ramped up from counterculture to dominant culture. And Augustine didn't shrink from advocating force and torture to get compliance. It was Clement's and Ignatius' 300-year-old hierarchical model come full term, with the priesthood now backed by the supreme army of the world.

Jim Petersen aptly summarizes this hair-raising shift:

> Thus, according to Augustine, the state needed the church to transform society, and the church needed the state to enforce that transformation. That was a fearsome arrangement. Nonetheless, it endured over the next thousand years as the foundational concept of the Middle Ages, a period often characterized by despondent passivity. Consumed with anxiety over their eternal destinies, and believing that the church held control over them, people resigned themselves to awaiting their fate... .
>
> Supported by Augustinian theology, the clergy exerted unbelievable power throughout the Middle Ages. Heaven and hell were in their hands. Thus, not only had the average believer forfeited ministry to the clergy, but access to personal salvation was in the hands of the clergy as well. The possibility that God's people might function [in world-changing freedom] had been destroyed. The average believer was encircled by the institutional church.[18]

The total subjugation of the layman marked the end of Act I of the Christian drama. For the next 1,100 years, open Christianity was banished to private homes and forest clearings filled with children of God eager to enjoy true fellowship, share their lives, sing together, learn the Bible, and worship unoppressed by the state-backed clergy.

Nowhere to Go But Down

It's not only lonely at the top, it's slippery.

In 410, only 30 years after the state started shoving the Christian religion down everyone's throats, the Visigoths looted Rome. In 430, Augustine died of a fever while the Vandals were besieging his city of Hippo, and 25 years after his death, they destroyed Rome. In 476, the last emperor fell, and Rome became, for a short while, little more than a cow pasture.

With 1,500 years of hindsight, it's easy to moralize about the fall of Rome. But surely some blame must fall on the weak emperors, the weak citizens (a subjugated mass of make-believe believers), and the decaying church—especially the church.

When ordinary people began putting leaders on a pedestal, the leaders responded by laying this authority base for themselves:

1. There are now two categories of Christian believers, clergy and laity. The job description of clergy is to help the laity—as in, "We're from the Vatican, and we're here to help you."

2. If you're a layman, your job is to observe all rites and rituals and do as you're told.

3. We clergy are above the Bible. It means whatever we say it means, and we're never wrong.

Starting from that untouchable pinnacle, gravity took over. Corrupt beliefs and practices sprouted like dandelions:[19]

Year	Tradition
140	Pope Hyginus declares clergy distinct from laity
150	Sprinkling instead of immersion
200	Clergy called "priests"
200	Origen brings in Greek syllogistic theology, starting with Plato
200	Former pagan orators bring sermons into the church
211	Prayers for the dead mentioned by Tertullian
250	The perpetual virginity of Mary
250	Infant baptism (becomes dogma in 416)
258	Holy water mentioned by Cyprian
270	Monasticism
320	Wax candles and incense
320	Pastors salaried (by the state)
375	Veneration of angels and dead "saints"
375	Use of images and icons
378	Damascus I becomes "Pontifex Maximus." In 451, Leo I takes the title of "pope" and confers it on all previous bishops of Rome posthumously. In 606, Boniface III becomes "Universal Bishop."
380	Christianity compulsory
394	The mass
402	Innocent I calls himself "Ruler of the Church of God"
405	List of forbidden books (the most formal list published in 1559)
420	Purgatory proposed

431	Exaltation of Mary as "the Mother of God"
476	Indulgences for the dead
500	Priestly dress
526	Extreme unction
590	Purgatory confirmed
600	Prayers directed to Mary, dead saints, and angels
709	"Kiss my foot!" becomes more than an insult, as people begin kissing the pope's foot
787	Veneration/worship of images and relics authorized
819	Feast of the assumption of Mary
858	Wearing of papal crown (Nicolas I)
859 lish	*Pseudo-Isidorian Decretals* (forged documents used to establish papal claims to temporal powers—biggest forgery in history)
869	Western and Eastern churches (Rome and Constantinople) mutually excommunicate each other
995	Dead "saints" canonized
1045	Gregory VI elected pope after paying Pope Benedict IX to resign
1074	Celibacy of the priesthood
1080	Reading of the Bible in a common language first forbidden (other actions: 1199, 1229, 1233, 1408, 1564, 1816, etc.)
1184	The Inquisition begins, eventually killing many millions
1190	Indulgences sold (forgivene$$ of in)
1208	The Rosary—praying with beads
1215	Transubstantiation (wafer and wine changed into body and blood of Christ by priestly incantation)
1215	Confession to a priest instead of God
1220	Adoration of the wafer (host)
1245	Limbo invented for dead, unbaptized infants
1300	Stained glass becomes popular
1342	Treasury of Merits (credit for good deeds made transferable)
1414	The cup forbidden to the people at communion
1484	Innocent VIII (those guys knew how to pick names) orders extermination of the Waldenses
1546	Council of Trent affirms Latin as language of the mass, decrees absolute power of the pope over the whole earth, gives tradition equal authority with the Scriptures, proposes seminaries
1547	Rejection of justification by faith alone
1564	Immorality in southern Europe deemed to be caused by nude statues, so orders issued to retrofit fig leaves everywhere
1572	Solemn mass celebrated for the St. Bartholomew's Day massacre of 60,000 Huguenots
1854	Immaculate Conception (Mary born sinless)
1870	Papal infallibility

1931   Mary named "mediatrix" (gives favors not granted by God—
        and faster than Jesus!)
1950   Assumption of Mary to heaven
1954   Mary named Queen of Heaven

And thus did the original shape of the church disappear under 18 centuries of ecclesiastical pixie dust.

Did the Flame Ever Die?

No.

Even under the heaviest persecution by a distorted Christian establishment, there was never a time when open Christianity was totally extinguished. Amazingly, there was always a remnant of believers somewhere trying to live free, to:

• worship God spontaneously, from their hearts, rather than in the codified words of frozen liturgy
  • share their joys and struggles rather than sitting in silence
  • confess their sins to one another rather than to a priest
  • discuss what they knew of Scripture or apostolic tradition
  • eat together in homes, often sharing communion without a priest
  • survive spies, pressure, persecution, and murder.

Adolph Schmidt, possibly the greatest authority on the history of Christian dogma, has said:

> During the twelve centuries that went before the posting of Luther's theses, it never lacked for an attempt to do away with the State Church/priest church and to reinstitute the apostolic congregations.[20]

Quite a statement—and he is not alone. I should point out that although most freedom-seeking groups were not what we would call full-blown house church movements, most shared several of the six goals listed above.

The greatest alternative to Rome was the vigorous Celtic Christianity, which starting from the north did much more to evangelize Europe than Catholicism starting from the south. During the darkest of the Dark Ages, Celts kept the fire of the gospel burning.

The records of most non-Roman groups, however, have not survived. Evidence of their very existence is often like the faint tracks left by atomic fragments from a particle accelerator. The strongest evidence is indirect: the Catholic reaction to them. Historian Leonard Verduin said:

The medieval church of Christendom, the Catholic Church, created a special order. They were known as the Dominicans. The reason they created them was they thought that would be a way in which they could offset the influence of the underground church, the remnant. And so they did everything that the others did. They wore the same clothing. They went two by two. They went preaching out in the countryside. Their only difference was that they tried to support the central church, whereas the remnant tried to replace that central church. But that there always were these people is beyond any doubt.[21]

Dominican-style competition worked nicely. But diplomatic threats were sometimes faster and cheaper. And if neither worked, brute force always kept the numbers of "heretics" down to manageable proportions—that is, until ...

The Dawn of the Reformation

Like the moles in the arcade game, underground, holy-living gatherings kept popping up—inside and outside of Catholicism—and kept getting hammered into oblivion.[22]

Eventually, though, the System became so brimful of corruption that it began to spring leaks. Inside the Church, new orders, monasteries, and movements broke forth, while outside, a few brave souls willing to be martyrs arose here and there, each setting new standards of grace and glory. Prior to Luther, the most noted were:

• Waldo, a wealthy merchant of Lyons, France, who in 1176 sold everything and led many followers to join him in preaching in the countryside. The Waldensians, the "Poor Men of Lyon," hit hard at corruption in the Church and things like prayers for the dead. They insisted that any righteous man could hear confessions and celebrate the eucharist (communion). They even sent women out to preach, including a few ex-harlots. Pope Lucius III excommunicated them in 1184 as heretics, and they were persecuted nearly to extinction.

• John Wycliffe, "The Morning Star of the Reformation," who translated the Bible into English and sent out poor, less-than-educated men to preach on the highways and byways of England. He also stomped on indulgences, pilgrimages, masses for the dead, transubstantiation, and other excesses, and even suggested that the pope was the Antichrist. This did not set well in Rome. But he was lucky: The Great Schism that produced two rival popes from 1378-1415 left them too busy hurling curses at each other to pay the usual attention to heretics. He died in peace, thanks to the protection of Edward III. His followers, the Lollards, grew to a point where half of England was either Lollard or pro-Lollard, but then were persecuted down to manageable numbers.

• Jan Hus, a very popular Bohemian-Czech reformer, who wanted to clean up the church, restore free preaching of the gospel, and allow communion wine for the laity. He was promised safe passage to Rome, then betrayed and burned at the stake in 1415.

• William Tyndale, who produced both a Greek New Testament with notes and an excellent new English Bible. Appalled at clergy ignorance of the Bible, he taught at Oxford and Cambridge and lit fires across Britain for the study of God's Word. The church tried to straighten him out with no success. One supposed theologian sent to convert him made a remark so stupid that Tyndale replied, famously, "If God spares my life, ere many years I will cause that a boy that driveth the plough shall know more of the Scriptures than thou dost." From about age 30 on, he lived in exile, on the move as a hunted man, and was strangled and burned in 1536.

And Then Came Luther

Reformers finally tired of being slaughtered and began to cut deals with discontented kings and princes, becoming their mouthpieces to criticize the church in return for protection.

Such was the case with Frederick the Wise, Duke of Saxony, under whose wing a young Augustinian monk named Martin Luther was allowed to take refuge. Without Frederick, Luther would have been turned into a little pile of carbon by age 34. But Frederick had the biggest army in Europe and was royally peeved at not having been made pope. It was a marriage made in heaven.

Luther's big gripe was the sale of indulgences, which had gone way beyond bingo games or even Girl Scout cookies as a means of raising funds for Holy Mother Church. So on Halloween of 1517, he pulled off history's biggest trick-or-treat stunt by nailing to the Wittenberg church door a list of 95 points he wanted to debate, and they were all about indulgences.[23] Unknown to Luther, enterprising publishers copied and began printing his 95 theses all over Europe. The rest is history.

Luther set up a Protestant state church. He popularized the pulpit and the 11 A.M. worship hour. And he invented the biggest success secret of the evangelical church: the pastor's wife.

The Lutheran church brought a new dimension to Christianity, a whole new culture. The changes he wrought were so broad that they raise the question, "Where did he get all those ideas?" Verduin answers:

> There is conclusive evidence that all the reformers—Luther and Zwingli and Calvin ... knew about the remnant. They knew its thought pattern and they knew its way of living, and they loved it. They were going to try to copy it. I find Luther saying things early in his career that couldn't possibly have come from any other source but from the underground church.
>
> The same is true of Zwingli... . Calvin was also converted to the underground church first."[24]

The clearest example is Luther's proposal in 1526 of a "third order of service" to complement the big services in Latin and German (which he disdained as public shows for the ignorant and unconverted):

> The third kind of service should be a truly evangelical order and should not be held in a public place for all sorts of people. But those who are seriously determined to be Christians and who profess the gospel with hand and mouth should sign their names and meet apart in a house somewhere to pray, to read, to baptize, to receive the sacrament, and to do other Christian work.[25]

Alas, Luther never followed through on house churches:

> But as yet I neither can, nor desire to begin such a congregation ... for I have not yet the people for it, nor do I see many who are urgent for it. But if I should be requested to do it and could not refuse with a good conscience, I should gladly do my part and help as best I can.[26]

Downhill from There

After that time, however, the fearless Luther caved, yielding to state pressure and qualms about losing the whole movement to the Anabaptists. Wolfgang Simson summarizes the reversal and slide:

> He is even directly responsible for the martyrdom of many thousands of Christians who did not go along with his teachings—Luther's contribution to the spirit of the Inquisition. From 1530 he maintained that all Christians

who publicly preached and taught the word of God without being [licensed] pastors should be put to death, even if they taught correctly.[27] But Luther was not happy with his achievements. At the end of his life he wrote: "Amongst thousands there hardly is one true Christian."[28]

After 1530 it was bad. For instance, when Caspar Schwenckfeld, a close disciple, kept on planting house churches and Bible study groups across Europe, Luther turned on him with bitter hatred, persecuting him like a hunted animal. Simson comments: "When Schwenckfeld died in Ulm in 1561, Lutheran pastors tried to bring his many disciples back into the churches by force, and if they were not willing, had them thrown in jail and their children taken from them."[29]

John Calvin sometimes displayed the same ill temper—with similar grisly results. I'll spare you the details. Overall, the Reformation was a cold experience. For the next 200 years, the Catholics ran circles around the Protestants in missionary work.

While the Protestant Reformers were fighting the Catholics on one front, they were busy trampling the true remnant on the other. Mostly, that remnant was the Anabaptists, a loose-knit, Biblical/social movement that took up where the Waldensians left off. While the Anabaptists benefited from the "cover" provided by the Lutherans and Calvinists, shielding them from some of the traditional Roman onslaughts, they also believed in nonresistance and so got hit from both directions. It was not a pretty sight—but they survived.

The Reformers changed some key doctrines and dumped a lot of theological millstones. But one tenet they didn't change was the time-honored *Kill thy neighbor.*

Same Song, 83rd Verse

Some of the changes were a bit cosmetic or semantic. For instance, if today you call a Protestant pastor a priest, most parishioners will bristle. Yet a priest he is. Take a look at Gene Edwards's list of priestly duties for Catholic and Protestant pastors:

Catholic	Protestant
1. Marry the young	Ditto
2. Bury the dead	Ditto
3. Hear confession	Preach the Bible
4. Bless community events	Ditto
5. Baptize babies	Ditto
6. Visit the sick	Ditto
7. Collect money for the poor and the church	Ditto

The Worst Cataclysm in History

The events you've read about in this appendix add up to a world-wide disaster that dwarfs any tragedy you have ever heard of. Some numbers:

• The combined loss of life perpetrated in the name of Christianity, counting all the crusades, wars, and persecutions in 2,000 years, is well over 25 million.

• Nazi Germany caused perhaps 21 million deaths.

• The Red Chinese have killed 40 million at the very least.

• Soviet Communism left about 66 million dead.

Now think about this: *What if the church had never turned itself into an institution? What if we had remained a Christ-centered fellowship, bringing each believer the joy, peace, love, mutual commitment, and spiritual empowerment you've seen in this book?*

Despite the urban myth you've heard about most of the people ever born being alive today, it's not so. Since A.D. 100, roughly 60 billion people have walked the earth. (See www.prb.org. Under Focus Areas, click on Population Trends. Under Highlights, click on "How Many People Have Ever Lived on Earth-")

Now think about this:

If the church had continued as a warm, attractive family, growing in freedom and responsibility, how many of those 60 billion would have turned to the Lord, found eternal life, and entered the kingdom?

Go ahead, take a guess. I recognize that playing "what-if" with world history is speculative in the extreme. A basic change in the first-century Christian movement would have tripwired changes in wars, exploration, culture, science, famines, economics, etc. (For just one example, Islam would never have begun! The church in North Africa was once the strongest in the world, but well before Mohammed, it became so rigid and weak that it had to import its bishops and teachers from Europe. It was a pushover for the Muslim warriors.)

But if you make the simple assumption that population growth would have run roughly parallel to what it actually did, then we may at least hazard a guess. *Based upon what we know about successful missions work and church growth when things are being done right, we may reasonably conjecture that keeping the church open could have saved 30 to 50 billion of us from living stunted lives ending in eternal deaths.*

These are the saddest numbers of all time, and I do not enjoy adding them up. I do so only to make a point: The choice between an open or closed church system is not a matter of taste or personal preference. It is a matter of billions of lives and deaths.

As far as I know, Luther never repudiated his belief in the *priesthood* of all believers, but he never quite put into practice the *ministry* of all believers, either. And in later years, he began to tap dance around the whole issue.

Luther's reputation with the common folk went south after the Peasants' Revolt, when, fearing he might be blamed for the war, he took the side of the nobles, urging them:

> If the peasants are in open rebellion, then they are outside the law of God. Therefore if you are able, slash! Strike down! Kill [those who rebel] openly and secretly, remembering that there can be nothing more venomous, harmful, or devilish than a rebel.... Let there be no half measures ... leave no stone unturned. To kill a rebel is to destroy a mad dog....
>
> A prince can enter heaven by shedding of blood more certainly than by means of prayer.[30]

It was a shabby ending for one of the greatest men ever to walk the face of the earth.

Reformation II: The Reformation of the Heart

Except for the Anabaptists and kindred types, the Reformers failed to repent of the spirit of violence or to change the strangling, top-down structure of the church.

But the dam had burst. Small-group movements began to rise up in a swarm of house churches, cell churches, conventicles, class meetings, collegia, societies, and other attempts at freedom. Inside and outside of Catholic, Lutheran, Reformed, Anglican/Puritan, and other traditions, little bands of disciples began to experience the presence of Christ in living rooms, forests, haymows, and church buildings across Europe and in America. I cannot begin to list their names because it would launch me on a very long essay. Besides, we now have a slender but excellent book on the subject: Peter Bunton's *Cell Groups and House Churches: What History Teaches Us* (Ephrata, PA: House to House Publications), 2001.

Let it suffice to say that when the Wesleys, George Whitefield, Jonathan Edwards, Cotton Mather, and others in the eighteenth century began to turn large numbers to Christ, they were building upon a proven base. John Wesley's "class meetings" alone were enough to turn the course of civilization by instilling responsibility, sound judgment, and shining hope in the hearts of the lower classes, and thereby, it is often said, saving England from a repeat of the bloody tragedy of the French Revolution. His was truly a Reformation of the Heart; the usual name for it is *The Great Awakening.* In four waves, it crossed the Atlantic and brought the conversion of 10% to 20% of the population of America—a worthy goal for our day!

Reformation III:
Giving Jesus His Church Back

I call it The Transformation. Or The Empowerment.

The revolution now upon us is a complete paradigm shift, taking us back to the time of Christ. It is going to be a lot bigger than the Reformation. Even bigger than Wal-Mart.

It is, at last, the Reformation of Structure—not just flattening the pyramid a little, but turning it upside-down so that the true leaders are the servants, lifting up and equipping those they serve. Modern linguists have discovered that Augustine was right: *Overseers* in the New Testament were probably more *guardians* of the flock than its *supervisors.* Our perspectives are shifting rapidly.

Yet despite our continual references to the New Testament churches, we are not engaged in a quest for the perfect church in any golden era, even Bible times. The early church is our prototypye, not our goal or ideal. We've already surpassed it in some ways. For instance, today's massive quantities of miracles and the growth in kingdom numbers are beyond anything in recorded history. In faith, we are working toward a future that is the substance of things we've hoped for.

We have asked for and received kings—too many of them. Now we have the Real King, and He is taking the reins as Lord of Lords. The kingdom is now, and now is the time to take your place in it.

1. Moved forward about 44 years because of a new dating system. See www.lamblion.com/other/religious/RI-19.php.

2. My personal opinion is that the most damaging spirits to infect the early church were, consecutively, religiosity, control, pride, and fear/insecurity. All four still beset the traditional church.

3. As translated in *The Early Christian Fathers* by Henry Bettenson (Oxford Univ. Press, 1996), chapter 40, p. 32.

4. His letter to the Smyrnaeans I, in *Ante-Nicene Fathers,* American Edition, Volume 1, edited by Alexander Roberts and James Donaldson, 1885, chapter 40, "Honour the Bishop."

5. From Ignatius' letter to the Ephesians, vi, 1.

6. Ignatius' letter to the Magnesians, in Bettenson, *op. cit., The Early Christian Fathers,* pp. 42-44.

7. Ignatius' letter to the Smyrnaeans, 8:8-9, J.B. Lightfoot, translator.

8. Jim Petersen, *Church Without Walls: Moving Beyond Traditional Boundaries* (Colorado Springs: NavPress), 1992, p. 89. Monarchical bishops were not the general practice even in the major churches of that time, according to F.F. Bruce in his *New Testament History,* p. 418. Like Clement, Ignatius had a vivid imagination; though Ignatius referred to the great Polycarp as "the monarchical bishop of Smyrna," Polycarp just referred to himself as one of the elders.

9. Irenaeus, *Against Heresies,* book 3, chapter 3.

10. Tertullian, *De Ex. Cast.* 7 ANF.

11. Tertullian, *On Baptism,* 18:10-11.

12. Neander, Volume 1, *General History of the Christian Religion and Church,* 216.

13. By Pontius the deacon (c. 258, W), 5.268, 269.

14. Cyprian (c. 250, W), 5.398.

15. Tertullian (c. 197, W), 3.258. This is a paraphrase of a more lengthy quote.

16. Cyprian, *On the Unity of the Catholic Church,* 6.

17. E. Glenn Hinson, *The Early Church* (Nashville: Abingdon Press), 1996, p. 214f.

18. Jim Petersen, *op. cit.,* p. 93f.

19. This list is a blend of several lists, including those at www.catholic-concerns.com, www.compusmart.ab.ca/rprince/Chrono-1.htm, Wolfgang Simson, *op.cit.,* p. 60f., www.baptistlink.com/bible/catholicism.htm, www.biblicist.org/bible/popes.htm, and some of my own

research, but not enough to make it authoritative.

20. Leonard Verduin in *The Future Church: Lions in the Pews,* by David Bradshaw (Portal, GA: Open Church Ministries), 1993, p. 218.

21. Leonard Verduin, *loc. cit.*

22. Robert Lund quotes famed church historian Kenneth Scott Latourette as saying that "the main outlines of the Christianity of the year 500, even though altered in details, continued to be the chief characteristics of the Christianity of the year 1500." Lund goes on to comment, "In other words, after a millennium of utter religious nonsense, the Church, and the world, for that matter, was not much better off than when it had begun in the year 500... . More specifically, this age shows what happens when we mix spiritual weapons, principles, ideas, wisdom, structures, and practices with those that are humanly logical, earthly, religious, and carnal... . [The Church] resorted to politics, warfare, torture, intimidation, deceit, false doctrine, and a myriad of other anti-Biblical methods in order to 'expand' the Kingdom of God." (Lund, *op. cit.,* page 30f)

23. He had the choice of plenty of other issues. For instance, in that same year, in Coventry, England, "five men and two women were burned at the stake for the heresy of teaching their children the Lord's Prayer and the Ten Commandments in English." (Mike and Sue Dowgiewicz, *Restoring the Early Church,* p. 90.)

24. Leonard Verduin, *op. cit.,* p. 219

25. Martin Luther, *Vorrede zur Deutschen Messe,* 1526.

26. Ibid.

27. He also recommended that prophets and speakers in tongues should be drawn and quartered. (Vinson Synan, "2000 Years of Prophecy," *Ministries Today,* Sept/Oct 2004, p. 25.)

28. Wolfgang Simson, *Houses That Change the World* (Waynesboro, GA: OM Publishing), 1998, page 65.

29. *Op. cit.*, page 66.

30. Various translations can be found at www.libertyhaven.com/noneofthe above/alternatives/brightencorner.html and others.

Appendix Three

How to Raise the Dead
A Dozen at a Time

The commands of the Bible can be condensed to six words:
Love God,
bless others,
make disciples.

That's disciples, not converts. It's great to help people get saved, but they also need to solve their sin problems and achieve greatness of spirit.

Where do you start? You start by going to where they are. Right now, you probably know two or three hundred folks who are basically marking time, waiting for you to get in touch with them, to rescue them from their stunted lives, put them in touch with the Savior, and set their feet on a clear path to victorious living.

About 80% of Americans believe that Christ rose from the dead. They just haven't been able to connect that with any lifestyle option they've ever seen. A poll showed 93% of them would visit a church if asked, but only 16% had been invited.[1]

They have little idea of how much the Lord wants to do for them. They're vexed with troubles at work and at home, with issues of money and health, and with a vague discontent that has no name. But although they feel these things keenly, they seldom see the connection to sin. Even if they're religious, they don't see God as the obvious solution.

You, however, are quite aware that their *real* needs are to . . .

• be touched by the love of God, probably in a practical way, and have some wounds healed
• see Christ's glory and understand the good news
• break free from their past through genuine repentance—which may involve apologies, reconciliation, or restitution
• accept Christ as both Lord and Savior, thus going from death to life
• be assured of their salvation, new life, and new identity
• be accepted quickly and fully into a family of believers who are committed to helping them (and vice versa)
• get baptized, receive power over sin, straighten out their lives, and begin to enjoy a whole new lifestyle
• discover day by day how God meets their needs in Christ
• experience spiritual freedom and growth through the disciplines of prayer, giving, and study of the Bible and other helps
• be transformed by the renewing of their minds and daily obedience
• take their full place in the kingdom, using their gifts to become fruitful in service and loving witness.

I give you this list not to burden you with a program or agenda, but to help you grasp the big picture and free you from getting sucked into a sketchy set of priorities that could burn you out because it's too skimpy to work!

Build It, and They Will Come ... and Break Down the Doors or Climb in the Windows

You know many people who would give their right arm to have a life of power and miracles like you've learned about in these pages.

They would cross oceans and climb mountains to have a support team that would help solve their biggest problems, stand by them in trouble, be there for them day or night, and commit 100% to their success in life.

You, of course, understand that their biggest need is to be saved from hell and eternal death, but most Westerners are blind to that today. So most church planters have better luck *starting off* with the blessings and benefits of salvation rather than brimstone.

I'm not suggesting you water down the gospel to a feel-good message. I'm suggesting you start off at your friends' points of need, where you're more welcome. When Jesus sent out 70 of His disciples on their first mission, that's what He told them to do. As Argentine missions authority Ed Silvoso often says:

> The best way for them to experience the reality of God is through an answer to prayer that meets a felt need. When Jesus sent out the teams of evangelists in Luke 10:5-9, He told them first to speak peace over the house to be visited, then to meet the felt needs of the household by doing something like healing the sick. Then, and only then, were they to proclaim the kingdom of God.
>
> We have reversed the order by approaching people with whom we have no credibility to tell them about a God they don't know. If we followed Jesus' instructions and first provided people with a sense of peace and miraculous answers to prayer, then it would be easy to convert them.[2]

So much for big-picture generalities. Now if you're going to raise the dead a dozen at a time, it's time for some specifics.

15 Tips on Starting a Life-Giving, Self-Multiplying Church Network

This is not a rigid agenda, but a series of tips that can save you a whole lot of time and trouble.

1. **Make sure you have a real relationship with Jesus Christ.** Most folks in this country believe the Bible and pray. That won't cut it at the pearly gates. Before you start to do heavy work for the kingdom, make sure you're part of it. Maybe review Appendix One.

2. **Get clear on what you're doing.** Your goal is not to plant one church, light a cigar, and take early retirement, but to launch a major movement, to plant a rapidly multiplying network of loosely related rings that will transform lives and saturate every area they target with life-giving open fellowships.

Remember my Indian student Haroon, the one who had to deal with the cow spirit? He is a first-class apostle who from 1992 to 1997 planted 40 churches. Not bad at all. But in 1997 he began planting church-planting *movements*, and in the next four years he and his people started 346 churches! Instead of asking, *How can I expand my work?*, he began to ask, *What will it take to saturate my whole area with house churches?*

3. **Make a commitment.** Don't just slide into this half-heartedly. Pray something like this (with your spouse if you have one): "Lord,

you love everybody in this neighborhood (or office/school). You died to save them, and now You've put me here where I can touch their lives. So depending on You to prepare their hearts for Your message, I commit myself to pointing them toward You and helping them become part of a strong circle of brothers and sisters with You at the center."

4. **Get backup.** This is a tough one. Find two or three people, if you can, who will pray for you faithfully. It will make a big difference.

5. **Get sent.** If you are currently in a church that's sympathetic to the house church movement, ask them to bless you and commission you for this work. This will add to your sense of authority. But if you're not part of such a congregation, ask the Lord to guide you every step of the way.

6. **Start on the right foot. Pray!** As Ed Silvoso puts it, "Talk to God about your neighbors before you talk to your neighbors about God." Alvin Vander Griend of HOPE* suggests praying five blessings for five neighbors for five minutes a day, five days a week, for five weeks. And what could those blessings be? He makes BLESS an acronym:

Body: health, protection, strength
Labor: work, income, security
Emotional: joy, peace, hope
Social: love, marriage, family, friends
Spiritual: salvation, faith, grace.

Create your own prayer "neighborhood," whether it's neighbors, friends, colleagues, or just folks you bump into.

7. **Make contact.** Do whatever it is you like to do in building friendships. That may be golf, house repairs, chatting in the lunchroom, just hanging out, etc. A meal is always nice—either agenda or non-agenda. But in all cases, do something like asking them for any prayer request they may have. (As long as you sound more loving than nosy, they'll feel honored.) This will add a spiritual dimension to your relationship and give you something to build on.

NOTE: If your friend opens up quickly with a barrage of the standard questions *(What about evil? What about the sincere Hindu? Etc.),* answer as best you can, but remember, your goal is to love him into the kingdom, not to win a religious debate.

8. **Form an open fellowship if you can.** Even Paul, the master church planter, preferred to work with a team. Teamwork is better (and far faster in the long run) because you don't make as many mistakes when you have a broader perspective. And you don't spend as

---

* Houses of Prayer Everywhere has many helpful resource items. They're at P.O. Box 141312, Grand Rapids, Michigan 49514, (812) 238-9424, info@hopeministries.org, www.hopeministries.org.

much time trying to stretch yourself to do the work of an apostle, prophet, evangelist, pastor, teacher, and intercessor all rolled into one.

I'm not saying that church planting teams have *all* those gifts. They usually don't. But teammates will add tremendously to your breadth of understanding—and your power.

Teamwork is sometimes not an option if you're the only known Christian in your neighborhood ... or office or school or drinking club or witch coven or whatever you were in when you turned to Jesus or started getting serious about creating a home church movement. But if you have a choice, teams are best.

The problem with being a lone ranger church planter is that you are *the* star of the show, and the whole church tends to cluster around you—which sort of puts everybody else in a dependent status and marginalizes Jesus. So you have to work harder from day one to empower everyone, train leaders, hold meetings in *their* homes, etc. Also, if you stay too long, the group may collapse when you finally move on to start another church.

In contrast, teams often day-trip or travel to do their work, and they usually build their churches around a MOP (see below), not one of their own members.

9. **Keep it simple** by following the Holy Spirit. Sure, you need to know the principles in this book. That's why I wrote it. But if you go out to plant a church with a Bible in one hand and this book in the other, thinking *church, church, church,* you'll be dead in the water. Better that you read some good church books, leave them at home, and go out the door thinking *Jesus, Jesus, Jesus.*

Anything complex will break down. You may have a 160 IQ and a burning desire to download everything you know about eschatology, soteriology, ecclesiology, and flying saucers. Put a cork in it. Try not to do things that your one-week-old new disciple can't do. Don't even pray high-gloss prayers. Your disciples will be watching everything you do, and if you sound like Mr. or Ms. Slick, they will be too scared to go out and start their own churches. Ask yourself what you want: admiration or multiplication?

If the idea of "just go with the flow" of the Holy Spirit is too vague for you, it's OK to think up some set of steps or a track to run on. For example, some Christians in Manila follow four steps:

A. Praying every morning: "Lord, today send me someone who needs your help."

B. Asking general questions that allow for specific answers, like, "So how is the world treating you these days?" (Often, people will start telling you about a personal problem.)

C. Bragging on Jesus, telling what he's done for you. (If this sparks any sign of interest, follow on by saying that God loves them and wants to reveal His power in their lives, and so forth.)

D. Offering to pray for them—right now.

But don't just copycat this pattern, make up your own! And keep it simple.

10. Find a MOP. When Jesus sent out the 70 church planters in Luke 10, He told them not to go door to door. Jesus was smart. He knew that the folks at the second and third doors would quickly figure out that the disciples didn't exactly get a jubilant reception at the first door. And rejected merchandise is a hard sell.

So instead, He told them to build their work on a MOP, a *Man of Peace* (which can also be a woman of peace, like Lydia in Acts 16). This is someone who is open to the gospel and has influence and respect—and perhaps some wealth. When your MOP turns to Christ, your work is half done!*

11. Focus on the lost. Give top priority to non-Christians and nominal Christians. Sure, it's nice to reclaim church dropouts and revive them for kingdom work, but it's a lot more fun to resurrect the spiritually dead. And why cannibalize the traditional church when the sinner pool shows no signs of drying up? Newly saved saints are the best building blocks for your work, anyway. They come without institutional baggage.

Your second priority (a close second) should be those dropouts, the de-churched, the 23 million (in the U.S.) who have accepted Christ but don't find it worthwhile to regularly attend church anymore. Many of these burnt-out souls are quite ready to pay the price to step up to a higher spiritual plane and get the kind of peer-team support they never had before. They're looking for you—even if they don't know it yet.

Then you have the active pew-sitters. Over time, hundreds of frustrated but dutiful church members will find you and be eager to join you. That's OK. Accept them with open arms. However, if you seek them out or build your work on them, be aware that this type may lobby forever to get the group to meet the expectations gained from their good or bad experience in the pews. They may try to hijack your team for their own agenda. As Carol Davis overstates, "If you want a really powerful church start, find people of peace. Bar the Christians; don't let them in. They mess things up in the early stages."[3]

(Also, if deliberate sheep stealing becomes the strategy of choice throughout your network, the local pastors will be steamed, and that

---

* You yourself could perhaps function as a man of peace. But just remember the problem of building a church with yourself at the center.

fractures the spiritual unity you need to get God's blessing on the whole church of your community. *No matter how lousy a congregation is, you have no right to break it up.)*

12. **Learn to *enjoy* growth and multiplication.** Don't look upon church planting as a humongous new burden or project; learn to love it as your new lifestyle! That means:

• Pray for growth and expect it.
• Don't take charge, take responsibility; Jesus will build your church.
• Establish an atmosphere of mutual accountability.
• Center everything around Christ. Go deep.
• Show how to be an encourager. Create an atmosphere of love.
• Don't be hierarchical, but keep a shepherd's eye open for each person, to help him avoid trouble and move up spiritually.
• When someone turns to Christ, follow up zestfully and immediately; the first 24 to 48 hours are crucial to his future. See that the new believer is baptized right away and welcomed to share the Lord's supper (communion) with others—without a probationary period or preliminary indoctrination course.*
• Build to 10 or 15. Stay relational, not hierarchical; resist the temptation to incorporate and have a constitution.
• When the group feels like it's hitting a limit, bless and send out your best couple—or three or four strong people—to establish a new church plant. With enough time and spiritual growth, almost everyone should become able to split off and form their own pioneer work.[4] You can also divide the group, but that brings the perennial problem of who gets to stay with whom. It also allows some people to easily remain permanent followers, drifting feebly along behind others' leadership rather than learning to take action.
• Learn sacrificial giving with no browbeating.

13. **Pray some more!**
Alvin Vander Griend tells of an experiment done by a church in Phoenix, Arizona. Intercessors randomly selected 160 names from the local telephone book and divided the names into two equal groups. For 90 days they prayed for one group of 80 homes. The other 80 homes were not prayed for.

After 90 days, they called all 160 homes, identified themselves and their church, and asked for permission to stop by and pray for the

---

* Of course, if the commitment is weak and questionable, or there is a reluctance to take the step of - baptism, or there are unresolved issues of major ongoing sin, then a delay is appropriate. But many missionaries around the world have discovered over the years that even a chronic dropout rate of 95% will fall to about 0% if new believers are quickly drawn into the center of church life, especially including baptism and communion.

family and any needs they might be willing to share. Of the 80 homes for which they didn't pray, <u>only one</u> invited them to come in. Of the 80 homes for which they had prayed for three months, <u>69</u> invited someone to come over; of the 69, 45 invited them to come in.[5]

If you pray, God will do the heavy lifting!

14. **Stay balanced.** Open churches—without denominational straitjackets, fixed programs, and pyramidal locks on ministry—tend to slide toward one extreme or the other. Try to maintain a balance in:

• *Freedom vs. order.* In your meetings, err on the side of freedom. Trust the Spirit. But don't let things get so wild so often that people are driven away.

• *Freedom vs. teamwork among individuals.* Freedom is primary, but team Christianity requires a lot of working *together.* If everyone is doing his own thing, your team won't have much impact.

• *Apostolic leadership vs. upward mobility.* We must have strong leadership. But half the job of leaders is developing *more* leaders. So let new leaders bloom as fast as they can produce petals.

• *Congregational independence vs. networking.* Unlike cell groups, house churches are complete, free-standing churches. But if they aren't praying for each other, having joint meetings now and then, and sometimes cooperating in joint projects, they will be isolated, less-than-useful outposts of the kingdom.

• *Rapid multiplication vs. mature discipleship.* It's great to have a passion to get everybody saved as fast as possible. It's also great to take enough time to bring everyone in your ring to maturity. Do both.

• *Small vs. large gatherings.* Don't have joint gatherings more than every three to six weeks. People get too lazy.

• *Authority vs. authoritarianism.* A bossy attitude or controlling spirit is the weak leader's imitation of power.

15. **Join the growing worldwide networks of on-fire gatherings meeting in homes.** Loners are losers!

Subscribe to *House2House* magazine, the *Friday Fax,* and *Joel News International.* Join a house-church discussion group on the Web. Read some of the very helpful books you'll see in the bibliography. Why spend the rest of your life reinventing the wrong wheel? Or trying to ride a dead horse backwards? Devote more of your time to reading and less to shooting yourself in the foot.

Become part of the larger community of brothers and sisters in open churches by attending some regional house church conferences and training seminars. You'll meet many others who are doing what you're doing, you'll be greatly encouraged, and you'll return home feeling much less weird.

Stop Dreaming, Start Doing

If this were a movie, here is where the violins would come up as you wave good-bye and I ride off into the sunset. I've run out of appendices to badger you with and used up more paper than any sane editor should allow. The happy story is told, at least for the moment, and a priceless scarlet baton now rests in your hand.

A lot of people died to bring you the baton, my friend. Foremost among them is the Lord Jesus, who went to the cross all alone so that you and I could have life together—a highly abundant life filled with the Spirit's rich blessings and the much-needed support of loyal brothers and sisters.

The greatest praise goes to the Father, the **I AM** whom Moses encountered in the burning bush, who allowed the Trinity to be torn apart for three days in order to create a blood-washed family of loving people who will never die, but are daily overcoming sin and growing to understand Him in ways even the angels cannot.

So bow your head with me for a moment of reverential thanks for those millions of ancestors in the faith who died insisting that there was a higher way of life than what the establishment was offering at the time. May the horrors they suffered be not a caution for us, but an inspiration for the shining years ahead.

You face a future so bright it's almost blinding. The world you live in is filled with countless people being cured of nearly everything, and all these resurrections have left taxes as the only real certainty anymore. There's also the shimmering possibility that you yourself will be involved in miracles. Keep that in mind!

You now have at least some grasp of the great Engines of Change that God has given us to transform the world, quite possibly in our generation. And you live in a time when we're rocketing toward that Transformation so fast I can hardly believe it myself—and I did the research.

The kingdom has come—not fully, but suddenly and spectacularly. What is that kingdom? Everything controlled by the King, whether territory or institutions or people. And its people are called the church.

As one of the new saints in that body, you now have (I hope) a new empowerment—along with a new freedom, new identity, new sense of responsibility, new maturity, and new understanding of the gospel. Taken together, these amount to a new lifestyle your forebears could hardly have imagined, much less experienced.

Also by now, you should have a wide vision of Team Jesus and know a few of the thousands of great things you can do as a core apostolic. You're following in the footsteps of the One who gave Himself for us, so you'll learn to give and give until some days you'll

241

think you can't give one more drop of help to anybody. But the crying chorus of need never stops crying, so your own resources (emotional, physical, financial) soon run dry. You'll then learn to let Him pour His unlimited resources *through* you. "Give, and it will be given to you," Jesus said.

Your world is littered with millions of victims of sin and circumstance who face decay and death in the long term and shrunken lives in the short term. Even if they own all the major toys and never miss a tee time, they desperately need to be connected to Jesus Christ and discover His love and lordship. They're waiting for you to come along and show them how that's done. (They know it doesn't happen just by sitting in a pew.)

Here and there in the U.S., where team Christians have been willing to roll up their sleeves, stop playing the usual games, and reach out in unity, they have succeeded in moving the hand of God. Mightily. A friend who is a national prayer leader summarizes the typical impact this way:

> Government officials are given wisdom and guidance. Businesses are blessed. Crime rates go down. Healthy churches impact their communities... .
>
> [D]rug centers have closed, prostitution rings have moved out of neighborhoods, bars have shut down, crime rates have dropped, fractured neighborhood relationships have been healed, suicides have been prevented, marriages have been restored, workplaces have changed ... and individuals have given their lives to Christ.[6]

Freed of the usual claptrap and routine, simple believers like you and me can actually do such things—and more. This is the megashift we've been waiting for, and in your neck of the woods, you're the one who's going to make it happen ... if you're game!

For you, the cascade of events may flow quickly and with few glitches. Or you may have to face disinterest and pain and climb steep walls of resistance. Each person's path is unique. But wherever your path leads you, I guarantee you'll find it the most joy-filled adventure you've ever been on—because the joy is open-ended and never stops.

You're Entering a New World

Is your heart with me? Then somewhere in the process of reading this book, you jumped across a wide chasm, and you now find yourself hesitantly surveying your new surroundings. The vegetation may somehow look a little greener, but unfamiliar. And that's good.

242

Take a deep breath and smile. You're about to launch yourself on an invisible river that will carry you even farther away, into a new country where mysteries unfold like crimson roses and the clear air brings a new health to your mind and spirit. Take the hands of a few friends and strangers and draw them along with you as companions on your voyage through unexplored territories. Dangers lurk, and you'll need their help, as they'll need yours.

On your river journey, you'll face combat. You'll have to learn how to kill dragons now and then (which really isn't all that scary once you get the hang of it). Fighting evil is a messy thing, and you'll get your share of dragon bites, but that's just part of a mission to save lives, break down gates of darkness, and bring righteousness to corrupted lands.

It's not all combat, of course. At night, often enough, there will be campfires—and times to laugh and relax with your comrades in arms, who will grow in numbers year by year. But in the day, at most points where you put in to shore, you'll face fresh battles—*bigger* battles—and often you'll wonder, as you lick your wounds, if you're really winning or losing.

Someday, though—I swear it's true—you'll come around a bend in the river and see a sight that will dazzle you speechless: the capital city itself, spread out beyond a thousand miles with glistening gold boulevards and crystal-gold homes arrayed with blazing jewels in colors you've never seen, soaring into mountains as high as the city is broad.

As you approach the city's flower-laden dock, you will see coming to receive you a noisy throng with many familiar faces (looking strangely young) led by the King himself. When you disembark, He will stretch His arms toward you and say, "Welcome, loyal servant! I've been waiting for this day!"

Yet as you run to meet Him, He may turn His eyes upstream and exclaim in joyful tones, "I see you've brought some friends!"

And looking back upriver, you'll discover, to your wonder, a mighty fleet of other vessels following in your wake.

---

1. Joni B. Hannigan, "Rainer: People need to be reaching lost for Jesus," citing a study by Thom S. Rainer, dean of the Billy Graham School of Missions, Evangelism and Church Growth at the Southern Seminary, at *www.pastors.com/article.asp? ArtID=4102* or call (877) PASTORS and ask for Article ID=4102.

2. Ed Silvoso, "How to Reach All the Lost in Your City," *Ministries Today*, March/April, 1997, page 32.

3. *Joel News International*, 329-4. Go to www.joelnews.org/news-en/jn329.htm. Then go to 329.4.

4. This is the promising new "G-12" pattern in many institutional "cell churches." The idea is that everyone grows to be mature and responsible. No permanent wallflowers. And the group does not split and grow from 12 to 24, but grows from 12 to 144. Note: An extraordinary feature of this model is that although each person in the group is expected to plant their own work, this is done "on the side." Everyone actually stays in their original base group semi-permanently. Thus they belong to two groups at any given time: their home group and their latest plant, where they are the founders. This allows you to launch whole new networks, but retain the luxury of being in the same group for many years, developing deep friendships with believers you know really well.

5. Douglas A. Kamstra, *The Praying Church Idea Book*, quoted in Felicity Dale, *Getting Started* (Austin: House2House), 2002, page 73.

6. Alvin Vander Griend in *Joel News Int'l* #400-2. Overseas, we also see another type of Transformation: economic. I was recently in Orissa, India, where the tribal village of Maliguda saw a sudden and overwhelming turning to Christ. At that point, they discovered diamonds in their hills! Members of the local Paraja and Dombo tribes have been out scooping up diamonds with just shovels, which has transformed the economy.

244

For Further Equipping

Symbols show ordering sources. See table below.

A. The Top Twenty

Any book on this list will give you an overall understanding of open churches. None are hard to read. Each is recommended by many of the movement's leaders, but the 1 to 20 ranking is my own.

1. *Houses That Change the World*, Wolfgang Simson (Waynesboro, GA: OM Publishing), 2001, 303 pp. A ground-breaking book from a brilliant thinker. Thorough, readable, and convincing as a tidal wave. Originally posted on the Web, it was downloaded 10,000 times and photocopied endlessly. This is *the* hot book today. ♥♣

2. *Organic Church: Growing Faith Where Life Happens*, Neil Cole (San Francisco: Jossey-Bass), 2005, 233 pp. This landmark work is a joy to read. The author is eloquent and brilliant in the way he splices in lots of great stories and illustrations. You will be thoroughly enlightened and motivated. Cole's teams have started over 800 organic fellowships–in homes, coffeehouses, offices, shops, bars, parks, and restaurants. *

3. *Revolution*, George Barna (Wheaton: Tyndale), 2005, 140 pp. America's leading pollster clearly describes the demographic aspect of the house church movement, showing that its drivers are a very distinct class of people: revolutionaries. A longtime chronicler of the traditional church, Barna has abruptly sided with the activists making radical changes in the practice of their faith. ✗

4. *The Meaning of Life*, James Rutz (Colorado Springs: Empowerment Press), 2006, 140 pp. A short but extremely broad book that touches upon Earth's origins, human history, Heaven, Hell, the problem of evil, 24 troublesome passages in the New Testament, and the church–tying these topics all together in the usual Rutz style. It offers a fresh rethink of these subjects, and it will likely convince you that the life you are living is far too small! Good for skeptical Christians and doubters as well. ♥

5. *Getting Started: A Practical Guide to Planting Simple Churches*, Felicity Dale (Austin: House2House Ministries), 2003, 180 pp. Dr. Dale's spiral-bound manual is not only practical, but inspirational. If you aren't sure of the steps to building a simple church network, this is a great book for individual or group study. ◊✗

6. *A Kingdom, A People & A River*, R. Maurice Smith (Spokane: The Parousia Network), 2006, 312 large pages. A one-book education, this wide-ranging, spiral-bound magnum opus of the eloquent Mr. Smith will keep you glued to the page all the way through. ◗

7. *Who Is Your Covering?* Frank Viola (Brandon, FL: Present Testimony Ministry), 1998, 106 pp. The answer to the question in the title is, "Jesus!" Gives smashing proof that the house church has a Biblical right to exist. ♥✗✳

8. *The Church Comes Home*, Robert & Julia Banks (Peabody, MA: Hendrickson), 1998, 260 pp. Rob Banks and his late wife, Julia, wrote this with tremendous authority, but also with great balance and moderation. Much practical help for church planters. ♥

9. *The Way Church Ought to Be/Volume I: Ninety-five Propositions for a Return to Radical Christianity*, Robert A. Lund (Albany, OR: Outside the Box Press) 2001, 464 big pages. This house church "encyclopedia" will tell you everything you ever wanted to know—plus 90% extra! ♥

10. *Rethinking the Wineskin: The Practice of the New Testament Church*, Frank Viola (Brandon, FL: Present Testimony Ministry), 2001, 203 pp. A companion volume to *Who Is Your Covering?* Proves that the traditional, institutional church is illegitimate. Airtight reasoning—except for the brief appendix, which greatly complicates the qualifications for anyone who plants a church. ♥✗✳

11. *Simply Church*, Tony and Felicity Dale (Austin, TX: Karis Publishing), 2002, 120 pp. A broad, highly readable introduction to the house church. ◊

12. *How to Meet in Homes*, Gene Edwards (Jacksonville: The SeedSowers), 1999, 135 pp. Often viewed as the voice of the U.S. house church, Gene is also its biggest critic! He is the ultimate house church purist. His folksy, in-your-face style is uniquely charming or irritating, depending on how attached you are to the traditional church system. ♥☆

13. *Toward a House Church Theology*, ed. by Steve Atkerson with 12 contributors (Atlanta: New Testament Restoration Foundation), 1996, 183 pp. Lively discussions of 32 house-church issues. Lots of information you can't find elsewhere. Each chapter was originally written as a journal article, and thus has almost the punchy tone of a debate. ♣♥

14. *Cultivating a Life for God*, Neil Cole (Carol Stream, IL: Church Smart Resources), 1999. The basic strategy of the most fruitful planter of house churches in America: intimate groups of three that power and multiply networks. ∗

15. *House Church Networks: A church for a new generation*, Larry Kreider (Ephrata, PA: House to House Publications), 2001, 118 pp. Larry is the only person I know of who draws great respect from both traditional and house-church Christians. In this work, he uses his wide, successful experience to show how house churches and tradition-based cell churches can not only coexist, but complement each other and build each other up. ♥

16. *An Army of Ordinary People*, Felicity Dale (Austin: House2House Ministries), 2005, 280 pp. A collection of inspiring stories of people who have planted simple churches. ◊✗

17. *God's Simple Plan for His Church—and Your Place in It: A Manual for House Churches*, Nate Krupp (Woodburn, OR: Solid Rock Books), 1993, 173 pp. An easy-to-scan overview that touches upon all the main issues connected to what a house church should be, such as what to do with kids, how to handle blabbermouths, etc. Plenty of Bible footnotes. ♥

18. *The Church in the House: A Return to Simplicity*, Robert Fitts (Salem, OR: Preparing the Way Publishers), 2001, 113 pp. A simple, outline-type book that beginners can digest in one evening. ♥

19. *Radical Renewal: The Problem of Wineskins Today*, Howard A. Snyder (Houston: Touch Publications), 1996, 223 pp. A rewrite of the 1975 classic, *The Problem of Wineskins*, which was in print for over 20 years. An in-depth book that will make you think—as will any of Snyder's books. ♥✦

20. *Pagan Christianity: The Origins of Our Modern Church Practices*, Frank Viola (Brandon, FL: Present Testimony Ministry), 2003, 304 pages. A hard-hitting, heavily footnoted book that systematically uncovers the pagan origin of every church tradition you can think of. Unanswerable! ♥✗∗

Honorable Mention

The most significant recent publishing event is not a book, but a magazine, *House2House*. This quality publication is already a landmark of the movement, having zoomed from 0 to 50,000 copies in its first year. It is a launch pad for breakthrough strategies, a trusted clearinghouse for opinion, and a much-needed centering influence. A "must read." Find it at www.house2house.tv or phone (512) 282-2322. (Free, but donations helpful.)

The following books should not be thought of as lesser in quality than those above. Most of them simply have a different focus.

B. General Interest Books on the Church

Against Great Odds (video), 29 minutes. Documents the growth of underground house churches in Ethiopia from 5,000 to 50,000 people during ten years of Communism. Gateway Films, item 4079, Box 540, Worcester, PA. Phone (800) 523-0226.

Awakening Cry, Pete Greig (London: Silver Fish Publishing), 1998. A lively, youthful perspective on holiness, revival, and church/social reform. Lots of good stories and fascinating, underlinable stuff.

The Blueprint, Clifford H. James (Warr Acres, OK: Living Water Publishing), 2000. An introduction to the house church in a warm, personal tone. +

Cell Groups and House Churches: What History Teaches Us, Peter Bunton (Ephrata, PA: House to House Publications), 2001. A brief (109-page) history of small groups starting with the Reformation. ✦∴

Church Multiplication Guide: Helping Churches to Reproduce Locally and Abroad, George Patterson and Richard Scoggins (Pasadena: Wm. Carey Library), 2002. Tested, internationally proven methods from two top veterans. †

Church Planting Movements, David Garrison (Richmond, VA: International Mission Board of the Southern Baptist Convention), 1999, free. Also available online at www.imb.org/CPM. A report on worldwide progress in house churches and very similar movements. The most exciting 260 pages you can find. Also free at www.imb.org/CPM is a terrific 12-minute video by the same title. ✓

Church Without Walls, Jim Petersen (Colorado Springs: Navpress), 1992. Tactfully sorts out Jesus from church tradition. ♥∴

Ekklesia: To the Roots of Biblical Church Life, ed. by Steve Atkerson (Atlanta: New Testament Restoration Foundation), 2003. Addresses apostolic tradition, the Lord's supper, interactive meetings, women's silence, church discipline, children in church, etc. ♣♥

The Future Church: Lions in the Pews, ed. by David Bradshaw (Portal, GA: Open Church Ministries), 1993. An 8-tape, 12-hour, $65 album of interviews with 65 diverse leaders, each of whom echoes some theme related to the house church movement. Includes a full, 250-page transcript. ♥

Getting Started: Planting and Multiplying House Churches, Felicity Dale (Austin, TX: House 2 House Ministries), 2002. A fine house church intro. The last half is practical advice from the highly experienced author. ◊

The Global House Church Movement, Rad Zdero (Pasadena: William Carey Library), 2004. A finely balanced introduction to the house church—from an experienced leader. †

Going to Church in the First Century, Robert Banks (Jacksonville: The SeedSowers), 1980. A fictional trip back in time to early Rome, as a sophisticated traveler from Philippi narrates the story of his first visit to the home of Aquila and Priscilla. ☞☆

Going to the Root: 9 Proposals for Radical Church Renewal, Christian Smith (Scottdale, PA: Herald Press), 1992, 176 pp. In addition -to the usual concerns, this book adds the social element, both with the church and outside, in social outreach. ♥☞

The House Church: A Model for Renewing the Church, Del Birkey (Scottdale, PA: Herald Press), 1988. ☞∴

In Search of a New Wine Skin, Dan Hubbell (Winnsboro, Texas: Hubbell Publishing), rev. 1999. A blow-by-blow account of what happened to Hubbell, once a distinguished traditional pastor, when God called him into house church ministry. You'll be appalled—and then delighted by the happy conclusion (and the many lessons learned). ±

Jaded: Hope for believers who have given up on church but not on God, A.J. Kiesling (Grand Rapids: Baker Books), 2004. Lots of stories of very reluctant church dropouts. You'll identify with them—and enjoy the excellent running commentary. ∴

Meetings in His Kingdom, Mike Peters, free on the Web at www.yourkingdomcome.com/meetings.htm. Good book on the format of different types of meetings and how to let the Holy Spirit run them.

Missionary Methods: St. Paul's or Ours, Roland Allen (Grand Rapids: Eerdmans), 1954. A classic. ∗∴

The New Reformation: Returning the Ministry to the People of God, Greg Ogden (Grand Rapids: Zondervan), 1990. ∴

The New Testament Order for Church and Missionary, Alexander Rattray Hay. The 1947 classic precursor to many of today's house church books. Musty but clear. Good depth. ☞

The Open Church: How to Bring Back the Exciting Life of the First Century Church, James H. Rutz (Portal, GA: Open Church Ministries), 1992. A fun read, but marred by its aim: to morph traditional churches into open churches—which we found nearly impossible. Still quite good if you ignore Part III: "How to Open Your Church Without a Crowbar." ♥

Paul's Idea of Community: The Early House Churches in Their Cultural Setting, Robert and Julia Banks (Peabody, MA: Hendrickson), 1994. About the freedom of Christians and the early house churches. ∴

Real Christianity: The Nature of the Church, R.J. Dawson (Enumclaw, WA: Winepress Publishing), 2001. An impassioned plea for the house church, by a man who knows how to write. Good depth, many Bible references. ✗

The Reformers and Their Stepchildren, Leonard Verduin (Sarasota: Christian Hymnary Publishers), 1991. An analysis of the rift between the Anabaptists and reformers like Luther and Calvin. ☞
Resident Aliens, Stanley Hauerwas and Will Willimon (Nashville: Abingdon), 1989. Breaks apart many of the traditional church paradigms. ∴

Restoring the Early Church, Mike and Sue Dowgiewicz (Colorado Springs: Restoration Ministries), 1996. An intro to the open church. But instead of the usual contrast between traditional and house church models, their contrast is between Greek and Hebraic. ❖∴

The Spontaneous Expansion of the Church and the Causes Which Hinder It, Roland Allen (Grand Rapids: Eerdmans), 1962. A classic, now free on the Web at www.gospeltruth.net/allen/spon_expanofch.htm.

The Torch of the Testimony, John W. Kennedy (Jacksonville: The SeedSowers), 1965. This little-known book is the only history of those Christian groups outside of the institutional church for 2,000 years. Quite an education. ☛☆

2000 Years of Charismatic Christianity, Eddie L. Hyatt (Lake Mary, Florida: Charisma House), 2002, 225 pp. A detailed answer to the misconceived question, "How come there weren't any miracles from the early Second Century until the modern Pentecostal movement?" This scholarly but fast-moving book gives many examples of miracles in every era. ✗

Waking the Dead, John Eldredge (Nashville: Thos. Nelson), 2003. Great, uplifting book that will widen your understanding of life. If chapters 4 and 5 of *MEGASHIFT* are the framework of an open fellowship, this book is its burning heart. ♥

C. Cell Churches

Making Cell Groups Work, M. Scott Boren and Don Tillman (Houston: Touch Publications), 2002. Two years of intense research have finally uncovered why some churches are able to make cells work and others aren't. A landmark book with implications for house church leaders. ✦

Where Do We Go from Here?, Ralph W. Neighbour, Jr. (Houston: Touch Publications), 2000. Updated version of the classic that launched thousands of cell churches. ✦

The Second Reformation, William A. Beckham (Houston: Touch Publications), 1995. The perfect companion volume to *Where Do We Go from Here?* ✦

D. Related Topics and Background Help

Acts of the Holy Spirit, C. Peter Wagner (Ventura, CA: Regal), 2000. Not a house church book, but an exciting, 556-page commentary on the book of Acts. You'll never again think of a commentary as "boring"! A great foundation for your ministry. =

Apostles and Prophets: The Foundation of the Church, C. Peter Wagner (Ventura, CA: Regal), 2000. Both apostles and prophets are crucial to the new Christianity. But sad to say, their function was *terra incognita* for the church until the 1990s. As George Barna has noted, "As long as the Church persists in being led by teachers, it will flounder." =

Apostles and the Emerging Apostolic Movement, David Cannastraci (Ventura, CA: Regal Books), 1996. How God is starting to use apostles today. (Update of *The Gift of Apostle*) ♥

Biblical Eldership: An Urgent Call to Restore Biblical Church Leadership, Alexander Strauch (Littleton, CO: Lewis & Roth Publishers), 1995. Fills a big vacuum in the literature on elders. ∴

City Reaching: On the Road to Community Transformation, Jack Dennison (Pasadena: Wm. Carey Library), 1999. How churches are working together to reach their cities. ✗

Climb the Highest Mountain, Gene Edwards (Jacksonville: The SeedSowers), 1984. How to face and handle a church split or crisis. ☆

Commitment to Conquer: Redeeming Your City by Strategic Intercession, Bob Beckett with Rebecca Wagner Sytsema (Grand Rapids: Chosen Books), 1997. The story of one of the cities in the *Transformations* video, showing how spiritual warfare works in practice. =

Common Sense: A New Approach to Understanding Scripture, David Bercot (Tyler, TX: Scroll Publishing), 1992. A return to ancient ways of looking at the Bible. Can be unsettling! ✗

Connecting, Larry Crabb (Nashville: W Publishing Group), 1997. An intensely personal plea for forming true, deep relationships. ♥∴

The Cry for Spiritual Fathers and Mothers, Larry Kreider (Ephrata, PA: House to House Publications), 2000. We live in a largely fatherless generation. The answer lies in this unique, warm, book, which renders moot much of our wrangling about eldership, authority, and overseers. ✦

DAWN 2000: 7 Million Churches to Go, Jim Montgomery (Pasadena: William Carey Library), 1991. Out of the hundreds of current plans to evangelize the world, this is probably the one that will have the most impact. See also his 1997 sequel (same publisher), *Then the End Will Come.* Eye-opening and encouraging. ♣†

God Guides, Mary Geegh (Lansing: Pray America), 2000. A unique, life-changing little book on a practical way to listen to God. ♥

Gospel of Victory: The Revolutionary Keys of the Early Church Gospel, James E. Leuschen (Spokane: Restoration of Hope Ministries), 1999. In only 62 pages, this significant book restores the resurrection as the key part of the gospel's success. ▼

Our Father Abraham, Marvin Wilson (Grand Rapids: Eerdmans), 1989. The best book on understanding Christianity through its Jewish roots. ♥

Out of Bondage, Tim Mather (Portal, GA: Open Church Ministries), 2005, 164 pp. Right from its rocketing start in the opening pages, this book will open your eyes to perhaps the biggest spiritual problem in Christianity: the spirit of control. Tells how to recognize it and break it. ♥

Overcoming the Religious Spirit, Rick Joyner (Charlotte: MorningStar Publications), 1996. A 61-page booklet that nails a basic problem few people even recognize. ♠

Pastoring by Elders, Mike and Sue Dowgiewicz (Colorado Springs: Restoration Ministries), 1998. The amount of nurturing and shepherding that needs to be done in the church is at least ten times what one "pastor" can provide. Mike and Sue show how elders can and must take on that role. ❖

Prayer: Conversing with God, Rosalind Rinker (Grand Rapids: Zondervan), 1987. This is the best-selling classic on conversational prayer, written by a friend and mentor, the late Ros Rinker. Practical. ∴

Prophetic Deliverance, Timothy C. Mather (Portal, GA: Open Church Ministries), 2000, 208 pp. Deliverance from demons was never like this. Mather and his wife Katie, now on the staff of Covenant Bible Institute, have performed over 5,000 deliverance sessions–entirely without the "standard" physical manifestations and noise. Combining the gifts of prophecy and deliverance, this calm new approach will solve more deep-seated problems than you would imagine. A fascinating read that will change your life. ♥

Shaking the Heavens, Ana Méndez (Ventura, CA: Renew Books), 2000. A startling book from a former voodoo priestess who has led many decisive battles in her native Mexico and elsewhere. Will definitely advance your understanding of spiritual warfare principles. ✗

Their Blood Cries Out: The Untold Story of Persecution Against Christians in the Modern World, Paul Marshall (Dallas: Word Publishing), 1997. Worldwide church unity must not be based on denominations, doctrine, and token cooperation, but on mutual support, intercessory prayer, and informed interaction. House church people must take the lead in reaching out to our persecuted brothers and sisters. ∴

Thus Saith the LORD?, John Bevere (Lake Mary, FL: Creation House), 1999. How to discern when a "prophecy" is just hot air—or worse. ∴

Transformations and *Transformations II*, George Otis (Lynnwood, WA: The Sentinel Group), 1999 & 2001. Two videos. The former may qualify as the best video ever made. Shows how revival can be so far-reaching that the very nature of a town or city is transformed. Seen by 50 million in 25 languages. Highly encouraging! Get out the popcorn and the Kleenex. ♣=

The 2 Minute Miracle: Releasing God's Power, Protection and Prosperity with Spoken Blessings, M. Lynn Reddick (Portal, GA: Portal Publishing Company), 2003, 96 pp. This little book will open up to you a whole new world of power. The long-lost Biblical treasure of blessing will enable you to change lives, guaranteed. ♥

Upside Down: The Paradox of Servant Leadership, Stacy T. Rinehart (Colorado Springs: Navpress), 1998. On servant leadership. ∴

The Voice of God, Cindy Jacobs (Ventura, CA: Regal), 1995. A warm and charming explanation of how God speaks to us today—by the most noted prophetess in America. Very helpful. =

Will the Real Heretics Please Stand Up, David Bercot (Tyler, TX: Scroll Publishing), 1989. Reveals how the earliest Christians thought about many issues we face today. An amazing book—guaranteed to shake up your beliefs on various matters. Not for the faint of heart. ♥

You May All Prophesy, Steve Thompson (Charlotte: MorningStar Publications), 2000. A practical book written especially for those who have never prophesied but would like to. ♠

Sources for Above Books

Because so many of the cited works are from small publishers and not in bookstores, you may find this source guide helpful:

✗ Amazon.com

= Arsenal Christian Booksellers, 5775 N. Union Blvd., Colorado Springs, CO 80918, www.arsenalbooks.com. (888) 563-5150

∴ Christianbook.com

* Church Multiplication Associates, 1965 E. 21st Street, Signal Hill, California 90806, toll-free: (877) 732-3593, www.cmaresources.org

+ Clifford James, (405) 722-7428, hisservants@theearlychurch.com

◊ House2House Ministries, www.house2house.tv or phone (512) 282-2322

± Hubbell Publishing, Box 673, Winnsboro, Texas 75494

✓ Int'l Mission Board Resource Center, P.O. Box 6767, Richmond, Virginia 23230-0767, (800) 866-3621

♠ MorningStar, www.MorningstarMinistries.org, (800) 542-0278, (336) 651-2400

♣ New Testament Restoration Foundation, 2752 Evans Dale Circle, Atlanta, Georgia 30340, ntrf.org

♥ Open Church Ministries, 304 Grady St., P.O. Box 399, Portal, Georgia 30450, www.openchurch.com, openchurch@angelfire.com, (888) OPEN-123, (912) 865-9811, fax (912) 865-9812

▶ The Parousia Network, P.O. Box 18793, Spokane, WA 99228, www.parousianetwork.com

✱ Order from www.ptmin.org.

▼ Restoration of Hope Ministries, N. 3617 Normandie, Spokane, Washington 99205, (509) 325-2964

❖ Restoration Ministries, 205 N. Murray Blvd. #68, Colorado Springs, Colorado 80916, (888) 229-3041

☞ Searching Together, P.O. Box 377, Taylors Falls, Minnesota 55084, (651) 465-6516, fax: (651) 465-5101

☆ The SeedSowers, P.O. Box 3317, Jacksonville, Florida 32206, www.seedsowers.com, info@seedsowers.com, (800) ACT-BOOK

♣ The Sentinel Group, P.O. Box 6334, Lynnwood, Washington 98036, www.sentinelgroup.org, (800) 668-5657

✦ Touch Outreach Ministries, 10055 Regal Row, Suite 180, Houston, Texas 77040, www.touchusa.org, (800) 735-5865

† William Carey Library, c/o Gabriel Resources, P.O. Box 1047, Waynesboro, Georgia 30830, www.WCLBooks.com, toll-free: (866) 732-6657

In addition, www.simplechurchbooks.com is a focused site, selling 48 of the best titles related to the house church.

House Church Websites

Our websites are multiplying, too. The sites in this list (not in any order) have links to many more sites. An ocean awaits you. Dive in, enjoy the swim, and be refreshed.

But the important thing about house-churching is just to DO it. Invite people to a whole new life in Christ and meet with them for fellowship, Bible study, and sharing the Lord Jesus. Pray and expect that God will add to your number. *Don't chicken out and spend the next six months wading around on the Web, reading about house-churching instead of doing it.*

When you run into speed bumps, or need wisdom or encouragement, come back here for another swim. These folks have been through most of the known problems—and turned into overcomers!

www.megashift.org
We've positioned this first simply because it's the official forum for readers of this book who want interaction and updates on matters raised in these pages. Our former website, www.megashift.com, was taken from us by error and given to a non-Christian portal. Until this is restored, please use www.megashift.org.

www.house2house.com
One of the very best sites. Includes *House2House* magazine online. Great articles and letters. Important feature: has an ever-growing directory of house churches, including other people interested in starting one in your area. Your home church can have a home page on this website too!

www.hccentral.com
Great site, very complete. Even includes solid teaching on theological subjects for new folks.

www.house-church.org Good website. Solid teaching, interesting writing.

www.homechurch.org *or* www.housechurch.org
Excellent! Be sure to click on BASICS and read especially the letters about "start-ups." Even better is the FORUMS section, listing every home church topic and question you could think of. There is a fine bibliography under RESOURCES.

www.openchurch.com
Open Church Ministries is the parent ministry of MEGASHIFT. Click on THE CONCEPT for a clear-eyed, delightful story by Jim Rutz of what God would like to do in the traditional church of today.

www.parousianetwork.com
Network of home and cell churches. Click on CURRENT EVENTS for up-to-date articles in dozens of areas affecting our lives as Christians. Click on MORE HOUSE CHURCH RESOURCES, then *HOUSE CHURCH PLANTING* by Joseph Cartwright.

www.outreach.ca/cpc
Comprehensive site on every aspect of house churches. Click on
HOUSE CHURCHES. Concentrates on Canada.

www.dawn.ch
Click on HOUSECHURCH. Short and to the point. Great classic site. See
also dawnministries.org.

www.cmaresources.org
A practical site by the sophisticated people at Church Multiplication
Associates, who are doing an outstanding job of planting new house
churches. They are the most prolific U.S. church planters.

www.geocities.com/redwookie
Has "Earth's Mightiest Alternative Christian Link Portal," with 1,483
links. A jungle with rabbit trails for everyone.

www.IWantMeaning.com
The website supporting James Rutz's book, *The Meaning of Life.*

www.parousianetwork.com
The website of Maurice Smith, one of the most eloquent and far-ranging writers in the house church community.

www.koinonianet.net
A good selection of articles by solid people.

www.dcfi.org
A sound list of resources for establishing house churches and also cell
churches.

www.radchr.net
Good books and training sessions on house churches.

www.homechurch-homepage.org
Great website with lots of in-depth articles and good editing.
Discussions are time-consuming but lively. Even has a page for house
church music folks.

www.openchurches.org
Good site, good articles.

www.livingtruth.com/newcovenant/newcov.htm
Articles of amazing depth—really interesting insight on ideas, like
how we can include children, the community of God, and how to live
with Him in ordinary matters of life.

www.ptmin.org
Well-written, deeply thought books, articles, messages, and resources,
including an exceptional article on the role of women in the church.
By Frank Viola.

http://members.tripod.com/~lotsofinfo/index.html
Popular site on how to feed hungry house church people on a shoe-string budget!

www.atlantaconference.com
Tiny website with lively testimonies (and a picture!) of what a house church is like.

www.cwowi.org
Unusual website of a former megachurch pastor who was called by direct revelation to start house churches.

www.churchrestoration.org
These folks may be willing to come help you get started! Also, very extensive Scripture references and teachings on house churches and related subjects.

www.geneedwards.com
Gene Edwards is sometimes called "Mr. House Church." His high-drama, first-person books (the combined gospels as if told by Jesus, Acts as told by the participants) have sold by the hundreds of thousands in many languages. His writings to brokenhearted Christians are tear-stained classics.

www.missionresources.com/house.html
A huge referral site with links listed by subject.

www.thirddaychurches.com
A well-rounded site by an experienced church planter.

www.ntrf.org
Thorough answers to tough house church questions.

www.homestead.com/mentorandmultiply/Patterson.html
Loaded with helpful material from a wise and highly experienced church planter.

www.vineyardcentral.com
A real, live, happening site. Includes a living-together Christian community.

www.bruderhof.org
Great if you want a live-in community with all things in common.

www.home-church.org
You get the benefit of 30 years' experience from this cluster of home churches. Note the archives of the best of *Voices* magazine under "Does HCDL have other resources I might find useful?"

www.searchingtogether.org
Hosted by an experienced house church scholar.

www.gty.org/~phil/hall.htm
An award-winning site with lots of data on church history, past Christian leaders (with pictures), creeds, etc. Disputatious but very valuable.

www.tallskinnykiwi.com
Extremely far-ranging, fast-moving website by Andrew Jones, one of the most avant garde thinkers connected to the open fellowship movement. High entertainment value, but may be obscure for many. *Warning:* His site will pull you in 90 directions!

www.robertfitts.com
A veteran house church pioneer lays it all out in simple, understandable terms. If you're feeling overwhelmed by the complexity of life in the midst of a megashift, this is your site!

www.ccel.org
Has a good library of ancient classics.

www.shareonhousechurch.net
An umbrella site for Europe. Also has subsites for Germany, Austria, Switzerland, and the Netherlands.

www.healingcommunities.org
An authoritative site on the home church as a total healing ministry. English and Spanish.

www.OdrosNuevos.org
A Spanish site worth a visit for the graphics even if you can't read it.

www.LifeShare.ch
Life Share Network is a Swiss site in German, Italian, and English.

www.VrijeChristenen.tk
A Belgian site.

www.homefellowshipleaders.com
A clean site with simple, nuts-and-bolts instructions by Harold Zimmerman, who has started over 800 house churches across Russia.

www.cofcare.org
Has a nice, long definition of "church" under Scriptures/Definitions.

www.rememberchrist.com
A well-done site with some good links and articles.

*D*id MEGASHIFT speak to you? Would you like to take a giant step up in your life? Then consider these options ...

1. Visit www.megashift.org. We have put a lot of work into this interactive, state-of-the-art website:

A. Watch our fast-moving opening video, *A Journey into the Heart of God.* It recaps all of human history in three minutes!

B. Be sure to sample *My Own Personal Worship Space.* There is nothing quite like it on the web. Along with scriptures, prayers, and scenery, it offers you a choice of various kinds of music: hymns, praise & worship, classical, Christian pop, movie themes, and more.

C. You will find more miracle reports and brief articles that will help you grow spiritually.

D. Our "Great Links" page will link you not only to related websites, but to the *best articles* on those sites, saving you the trouble of fishing around to find the "good stuff."

E. Five of our hottest articles are available to you free upon request in our freebies section. Great reading!

2. If you mooched this copy of MEGASHIFT from a friend, be a good sport, give it back, and get your own copy, either at your local Christian bookstore or through Open Church Ministries, www.openchurch.com or (888) OPEN-1-2-3 or (912) 865-9811 or 304 Grady St., P.O. Box 399, Portal, Georgia 30450.

3. Full academic training for non-professional, non-clerical ministry is available at Covenant Bible Institute (same contact information as above or Info@CovBible.org).

4. If you would like help or information on building a network of open fellowships, call or write Open Church Ministries or visit www.openchurch.com/wanthelp.

5. For seminars or group training in your area, call OCM or write us at info@openchurch.com.

6. To schedule media interviews with Jim Rutz, please contact the Publisher: Empowerment Press, (719) 277-6635.

7. Financial help is *always* needed! You may designate "For Megashift" in a check to Open Church Ministries or call them with a phone donation. Blessings on you!

Two Roads Diverged in a Yellow Wood

... and Jim Rutz didn't care much for either one.

Early in life, he decided that roads were boring, so he embarked on a quest for a short cut to the heart of the universe, a center of wisdom where everything would make sense and problems would tend to get solved rather than getting worse.

It wasn't easy. Being a dogged scholar, he managed to compress five years of college into eight—and then spent forty more long years hacking through the cultural underbrush. Now at last he has cleared a path to a dazzling spiritual mountaintop that few even knew existed. The view from there will make you blink in disbelief.

It's a wide-open place where people like you dump their heaviest hangups, turn into free and powerful spearheads of worldwide change, and get connected with God and man in ways that almost defy description. It's a swarm of battles and struggles, but also a place where hundreds of people have recently been raised from the dead...all duly documented in MEGASHIFT. Many types of miracles abound.

With this book, Rutz (rhymes with klutz, he says) has become the main chronicler of that new Kingdom, and he wants very much to help you get there and take your part—a very active part—in the extreme adventure of transforming the human race.

Never before have you faced a bigger opportunity. Never before has the King of Heaven allowed such a megashift of His power to mere mortals. And never again will you have such a golden chance to join with Rutz and others in lifting hundreds of millions of hearts to a place they've never been.